Cloud Computing Applications and Techniques for E-Commerce

Saikat Gochhait
Symbiosis Institute of Digital and Telecom Management, Symbiosis International University, India

David Tawei Shou
University of Taipei, Taiwan

Sabiha Fazalbhoy
Symbiosis Centre for Management Studies, Symbiosis International University, India

A volume in the Advances in
Systems Analysis, Software
Engineering, and High Performance
Computing (ASASEHPC) Book Series

Published in the United States of America by
    IGI Global
    Engineering Science Reference (an imprint of IGI Global)
    701 E. Chocolate Avenue
    Hershey PA, USA 17033
    Tel: 717-533-8845
    Fax: 717-533-8661
    E-mail: cust@igi-global.com
    Web site: http://www.igi-global.com

Library of Congress Cataloging-in-Publication Data

Names: Gochhait, Saikat, 1974- editor. | Shou, David Tawei, 1962- editor. |
    Fazalbhoy, Sabiha, 1977- editor.
Title: Cloud computing applications and techniques for E-commerce / Saikat
    Gochhait, David Tawei Shou, Sabiha Fuzalbhoy, editors.
Description: Hershey, PA : Engineering Science Reference, 2019. | Includes
    bibliographical references and index. | Summary: "This book examines the
    application of cloud computing in business"-- provided by publisher.
Identifiers: LCCN 2019027704 (print) | LCCN 2019027705 (ebook) | ISBN
    9781799812944 (hardcover) | ISBN 9781799812951 (paperback) | ISBN
    9781799812968 (ebook)
Subjects: LCSH: Cloud computing. | Electronic commerce.
Classification: LCC QA76.585 .C5727 2019 (print) | LCC QA76.585 (ebook) |
    DDC 004.67/82--dc23
LC record available at https://lccn.loc.gov/2019027704
LC ebook record available at https://lccn.loc.gov/2019027705

This book is published in the IGI Global book series Advances in Systems Analysis, Software Engineering, and High Performance Computing (ASASEHPC) (ISSN: 2327-3453; eISSN: 2327-3461)

British Cataloguing in Publication Data
A Cataloguing in Publication record for this book is available from the British Library.

All work contributed to this book is new, previously-unpublished material.
The views expressed in this book are those of the authors, but not necessarily of the publisher.

For electronic access to this publication, please contact: eresources@igi-global.com.

Advances in Systems Analysis, Software Engineering, and High Performance Computing (ASASEHPC) Book Series

ISSN:2327-3453
EISSN:2327-3461

Editor-in-Chief: Vijayan Sugumaran, Oakland University, USA

MISSION

The theory and practice of computing applications and distributed systems has emerged as one of the key areas of research driving innovations in business, engineering, and science. The fields of software engineering, systems analysis, and high performance computing offer a wide range of applications and solutions in solving computational problems for any modern organization.

The **Advances in Systems Analysis, Software Engineering, and High Performance Computing (ASASEHPC) Book Series** brings together research in the areas of distributed computing, systems and software engineering, high performance computing, and service science. This collection of publications is useful for academics, researchers, and practitioners seeking the latest practices and knowledge in this field.

COVERAGE

- Computer Networking
- Computer System Analysis
- Computer Graphics
- Enterprise Information Systems
- Engineering Environments
- Distributed Cloud Computing
- Virtual Data Systems
- Human-Computer Interaction
- Network Management
- Metadata and Semantic Web

IGI Global is currently accepting manuscripts for publication within this series. To submit a proposal for a volume in this series, please contact our Acquisition Editors at Acquisitions@igi-global.com or visit: http://www.igi-global.com/publish/.

Titles in this Series

For a list of additional titles in this series, please visit:
http://www.igi-global.com/book-series/advances-systems-analysis-software-engineering/73689

Soft Computing Methods for System Dependability
Mohamed Arezki Mellal (M'Hamed Bougara University, Algeria)
Engineering Science Reference • ©2020 • 293pp • H/C (ISBN: 9781799817185) • US $225.00

Grammatical and Syntactical Approaches in Architecture Emerging Research and Opportunities
Ju Hyun Lee (University of New South Wales, Australia) and Michael J. Ostwald (University of New South Wales, Australia)
Engineering Science Reference • ©2020 • 351pp • H/C (ISBN: 9781799816980) • US $195.00

Tools and Techniques for Software Development in Large Organizations Emerging Research and Opportunities
Vishnu Pendyala (Cisco Systems Inc., USA)
Engineering Science Reference • ©2020 • 240pp • H/C (ISBN: 9781799818632) • US $195.00

Fundamental and Supportive Technologies for 5G Mobile Networks
Sherine Mohamed Abd El-Kader (Electronics Research Institute, Egypt) and Hanan Hussein (Electronics Research Institute, Egypt)
Information Science Reference • ©2020 • 360pp • H/C (ISBN: 9781799811527) • US $225.00

Deep Learning Techniques and Optimization Strategies in Big Data Analytics
J. Joshua Thomas (KDU Penang University College, Malaysia) Pinar Karagoz (Middle East Technical University, Turkey) B. Bazeer Ahamed (Balaji Institute of Technology and Science, Warangal, India) and Pandian Vasant (Universiti Teknologi PETRONAS, Malaysia)
Engineering Science Reference • ©2020 • 355pp • H/C (ISBN: 9781799811923) • US $245.00

For an entire list of titles in this series, please visit:
http://www.igi-global.com/book-series/advances-systems-analysis-software-engineering/73689

701 East Chocolate Avenue, Hershey, PA 17033, USA
Tel: 717-533-8845 x100 • Fax: 717-533-8661
E-Mail: cust@igi-global.com • www.igi-global.com

Table of Contents

Detailed Table of Contents

Chapter 1
    Saadia Karim, Institute of Business Management (IoBM), Pakistan
    Tariq Rahim Soomro, Institute of Business Management (IoBM),
        Pakistan

Cloud computing is a distributed environment for multiple organizations to use remotely and get high scalability, reliability on anytime, anywhere, and pay-as-you-go concepts. An organization has to create data centres to store, manage, and process the information to achieve benefits from data and make decisions. Cloud gives organizations a successful approach that leads to profit without maintaining the cost of data centres and technical staff to manage the services. Cloud has different types of architectures, types of clouds, and cost packages for using the cloud. These services can be scaled up or down when required by an organization. Cloud has unbeatable future because IT world is acquiring it and giving a boost to their businesses. Many cloud providers are using it and the remaining are moving to cloud. Cloud computing also gives birth to edge computing, fog computing, and many more zero downtime solutions.

Chapter 2
    Saikat Gochhait, Symbiosis Institute of Digital and Telecom
        Management, Symbiosis International University, India
    Shariq Aziz Butt, University of Lahore, Pakistan
    Tauseef Jamal, PIEAS University, Pakistan
    Arshad Ali, University of Lahore, Pakistan

The software industries follow some patterns (i.e., process model to develop any software product). Agile methodology is the most famous and used process model. It is a trend to develop efficient software products with high client satisfaction. In this chapter, the authors discuss agile methodology and its components, benefits, and drawbacks while using the cloud computing in agile software development, existing frameworks for agile-cloud combination, and some security measures.

Chapter 3

Shah Rukh Malik, Government College University, Pakistan
Mujahid Rafiq, The Superior University (Defence Road Campus),
*   Lahore, Pakistan*
Muhammad Ahmad Kahloon, The Superior College (University
*   Campus), Lahore, Pakistan*

In this chapter, the authors focus on the most fundamental barrier in the e-commerce application's adoption: security. The most significant or important aspect to explore in cloud computing is how to keep the data secure in the most efficient way with cutting-edge technologies. Cloud computing has taken its place by providing its convenient services like on-demand service, pay-per-use, rapid elasticity, resource pooling, and other lucrative facilities. In this chapter, the authors will firstly describe the introduction related to cloud computing, major characteristics, types, and a few security concerns and issues in cloud computing. Furthermore, they discuss the introduction of e-commerce applications, how it is interlinked with cloud computing, and what the possible threats are. Moreover, what the possible solutions could be are discussed, so that we can secure data on both user side as well as on the server side. The authors suggest some existing solutions at the end of the chapter.

Chapter 4

Shweta Kaushik, ABES Engineering College, Ghaziabad, India
Charu Gandhi, Jaypee Institute of Information Technology, Noida, India

Today's people are moving towards the internet services through cloud computing to acquire their required service, but they have less confidence about cloud computing because all the tasks are handled by the service provider. Cloud system provides features to the owner to store their data on some remote locations and allow only authorized users to access their data according to their access capability. Data security becomes particularly serious in the cloud computing environment because data are scattered in different machines and storage devices including servers, PCs, and various mobile devices such as smart phones. To make the cloud computing be adopted by enterprise, the security concerns of users should be rectified first to make cloud environment trustworthy. The trustworthy environment is the basic prerequisite to win the confidence of users to adopt this technology. However, there are various security concerns that need to be taken care of regarding the trust maintenance between various parties, authorized access of confidential data, data storage privacy, and integrity.

Chapter 5
Ravindra Kumar Singh Rajput, Suresh Gyan Vihar University, India
Dinesh Goyal, Poornima Institute of Engineering and Technology, India

Every software application has its own minimum set of requirements like CPU, storage, memory, networking, and power. These have to be integrated into a specific configuration to allow the smooth functioning of the software application. When data traffic becomes higher than expected, higher resources are required. There may not be enough time to provision new resources manually; in such cases, an auto-scaling system is required for managing these situations. Cloud computing means using data, programs, and other resources pooled in the data center and accessed through the internet instead of the user's computer. In the chapter, the authors discussed some aspects related to cloud computing like cloud workload, load balancing, load balancing algorithms, scaling techniques, and auto-scaling to fulfill cloud workload balancing requirements.

Chapter 6
Abhineet Anand, Chitkara University Institute of Engineering and
*   Technology, Punjab, India*
Arvindhan Muthusamy, Galgotias Universirty, India

Cloud computing is a new technique that has been widely spread recently due to the services provided to users according to their need. Being a pay-for-what-you-use service, it provides a much-encapsulated set of services. Cloud computing acts as a main attraction for the business owners. Whether they are big or small, they can choose from the required services. Management of heavy flow data is very likely to be managed under this with the confidentiality and security of the data attached. Having all these features may attract everyone, but every technique always comes with some issues. The main aim of this survey chapter is to gain a better understanding of security issues that can occur in cloud computing.

Chapter 7

    Reimar Weissbach, Technical University of Munich, Germany
    Alexander Bogislav Herzfeldt, Technical University of Munich, Germany
    Sebastian Floerecke, University of Passau, Germany
    Christoph Ertl, Technical University of Munich, Germany

In the complex and opaque cloud business ecosystem, service providers face several
challenges. The fastest growing field of IaaS is evolving towards a commodity market,
resulting in an increasing price competition. By first examining current challenges
for cloud service providers, giving a theoretical background on value facilitation
with a focus on the areas of value creation, and describing a state-of-the-art cloud
ecosystem model, a sound understanding of the current situation is established.
The role of value facilitation and standardization as core capabilities for successful
IaaS providers are discussed and identified as being crucial for successful long-
term survival in the competitive ecosystem. Additionally, learnings from expert
interviews are analyzed, and five concrete recommendations for IaaS providers are
derived. These recommendations should serve the management of IaaS providers
in order to compare, challenge, and potentially adapt their current business models.

Preface

Many professional fields have been affected by the rapid growth of technology and information. Included in this are the business and management markets as the implementation of e-commerce and cloud computing have caused enterprises to make considerable changes to their practices. With the swift advancement of this technology, professionals need proper research that provides solutions to the various issues that come with data integration and shifting to a technology-driven environment. *Cloud Computing Applications and Techniques for E-Commerce* is an essential reference source that discusses the implementation of data and cloud technology within the fields of business and information management. Featuring research on topics such as content delivery networks, virtualization, and software resources, this book is ideally designed for managers, educators, administrators, researchers, computer scientists, business practitioners, economists, information analysts, sociologists, and students seeking coverage on the recent advancements of e-commerce using cloud computing techniques.

INSIDE THIS BOOK

In this regard, the first chapter is devoted to understanding of Cloud Computing that enable the delivery of cloud computing services such as; SaaS, PaaS and IaaS via a network.

The second chapter discusses on the cloud adoption in agile for enhance development with the help of virtual machines and use of cloud-based services for project management, issue management and software builds with automated testing.

The third chapter discusses on the Cloud Security in e-commerce applications based on the security and privacy issues related to cloud based E-Commerce to be explored more and on the network point of view as well as from application point of view, it should be analysed as cloud combining with E-Commerce is a good opportunity for the business industries.

The fourth chapter discusses on the cloud computing and data privacy in processing personal data in a transparent and complaint way to provide technological solutions aiming to provide to end-users the typical data collection and storage capabilities of data management systems but also, to help end-users regain control over their data.

The fifth chapter discusses on the Virtualization is a software that virtualizes your hardware into multiple machines while Cloud computing is the combination of multiple hardware devices.

The sixth chapter discusses on the Blockchain-as-a-Service platform enables developers, entrepreneurs, and enterprises to develop, test, and deploy blockchain applications and smart contracts that will be hosted on the BaaS platform.

The seventh chapter discusses on the contribution will build on the Passau Cloud Computing Ecosystem (PaCE Model) to create an understanding for the distributed and increasingly nontransparent cloud ecosystem as well as to highlight challenges and requirements for the roles in the dynamic ecosystem.

CONCLUSION

Such discussions within the cloud computing domain are ... since they have shown an effective and positive result which has put it in the top flight of ICT technologies i.e. flexibility in space and enormous support for infrastructure and software. This innovation has a great potential that increases revenue, expands business and creates new jobs that extend to large sectors beyond the business sector. It plays a vital role in enabling a smart economy. Without doubt it will be the fifth utility after water, gas, electricity, and telephony which are always-on and paid by usage of consumer.

Chapter 1
What Is Cloud Computing?

Saadia Karim
https://orcid.org/0000-0002-3113-4365
Institute of Business Management (IoBM), Pakistan

Tariq Rahim Soomro
https://orcid.org/0000-0002-7119-0644
Institute of Business Management (IoBM), Pakistan

ABSTRACT

Cloud computing is a distributed environment for multiple organizations to use remotely and get high scalability, reliability on anytime, anywhere, and pay-as-you-go concepts. An organization has to create data centres to store, manage, and process the information to achieve benefits from data and make decisions. Cloud gives organizations a successful approach that leads to profit without maintaining the cost of data centres and technical staff to manage the services. Cloud has different types of architectures, types of clouds, and cost packages for using the cloud. These services can be scaled up or down when required by an organization. Cloud has unbeatable future because IT world is acquiring it and giving a boost to their businesses. Many cloud providers are using it and the remaining are moving to cloud. Cloud computing also gives birth to edge computing, fog computing, and many more zero downtime solutions.

INTRODUCTION

The term 'cloud computing' consists of two words; first term 'cloud' means "over the Internet" as the Internet visualizes as available in clouds because no one exactly knows and no one worries to know from where the information is accessed, retrieved

DOI: 10.4018/978-1-7998-1294-4.ch001

and/or updated. The second term 'computing' refers to "use of computers" and jointly term 'cloud computing' refers to "remote computing" or "use of computing services over the Internet". Traditional computing using desktop, which is now changing to Internet computing helps users access, retrieve and/or update his/her work at any time (24/7), anywhere (ubiquitous). Users access, retrieve and/or update cloud services, which are available on demand and pay subscription charges known as "pay as you go" or a "utility". Cloud computing is one of the most vital scientific expansion in the last era. With no doubt, it is today's technology and tomorrow promise.

Cloud computing allows different customers and companies to share resources like storage, computing power, and interaction with services. In the early era, virtualization was an important discovery for sharing resources and computing. Currently, this concept increases Internet services, while reducing the cost and complexity of computing known as "cloud computing". In this chapter, an overview of cloud computing starting from the 1960s until the present day is discussed. The first section is all about a brief history of cloud computing. The second section of this chapter gives a brief knowledge about the cloud with the benefits of cloud computing, the security of cloud computing, and large players of cloud services available in the market; such as; Microsoft Azure, Google, Amazon, IBM, etc. and give a deep knowledge of services provided by them. The third and fourth sections will focus on the type of cloud computing architecture and types of cloud computing categories. Onwards, section fifth and sixth explains about applications and challenges of cloud computing. Finally, the last section will focus on future scope and future technologies of cloud computing.

HISTORY OF THE CLOUD COMPUTING

The cloud computing was born through the cycle of different practices done for storing, processing and connecting the computer to the Internet (García & Cusumano, 2006). The cloud computing concept gets on track since the 1960s, when the first time John McCarthy initiates the use of a time-sharing mainframe computer (Systems Kerridge Commercial, 2016) (Borko Furht, 2010). Later on, ARPANET (Advanced Research Projects Agency Network) developed by J.C.R. Licklider in 1969, the straight prototype to the Internet. Licklider promoted unified and unlimited ease of access to data and programs ("Cloud Computing History timeline | Timetoast timelines," n.d.) ("Cloud Computing and its Evolution Over Time 1969 to 2015," n.d.). In the 1970s, IBM released full time-sharing operating system name IBM VM, which has an admin panel that can control the activities of different environments to be present on a single physical machine, this upgrades the level of 50s-60s time-sharing system. Such more platforms as Cambridge CTSS, Multics (on GE hardware),

2

Figure 1. History of cloud computing

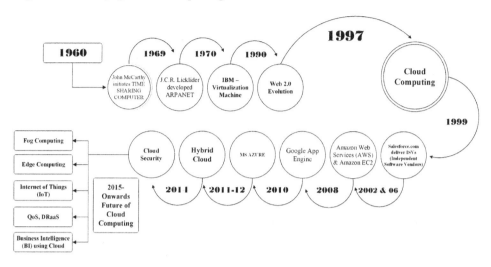

and the UNIX ports use the full time-sharing solutions. This change enables the telecommunication industry to take interest in time-sharing solutions, and initiate Virtual Private Network (VPN) and Web 2.0 evolution (García & Cusumano, 2006) ("Cloud Computing History timeline | Timetoast timelines," n.d.) ("Cloud Computing and its Evolution Over Time 1969 to 2015," n.d.) (Bojanova & Zhang, 2013) (Neto, 2011). The evolution of the network transforms traffic to a better network system. This advance shifting allows better network balance and high-speed bandwidth control. At that time (1997), "Cloud Computing" was coined by the University of Texas Professor Ramnath Chellappa as a new "computing paradigm", where computing borders are determined by a financial basis rather than technical limits (Ramnath Chellappa, 1997). Cloud computing becomes a hot solution for different organizations, like Salesforce.com in 1999. They presented enterprise applications solutions to end customers by Web portal. Salesforce.com improves the application over the Internet by delivering ISVs (Independent Software Vendors) solution to customers. The historical timeline of cloud computing (Agarwal, 2017) is shown in Figure 1 below with the future working of the cloud.

After 1999, the major change in cloud computing takes place in the form of Amazon, which steps in 2002, and introduces Amazon Web Services (AWS). AWS is providing advance level cloud services for storage and computations. Amazon also launches Elastic Compute Cloud (EC2) in 2006; EC2 provides the facility to small companies to rent computers on which they execute their applications. In 2007, Dropbox Inc. a cloud storage service created by MIT students for storing files with a synchronization feature on it. Whereas on the other hand, Force.com was initiated by Salesforce.com. Force.com gives an interface that allows customers to build, store, and execute their applications and websites on the cloud. In 2008, Google launched the Google App. Google App, a Technology Company that becomes the first pure entity into the cloud computing market. Google was a leading Internet company. Google enters into cloud market means a clear and major step towards the acceptance of cloud computing. As Google initiated the drastic pricing model that has a free entry-level plan with low-cost services among others, in the market. Furthermore, in 2010, Microsoft took a historical step towards cloud computing. Microsoft the largest software company initiates small, but significant swing toward Web as launching Azure. Azure has to provide the built-in solution with easy integration for the development of the Web and mobile apps ("Cloud Computing History timeline | Timetoast timelines," n.d.) ("Cloud Computing and its Evolution Over Time 1969 to 2015," n.d.) (Neto, 2011). Cloud gets a boost when so many vendors took an interest, which updates the level of cloud to the Hybrid cloud. In 2011 & 2012, Hybrid cloud gets into the market that uses the advantages of public and private cloud both on a single platform (Caitlin White, 2013). By the time of 2014, cloud security becomes a big issue for cloud vendors (Keith D. Foote, 2017) (Tariq Rahim Soomro & Sarwar, 2012). Currently, cloud computing is discussed with the new buzzwords, such as Fog computing, Edge computing, IoT (Internet of Things), etc.

WHAT IS CLOUD COMPUTING?

Cloud computing is similar to utility use in daily life. Utilities like electricity, gas, water, etc. paid as individual utilizes them. Cloud gives a utility that user use only, rather than owning it, but these resources are shared via the Internet and give "pay-per-use" or "pay-as-you-go" concept (Agarwal, 2017) (Lele, 2019a). The networks of computers make the cloud, where hardware and software needs of customers are fulfilled like data storage, recovery, and backup. Cloud provides a shared and distributed environment of resources among various customers, which enable access to network anywhere (ubiquitous), anytime (24/7). The cloud computing enables the user to control and upgrade the services up or down as per requirements without any investment in hardware, software, or human resource (Borko Furht, 2010) (Neto, 2011) (Agarwal, 2017) (Lele, 2019a). The cloud characteristics as compare to a desktop are large scale resources, high scalability, elasticity, self-service, shared & distributed pool of networks, dynamic resources scheduling, keeping user online & synchronize his/her applications (Sehgal & Bhatt, 2018) (Ahmad, Bakht, & Mohan, 2017) (Agarwal, 2017) (Nazir, Bhardwaj, Chawda, & Mishra, 2015) (Jajodia et al., 2014) (C.-Y. Huang, Hsu, & Tzeng, 2012) (Neto, 2011) (Sullivan, 2010) (Qian, Luo, Du, & Guo, 2009) as shown in Figure 2 below.

Figure 2. Cloud characteristics

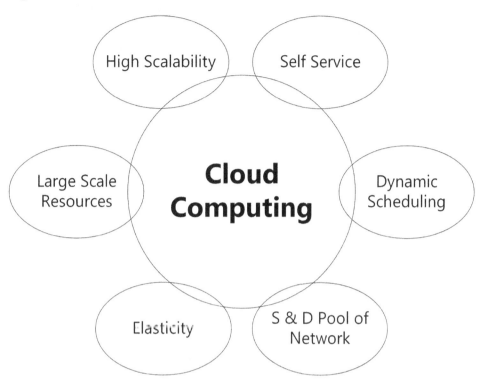

The necessary characteristics of cloud computing, as shown in Figure 2, gives acceptance and suitability over other computing models, are as follows:

1. **Large Scale Resources** empowers cloud computing to make large-scale computing power and resources available anytime, anywhere for a wide range of customers.
2. **High Scalability** is the key to managing a large amount of data loss when unexpected downtime or system failure occurs as well as cloud computing provides failover or disaster recovery solutions to the customer.
3. **The Elasticity** gives resources to rapidly scale up or down as per customer demand. The customers have the full accessibility to the resources, which can be purchased or upgraded when needed.
4. **Self-Service** promote customers to request and able to manage the computing competencies, for any type of workload without any human interference from the cloud service providers.
5. **Shared & Distributed Pool of Networks** empowers the computing resources like storage, processing, bandwidth, virtual network, etc. It should be managed

Table 1. Shows the cloud computing vendors and services provided by them ("Products & Services | Google Cloud," n.d.), (IBM Cloud Team, 2019), (Amazon, 2019), ("Cloud Marketplace - Hybrid Cloud Computing | Dell EMC US," n.d.), ("Cloud Service Provider Resources from Intel," n.d.), ("Choosing a Cloud Platform | Managed Cloud by Rackspace," n.d.)

Google	Infrastructure modernization	Data management	Application development	Smart business analytics & AI	Productivity & work transformation	Industry solutions	Role-based solutions
IBM	Managed	Advisory	Development	Migration	Integration	Security	Design
Amazon	Amazon EC2	Simple Storage Service (S3)	Aurora	Dynamo DB	RDS	AWS Lambda	VPC	Lightsail
Dell	Hybrid Cloud Platforms		Cloud-Enabled Infrastructure		Cloud Consumption		Cloud Consulting and Technology Services	
Intel	Security Enhanced Cloud Services		Data center optimization for CSPs		Grow Your Business with Differentiated Services		
Rackspace	Managed Hosting	Managed Cloud	Collocation	Application Services	Professional Services	Security & Compliance

as a pool of networks, which is shared by customers or having a distributed environment.

6. **Dynamic Resources Scheduling** map the workload of the customer and executes auto-scale up or down to have smooth working without any waiting time given by the cloud service provider.

The customers use these services and pay accordingly to the provider. Cloud has a different type of vendors such as Google, IBM, Sun, Amazon, Cisco, Dell, HP, Intel, Novell, Rackspace, and Oracle. Some of them with services detail is shown in Table 1 (Lele, 2019b), (Hille, Klemm, & Lemmermann, 2017). These vendors charge services from customers on the bases of the subscription model or utility model. These offering help customers to get services on very low pricing than conventional models in the software business. Table 1 shows the details about the services provided by different Cloud vendors in the market. Many more are also discussed in (Hille et al., 2017).

This makes a new concept of development and creation of products around the world. Another, benefit of the cloud is that it decreases the cost to run a data center, hire technical staff to maintain and give support to infrastructure (García & Cusumano, 2006), (Sullivan, 2010). Cloud computing gives access to data via the Internet, which involves a high risk of securing data. The cloud provider enables multiple layers of securities on the architecture design of the cloud and providers are more confident to say that the cloud is secure enough to store, upload, execute and manages the services (Ian Mitchell, n.d.), (Nick Antonopoulos, 2010).

ARCHITECTURE OF CLOUD COMPUTING

The cloud architecture is divided into two subdivisions as frontend and backend. These divisions are connected respectively, via the Internet. Customers use front-end and back-end used by a cloud system. Front-end means using computers and the required application to access the cloud. Whereas, the back-end has a cloud system like computers, storage, servers, data analyzer, bandwidth monitoring, and task schedulers. A cloud administrator called a central server, who manages these activities. The central server follows some protocols and special software known as Middleware. Cloud computing delivers basic three types of service plan to customers as Software as a Service (SaaS), Platform as a Service (PaaS), and Infrastructure as a Service (IaaS), as shown in Figure 3 below (Jadeja & Modi, 2012), (T R Soomro & Wahba, 2010). These service models are distinct from the top of the figurative pyramid, as follows:

Software as a Service (SaaS)

Software as a service is a model based on software applications hosted by the provider and available to customers via the Internet. SaaS support services oriented architecture (SOA) and Web services model, which change the mind of people to build, buy, sell, and utilize software applications, as seen in Figure 4. SaaS provides a "pay as you go" licensing model. Cloud provider sustains the security, accessibility, and performance of the software to customers. SaaS most often provides software solutions to the enterprise industry at a very low cost. SaaS cloud provider allows the customer to become free of installation, licensing, management, support of software applications. SaaS model gives support to user demands on even at high peak hours and able to execute a large number of business transactions in a protected and dependable environment. With the advancement of Web 2.0 & HTML5 standards, help SaaS vendors to give faster service to the customer as they are running software on their personal computers. For example, Google Play store, Google Docs, Google Gmail, Salesforce.com, Microsoft Office 365 and Customer Relationship Management (CRM) (Lele, 2019a), (Sehgal & Bhatt, 2018), (T R Soomro & Wahba, 2010), (Rashid & Chaturvedi, 2019), (Info & Deyo, 2008), (Hod, Professor CSE, & Sri Venkateswara, 2012), (M. Kumar, 2014), (Hill, 2013).

Figure 3. Shows the cloud architecture

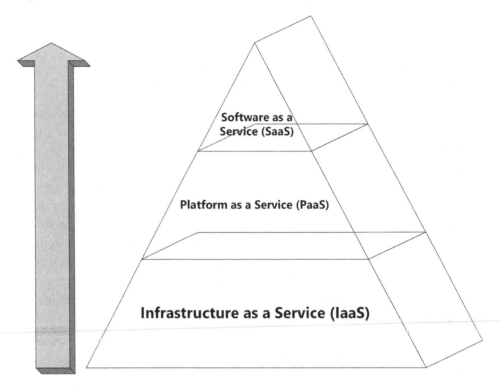

Platform as a Service (PaaS)

Platform as a service means developing a solution using the cloud, like having an operating system installed on the cloud. PaaS is a platform service architecture offered to customers by cloud vendors. PaaS cloud service rapidly changes the market as compared to the old times of platform, which need years of installation afraid and pieces of training. PaaS reduces the time to a day of installation. PaaS customers are developers who are creating and executing applications for a specific platform. Cloud online tools like middleware solutions and Application Program Interfaces (API) support the developers. PaaS customers get the benefit of lower cost expense, less risk management, and security features provided by cloud vendors. Some examples of PaaS vendors are Force.com, Amazon Web Services (AWS) & EC2, Google App Engine, Microsoft Azure platform (Lele, 2019a), (Sehgal & Bhatt, 2018), (T R Soomro & Wahba, 2010), (Rashid & Chaturvedi, 2019), (Hill, 2013). As shown in Figure 5, that PaaS offers Applications, data, and web user interfaces to be managed by customers and rest all architectural features are managed by cloud vendors.

Figure 4. Shows the Software as a Service (SaaS) cloud structure

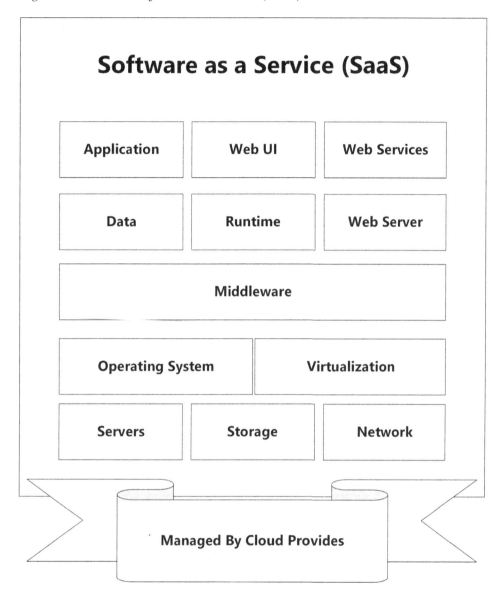

Infrastructure as a Service (IaaS)

Infrastructure as a service of the cloud is used to access the IT resources including applications, data, computing resources, and networks. IaaS on demand facility is very cost effective as compared to an old server of an organization. IaaS offers hardware solutions to customers in which physical resources like operating systems

Figure 5. Shows the platform as a service (PaaS) cloud structure

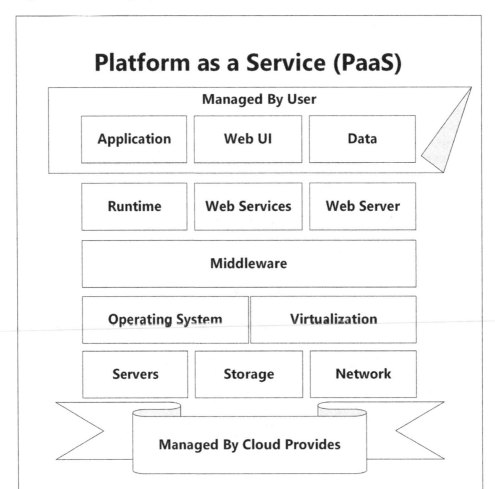

and middleware, is shared by virtualization to different end users. An IaaS customer uses the Application Program Interface (API) to access the virtual storage and servers and increase the control of the operating system. The customers have no control to manage the cloud infrastructure at own. For example, Amazon Elastic Compute Cloud (EC2) offers a large infrastructure and service to customers without any hesitation in management. GoGrid and Rackspace cloud are also providing IaaS. As shown in Figure 6, that IaaS offers an infrastructure facility to be managed by customers and rest all back-end features are managed by cloud vendors.

Figure 6. Shows the infrastructure as a service (IaaS) cloud structure

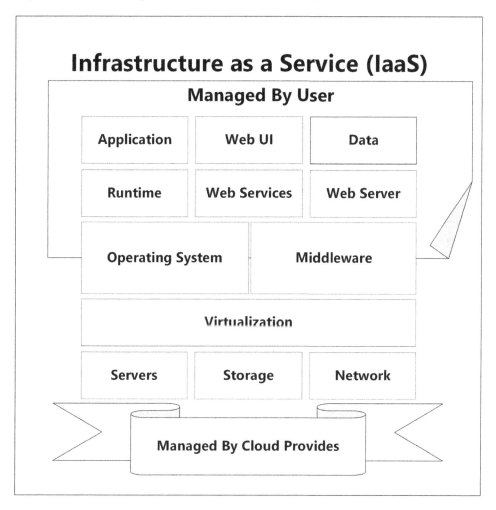

TYPES OF CLOUD

Cloud computing has four types of cloud based on their usage and deployment:

Public Cloud

Public cloud means general or universal access cloud. A complete infrastructure of computing is placed on the location of the cloud that manages the cloud services via the Internet, using Web services or applications. The public cloud infrastructure is detached from customer access and uses shared resources. These shared resources are susceptible to numerous attacks as resources of a single machine is used by different customers, but one thing is best in the public cloud that data is separated from others' data. Public cloud gives benefits to the organization to reduce hardware cost and increase the investment by providing the automatic backup and upgrades of applications and data. For example, the popular public cloud providers are Amazon Web Service, Google App Engine, and Microsoft Azure, and etc ("Types of Cloud Computing Explained | GlobalDots," n.d.), (Briscoe & Marinos, 2009), ("The Four Types of Cloud Computing Models," n.d.), (Dynasis, n.d.).

Private Cloud

Private cloud (or local cloud) refers to cloud computing on private networks. Private cloud gives the same benefits as the public cloud but uses dedicated resources including private hardware. Private cloud exclusively organized for organizations or customers for providing full access to host applications, services, development environments, and access control on data, while considering the security of data. For private cloud, an internal IT department setup requires that debug and manages the cloud infrastructure. Thus, the cost will be effective as compared to the public cloud and still need to pay for servers. The maintenance of private clouds like security, infrastructure, and backup becomes an extra job for an organization to do. The large enterprise organizations refer to private cloud as they have the expertise and budget to afford the private cloud. The private cloud providers enable the cloud functionality by using tools as vCloud Director, VMware, or OpenStack ("Types of Cloud Computing Explained | GlobalDots," n.d.), (Briscoe & Marinos, 2009), ("The Four Types of Cloud Computing Models," n.d.), (Huth & Cebula, 2011), (Dynasis, n.d.), (Gorelik, 2013).

Hybrid Cloud

A hybrid cloud means banding the advantage of Public and Private Cloud on a single platform. Hybrid is a combined platform, where customers can access internal as well as external services. A hybrid cloud combines elasticity and adaptability of the public cloud with the comfort level of the private cloud. The hybrid cloud merges the public cloud with the on-premises private cloud of an organization to give high security to application and get more benefit from both. For example, interaction with customers through Public cloud, while securing their data through a Private cloud. Hybrid cloud is offer by most popular providers as Google App Engine, IBM Cloud, Amazon Web Services (AWS), Rackspace, Microsoft Azure, and etc. ("Types of Cloud Computing Explained | GlobalDots," n.d.), ("The Four Types of Cloud Computing Models," n.d.), (Dynasis, n.d.), (Gorelik, 2013).

Community Cloud

A community cloud represents an exclusive use of cloud by the customer from an organization or country that has some shared resources like policies, security requirements, etc. The community cloud is present on or off the location of an organization without the interference of cloud vendors. The community cloud has a shared environment but within the premises of the organization or depending on the cloud relation built among two or more organizations. As it is owned by many organizations, it has less failure or downtime because it has a robust and flexible structure. The community cloud gives control and expediency, because of its self-governing distributed structure and it has a smaller footprint in the market as compared to cloud vendors, but it is a more growing and organic structure. It is shrinking the symbiotic relationship to support the demands of the community. Many big vendors like Google Cloud Platform, Amazon Web Services (AWS), Microsoft Azure, IBM Cloud, etc. are offering community cloud to organizations ("Types of Cloud Computing Explained | GlobalDots," n.d.), (Briscoe & Marinos, 2009), ("The Four Types of Cloud Computing Models," n.d.), (Huth & Cebula, 2011), (Dynasis, n.d.), (Gorelik, 2013). Figure 7 shows all four types of cloud in a glance.

APPLICATIONS OF CLOUD COMPUTING

Cloud Computing become one of the most dominant areas for computing online. Cloud computing has the scalability to reduce risk, auto-load balancing, providing customized segments to customers. These abilities make cloud computing an active component of an organization; numerous applications are available in today's world and some of them are as follows in Table 2.

Many applications are available in the market as a new way of presenting services to the customers. These changes open new paths of requirements and opportunities to fulfill in the growth of Cloud computing (Nick Antonopoulos, 2010), (Hill, 2013), (N. Kumar, Kumar Kushwaha, & Kumar, 2014), (Sareen, 2013), (Dhar, 2012).

CHALLENGES FACED BY CLOUD COMPUTING

All the various aspects of cloud computing like architecture, deployment, and advantages of using cloud computing are defined. However, the new concept of cloud computing brings some major challenges, which may cause trouble in the future if not taken care seriously. Some of the challenges are as follows (Rashid &

Figure 7. Shows the types of cloud

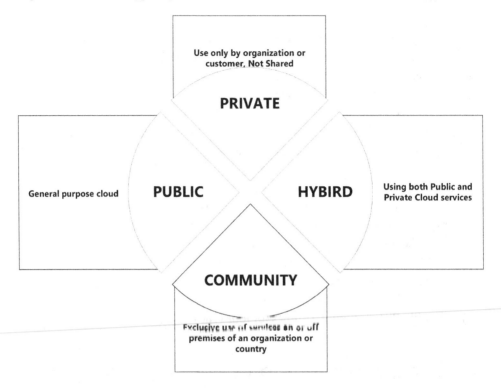

Chaturvedi, 2019), (Yang Chong, 2019), (Jonas et al., 2019), (Zhan et al., 2015), (Nazir et al., 2015) (Hill, 2013), (Huth & Cebula, 2011), (Dynasis, n.d.):

1. Security, Access Control and Privacy

Data security and privacy is a big issue in the cloud environment. How to assign access control over the data and to whom it will be given? How frequently password updates are done? Which type of recovery method is required for a password and account name? What about maintaining logs and providing audit access? Using secure protocol on the Internet (like Secure Socket Layer (SSL), Anti-Virus) and strong passwords, which are frequently changed, can help a lot in protected data from any misfortune.

Table 2. Different applications and cloud service providers- (Riahi, 2015), ("10 Best Learning Management Systems For Your Company - Financesonline.com," n.d.), ("Data Center Providers," n.d.), (EM360, 2018; technavio, 2018), (Williams Mike, 2019), (Liu, Wang, & Yao, 2016), (Drake Nate, 2019), (Lenart, 2011; Nguyen, Nguyen, & Misra, 2014), (Burney, Asif, & Abbas, 2016), (Fearn Nicholas, 2019), (Ohlhorst, 2018).

Applications	Cloud Service Providers
E-Learning	TalentLMS (https://www.talentlms.com/), Schoology (https://www.schoology.com/), Docebo (https://www.docebo.com/), SAP Litmos LMS (https://www.litmos.com/), Canvas LMS (https://www.canvaslms.com/), EduXpert (https://eduxpert.in/)
Search Engines & Social Websites:	Google.com, amazon.com, hotmail.com, Microsoft Azure, VMware, alibaba.com, facebook.com, linkedln.com, youtube.com, etc.
Data Centers	Google, Amazon Web Services, Digital Realty Trust, Equinix, Microsoft, China Telecom, IBM, NTT Communications.
Backups/Storage	IDrive Small Business, iCloud, Mega, One Drive, Backblaze Business, Mozy Pro, Google Drive, Box.
ERP Cloud	Oracle NetSuite (http://www.netsuite.com/portal/home.shtml), Saga Intacct (https://www.sageintacct.com/), SysPro (https://www.syspro.com/), SAP (https://www.sap.com/index.html), Epicor (https://www.epicor.com/en-us/)
Disaster Recovery	Microsoft Azure Site Recovery, Zerto IT Resilience Platform, Arcserve UDP Cloud Direct (is a Disaster Recovery as a Service)

2. Service Level Arguments (SLAs)

SLAs give cloud administrators full access on application to run several instances of the application on multiple servers or minimize or shut down any existing application without informing customers. This cause cloud computing as a challenge to customers because the customer gets difficulties to evaluate the SLAs schema of cloud providers. Cloud providers make a schema to protect the actions, while minimal guarantee to customers. So, this makes several important issues like outages, price, and data protection. The price is an important issue to consider before signing the agreement with the provider. SLAs give birth to a very basic question that if the account turns inactive then will they kept customer data? If yes, then how long?

3. Data Encryption

The security of data is also acquired by doing encryption. Encryption is performed in multiple ways such as easy level, middle level, very high or very complex level to secure the data. Cloud computing provider has different choices and decision for the customer to implement and for that they charge cost depending on the selection. For example, for giving access to the cloud, the Secure Socket Layer (SSL) encryption is provided by the vendors, which is a program using Web services APIs. Onwards, when the customer uses the cloud, it is decrypted and stored in the library for further processing and also next time use.

4. Cloud Interoperability

Interoperability gives access to the ability to band two to more systems together for the exchange of information and use that information for further exchange. In the public cloud, systems are closed to each other, but not band to share the information, sometimes it causes a lot to an organization to combine their IT system inside the cloud. To overcome this challenge, organizations and cloud providers have to create interoperable platforms, which enables the delivery of information between them. Many efforts are under observation to solve this matter, but until now this task is a challenging task in cloud computing.

5. Reliability and Availability

Cloud computing using Software as a service infrastructure, brings on-demand software to be provided by vendors. The quality of software needs reliability that customers can access the network at any time by zero downtime. Apple MobileMe cloud service is one of the examples that stores and synchronizes data on different devices, but Apple get embraced when the users are unable to access synchronize data and emails correctly. Some more vendors start introducing desktop applications such as Curl, Adobe AIR, and Google Gears. These solutions help in the absence of the Internet connection and synchronize when available.

6. Cloud Big Data Management

The data store on the cloud is really big data. It contains data in a structured, semi-structured or unstructured format. The data is store from the different spatial and temporal aspects in the cloud (Karim, Soomro, & Aqil Burney, 2018). The management of data in cloud infrastructure has objectives of confidentiality and auditability. Confidentiality of data can be achieved by securing data access using cryptography protocols and auditability can be achieved by securing application from misuse or dispose of, all by using remote attestation techniques. These facts make it difficult to manage with the traditional setup. Cloud providers are using new architectural frameworks like MapReduce, Hadoop, Apache, etc. These frameworks have different file systems like GFS, HDFS to distribute the processing, control the access patterns and securing of data as compared to traditional file systems. In this area, many researchers are working to explore the proper solution.

7. Energy Resource Management

Saving energy can benefit the economics of the data center's and also great environmental support for sustainability. Energy saving for the cloud data center is an important concern because it's estimated the cost of power and cooling increase the cost of total expenditure. The focus is to design efficient systems that will reduce the energy cost of data centers and also meet the environmental standards. The efficient design reduces the CPU speeds, turn off the unused devices by task scheduling and also a trade-off between applications perform and saving energy. Researchers and Global Energy Management Centre (GEMC) are working to gives companies efficient solution techniques for optimizing the cost, usage, and carbon footprint. For this, one concept is marketed named as Green Computing (Tariq Rahim Soomro & Sarwar, 2012).

8. Platform Management

The cloud platform has the challenge to manage the applications at scalable, flexible, and multi-tenant environments because of middleware used in cloud infrastructure. This will not allow the developer to develop, install, and synchronize their application on the cloud. For this purpose, the cloud vendors introduce the Platform as a Service (PaaS) infrastructure on which a developer or programmer can build his/her application and make it available to other users of an organization (intranet users). All the basic support is already configured in the platform that helps a lot in the development.

9. Server Consolidation

Server consolidation provides resource utilization, decreasing of power and maintaining the cooling requirements. This process is an efficient process, which maximizes resource and minimizes the energy consumption in the cloud environment. A live VM technique is usually used to maintain the consolidation process. This helps to switch off the unused server, so energy consumption will be saved. Many more heuristics are applying to solve this problem.

Figure 8. Shows the countries current cloud infrastructure usage and future usage ("Future of cloud computing: 5 insights from new global research | Google Cloud Blog," 2019)

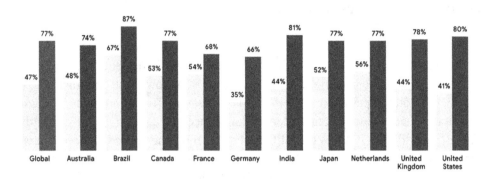

FUTURE OF CLOUD COMPUTING

As cloud computing becoming the need of an organization, the future of cloud computing is very bright. Cloud gives new computing concepts like the Internet of Things (IoT), Edge computing, Fog computing (Aljumah & Ahanger, 2018), (Sehgal & Bhatt, 2018), (Merlino, Dautov, Distefano, & Bruneo, 2019), Serverless environment (Jonas et al., 2019), Green computing (Tariq Rahim Soomro & Sarwar, 2012),, Disaster Recovery as a Services (DRaaS) (Ohlhorst, 2018), Quality of Service (QoS) (Heidari & Buyya, 2019), Mobile Cloud Computing and many more. As per survey analysis of 2019 ("Future of cloud computing: 5 insights from new global research | Google Cloud Blog," 2019) (Google Cloud, n.d.), cloud computing moves to lead enterprise technology over next decade with strong backend support. Globally, 47% of the IT industry is using cloud computing and in the next ten years (2029), this percentage will move to 77% of the usage of the cloud. Many countries are adopting cloud as shown in Figure 8.

Cloud computing focuses on improving the efficiency of the system, innovation, and decision-making, in organizations. Cloud computing services are ubiquitous and available anywhere, anytime, this makes cloud an essential need of an organization for future growing (Heidari & Buyya, 2019), ("Future of cloud computing: 5 insights from new global research | Google Cloud Blog," 2019), (Ahmad et al., 2017), (Google Cloud, n.d.), (Tariq Rahim Soomro & Sarwar, 2012), (Mirashe & Kalyankar, 2010).

CONCLUSION

This chapter of the book is emphases on Cloud Computing. In this authors, covers basic knowledge about cloud computing with the prior exploration of how cloud computing gets into the IT industry. Cloud computing has different types of architecture and types, which contains many challenges phased by the cloud providers and the solution to these challenges give a secure future of cloud computing. Readers will learn enough about cloud computing to explore more knowledge about cloud and usages of cloud in daily life. Before reading this chapter, if the reader doesn't have any knowledge about cloud then all knowledge is here and if readers are known to cloud, then again readers can explore more areas of cloud to work around.

Cloud computing is a buzz word of the new era of computing and coin by Ramnath Chellappa in 1997 but gets populated in 21 Century. Cloud means using resources like developing, managing, storing, analyzing data through the Internet at a vendor location, which seems to be unknown for customers or organizations. Cloud computing gives benefits over traditional systems of cost and management of the data center. In cloud computing, users can only pay to use the services and cloud providers are maintaining all requirements at their ends. For enterprise organizations or small business organizations, the cloud provides different cost packages based on infrastructures like Software as a Service (SaaS), Platform as a Service (PaaS), and Infrastructure as a Service (IaaS) and different types of cloud such as Public, Private, Hybrid, and Community. These enhancements work for customers or organizations to get benefits by reducing expenditure cost, utilization and achieve more profit. Cloud uses middleware to address the customer request. Cloud computing has task scheduler that schedule user applications or programs at a proper time interval, which customer demands and auto-load balancer that helps in balancing the application load on multiple devices, so the user can have the fast and correct information. There are different cloud providers available in the market such as Google Cloud, Amazon Web Server (AWS), IBM Cloud, Microsoft Azure, etc. They are helping to make cloud environments more reliable and scalable in the market. Many applications are available online to be accessible and paid according to the use of them like E-learning Portal, Data Centers, and Disaster recovery systems. The cloud gives many benefits, but also it has some challenges that are under the development phase and many companies with researchers are working on them. Security, access control and privacy of data is a big challenge for cloud providers to maintain with other more as data cryptography, interoperability of application or platform between servers for internal users of an organization, resources management, energy management, server level arguments parsing, and many more. As the cloud becomes the need of an organization, the future of cloud is very bright as it is giving a new concept of the Internet of Things (IoT), Edge computing, Fog computing,

Disaster Recovery system. Many companies are using cloud computing and some of them are still more towards cloud computing. Researchers and companies are joining together for the enhancement of cloud computing and cloud computing giving more areas to explore.

REFERENCES

Aazam, M., Harras, K. A., & Zeadally, S. (2019). Fog Computing for 5G Tactile Industrial Internet of Things: QoE-Aware Resource Allocation Model. *IEEE Transactions on Industrial Informatics*, *15*(5), 3085–3092. doi:10.1109/TII.2019.2902574

Agarwal, M. (2017). *Cloud Computing : A Paradigm Shift in the Way of Computing*. doi:10.5815/ijmecs.2017.12.05

Ahmad, I., Bakht, H., & Mohan, U. (2017). Cloud Computing – A Comprehensive Definition. *Journal of Computing and Management Studies*, *1*(1). Retrieved from https://journals.indexcopernicus.com/api/file/viewByFileId/234155.pdf

Aljumah, A., & Ahanger, T. A. (2018). Fog computing and security issues: A review. *2018 7th International Conference on Computers Communications and Control (ICCCC)*, 237–239. 10.1109/ICCCC.2018.8390464

Amazon. (2019). *Amazon - Cloud Products*. Retrieved April 15, 2019, from Amazon Web Services website: https://aws.amazon.com/products/?nc2=h_m1

10 . Best Learning Management Systems For Your Company. (n.d.). Retrieved April 25, 2019, from https://learning-management.financesonline.com/top-10-learning-management-software-solutions-for-your-company/

Bojanova, I., & Zhang, J. (2013). *Guest editors' introduction*. Retrieved from www.hibu.com

Borko Furht, A. E. (2010). *Handbook of Cloud*. doi:10.1007/978-1-4419-6524-0

Briscoe, G., & Marinos, A. (2009). Digital Ecosystems in the Clouds: Towards Community Cloud Computing. *3rd IEEE International Conference on Digital Ecosystems and Technologies (DEST 2009)*, 103–108. Retrieved from https://arxiv.org/pdf/0903.0694.pdf

Burney, A. M. A., Asif, M., & Abbas, Z. (2016). Forensics Issues in Cloud Computing. *Forensics Issues in Cloud Computing Article in Journal of Computer and Communications*, *4*, 63–69. doi:10.4236/jcc.2016.410007

Chellappa, R. (1997). *Cloud computing: an Emerging paradigm for computing.* Dallas, TX: INFORMS.

Chong, Y. N. (2019). Cloud Computing Challenges in a General Perspective. *Journal of Computing and Management Studies, 3.* Retrieved from https://64243b79-a-62cb3a1a-s-sites.googlegroups.com/site/jcomandman/NYC1319.pdf?attachauth=ANoY7cpjpe_BJkPXryTjeGoKmFInLc1svcZgVi3YHbpmKciM65WNCc_gYPdNSzs5jNaAa5UGOinNbxpNUmijXcxh2CfD0aAjt3_6IiUznVmi548SdKo235rNmchw56ps9in45z-Q8J3IjXqmHegSzVPRmduNdr0O442

Choosing a Cloud Platform | Managed Cloud by Rackspace. (n.d.). Retrieved April 15, 2019, from https://www.rackspace.com/cloud

Cloud, G. (n.d.). *Future of Cloud Computing Survey.* Retrieved April 25, 2019, from https://cloud.google.com/future-cloud-computing/

Cloud Computing and its Evolution Over Time 1969 to 2015. (n.d.). Retrieved April 1, 2019, from https://infooptics.com/cloud-computing-evolution-time/

Cloud Computing History timeline | Timetoast timelines. (n.d.). Retrieved April 1, 2019, from https://media.timetoast.com/timelines/cloud-computing-history

Cloud Marketplace - Hybrid Cloud Computing | Dell EMC US. (n.d.). Retrieved April 15, 2019, from https://www.dellemc.com/en-us/cloud/hybrid-cloud-computing/index.htm

Cloud Service Provider Resources from Intel. (n.d.). Retrieved April 15, 2019, from https://www.intel.com/content/www/us/en/cloud-computing/cloud-service-provider-resources.html

Data Center Providers. (n.d.). Retrieved April 25, 2019, from https://www.datacenters.com/providers

Dhar, P. (2012). *Cloud computing and its applications in the world of networking.* Retrieved from www.IJCSI.org

Dynasis. (n.d.). *Cloud-Computing-Public-Private-and-Hybrid.* Retrieved from www.DynaSis.com/ITility

EM360. (2018). *Top 10 most interesting data centre providers in the world | EM360.* Retrieved April 25, 2019, from https://www.em360tech.com/tech-news/top-ten/top-10-interesting-data-centre-providers-world/

Erl, T., Puttini, R., & Mahmood, Z. (2013). *Cloud computing : concepts, technology, & architecture*. Retrieved from https://books.google.com.pk/books/about/Cloud_Computing.html?id=czCiJ6sbhpAC&source=kp_book_description&redir_esc=y

Foote. (2017). *A Brief History of Cloud Computing*. Retrieved April 10, 2019, from DATAVERSITY website: https://www.dataversity.net/brief-history-cloud-computing/

Future of cloud computing: 5 insights from new global research | Google Cloud Blog. (2019). Retrieved April 27, 2019, from Google website: https://cloud.google.com/blog/topics/research/future-of-cloud-computing-5-insights-from-new-global-research

García, A. L., & Cusumano, M. A. (2006). *The Evolution of the Cloud The Work, Progress and Outlook of Cloud Infrastructure*. Retrieved from https://dspace.mit.edu/bitstream/handle/1721.1/100311/932065967-MIT.pdf;sequence=1

Gorelik, E. (2013). *Cloud Computing Models*. Retrieved from http://web.mit.edu/smadnick/www/wp/2013-01.pdf

Heidari, S., & Buyya, R. (2019). Quality of Service (QoS)-driven resource provisioning for large-scale graph processing in cloud computing environments: Graph Processing-as-a-Service (GPaaS). *Future Generation Computer Systems, 96*, 490–501. doi:10.1016/j.future.2019.02.048

Hill, R. (2013). Guide to Cloud Computer - Principles and Practice. Computer Communications and Networks. doi:10.1007/978-1-4613-1041-9

Hille, M., Klemm, D., & Lemmermann, L. (2017). *Cloud Computing: Vendor & Service Provider Comparison*. Retrieved from https://www.reply.com/Documents/Crisp_Vendor_Universe_Cloud Computing_250118_REPLY_englischeVersion_FINAL.pdf

Hod, Ss., & Professor, C. S. E. A., & Sri Venkateswara, M. (2012). Cloud computing : SAAS. *GESJ: Computer Science and Telecommunications, 4*(36). Retrieved from https://fenix.tecnico.ulisboa.pt/downloadFile/1126518382178096/1986.pdf

Huang, C.-Y., Hsu, P.-C., & Tzeng, G.-H. (2012). *Evaluating Cloud Computing Based Telecommunications Service Quality Enhancement by Using a New Hybrid MCDM Model*. doi:10.1007/978-3-642-29977-3_52

Huang, D., & Wu, H. (2017). *Mobile cloud computing : foundations and service models.* Retrieved from https://books.google.com.pk/books/about/Mobile_Cloud_Computing.html?id=1q2fAQAACAAJ&source=kp_book_description&redir_esc=y

Huth, A., & Cebula, J. (2011). *The Basics of Cloud Computing.* Retrieved from http://csrc.nist.gov/publications/drafts/800-145/Draft-SP-800-145_cloud-definition.pdf

Ian Mitchell, J. A. (n.d.). *Cloud Security- The definitive guide to managing risk in the new ICT landscape.* Academic Press.

IBM Cloud Team. (2019). *IBM Cloud services | IBM Cloud.* Retrieved April 15, 2019, from IBM website: https://www.ibm.com/cloud/services

Info, J. D., & Deyo, J. (2008). *Software as a Service (SaaS) A look at the migration of applications to the web.* Retrieved from http://www.isy.vcu.edu/~jsutherl/Info658/SAAS-JER.pdf

Jadeja, Y., & Modi, K. (2012). Cloud computing - Concepts, architecture, and challenges. *2012 International Conference on Computing, Electronics, and Electrical Technologies, ICCEET 2012,* 877–880. 10.1109/ICCEET.2012.6203873

Jajodia, S., Kant, K., Samarati, P., Singhal, A., Swarup, V., & Wang, C. (2014). Securing Mission-Centric Operations in the Cloud. Secure Cloud Computing. doi:10.1007/978-1-4614-9278-8

Jonas, E., Schleier-Smith, J., Sreekanti, V., Tsai, C.-C., Khandelwal, A., Pu, Q., … Gonzalez, J. E. (2019). *Cloud Programming Simplified: A Berkeley View on Serverless Computing.* Academic Press.

Karim, S., Soomro, T. R., & Aqil Burney, S. M. (2018). *Spatiotemporal Aspects of Big Data.* Applied Computer Systems. doi:10.2478/acss-2018-0012

Kavis, M. (2014). *Architecting the cloud : design decisions for cloud computing service models* (1st ed.). SaaS, PaaS, and IaaS. doi:10.1002/9781118691779

Kumar, M. (2014). Software as a service for efficient Cloud Computing. *International Journal of Research in Engineering and Technology, 3*(1), 2321–7308. Retrieved from http://www.ijret.org

Kumar, N., Kumar Kushwaha, S., & Kumar, A. (2014). Cloud Computing Services and its Application Nitin. *Advance in Electronic and Electric Engineering, 4*(1), 107–112. Retrieved from http://www.ripublication.com/aeee.htm

Lele, A. (2019a). Cloud Computing. In *Disruptive Technologies for the Militaries and Security* (pp. 165–185). Systems and Technologies. doi:10.1007/978-981-13-3384-2_10

Lele, A. (2019b). Cloud computing. In *Smart Innovation*. Systems and Technologies. doi:10.1007/978-981-13-3384-2_10

Lenart, A. (2011). *ERP in the Cloud – Benefits, and Challenges.* doi:10.1007/978-3-642-25676-9_4

Liu, K., Wang, H., & Yao, Y. (2016). On storing and retrieving geospatial big-data in the cloud. *Proceedings of the Second ACM SIGSPATIAL International Workshop on the Use of GIS in Emergency Management - EM-GIS '16.* 10.1145/3017611.3017627

Merlino, G., Dautov, R., Distefano, S., & Bruneo, D. (2019). Enabling Workload Engineering in Edge, Fog, and Cloud Computing through OpenStack-based Middleware. *ACM Transactions on Internet Technology, 19*(2), 1–22. doi:10.1145/3309705

Mike, W. (2019). *Best cloud backup of 2019 | TechRadar.* Retrieved April 25, 2019, from https://www.techradar.com/news/best-cloud-backup

Mirashe, S. P., & Kalyankar, N. V. (2010). Cloud Computing. *Communications of the ACM, 51*(7), 9. doi:10.1145/358438.349303

Munz, F. (2011). *Middleware and cloud computing.* Retrieved from https://books.google.com.pk/books/about/Middleware_and_Cloud_Computing.html?id=xStaYgEACAAJ&source=kp_book_description&redir_esc=y

Nate, D. (2019). *Best cloud storage of 2019: free, paid and business options | TechRadar.* Retrieved April 25, 2019, from https://www.techradar.com/news/the-best-cloud-storage

Nazir, M., Bhardwaj, N., Chawda, R., & Mishra, R. (2015). *Cloud Computing: Current Research Challenges.* doi:10.9790/0661/0811422

Neto, P. (2011). Demystifying Cloud Computing. *Proceeding of Doctoral Symposium on Informatics Engineering, 24*, 16–21.

Nguyen, T. D., Nguyen, T. T. T., & Misra, S. (2014). *Cloud-Based ERP Solution for Modern Education in Vietnam.* doi:10.1007/978-3-319-12778-1_18

Nicholas, F. (2019). *Best disaster recovery service | TechRadar.* Retrieved April 25, 2019, from https://www.techradar.com/best/best-disaster-recovery-service

Nick Antonopoulos, L. G. (2010). *Cloud Computing - Principles, Systems, and Applications.* Springer. doi:10.1007/978-1-84996-241-4

Ning, Z., Kong, X., Xia, F., Hou, W., & Wang, X. (2019). Green and Sustainable Cloud of Things: Enabling Collaborative Edge Computing. *IEEE Communications Magazine, 57*(1), 72–78. doi:10.1109/MCOM.2018.1700895

Ohlhorst, F. J. (2018). *The Best Disaster Recovery-as-a-Service (DRaaS) Solutions for 2019.* Retrieved April 25, 2019, from https://www.pcmag.com/roundup/342348/the-best-disaster-recovery-as-a-service-draas-solutions

Piper, B., & Clinton, D. (2019). *AWS certified solutions architect : study guide : Associate (SAA-C01) exam* (2nd ed.). Retrieved from https://books.google.com.pk/books/about/AWS_Certified_Solutions_Architect_Study.html?id=ocmGDwAAQBAJ&source=kp_book_description&redir_esc=y

Products & Services | Google Cloud. (n.d.). Retrieved April 1, 2019, from https://cloud.google.com/products/

Qian, L., Luo, Z., Du, Y., & Guo, L. (2009). *Cloud Computing: An Overview.* Springer. doi:10.1007/978-3-642-10665-1_63

Rafaels, R. (2015). *Cloud computing : from beginning to end, cloud technology, design, and migration methodologies explained* (revised). Retrieved from https://books.google.com.pk/books/about/Cloud_Computing.html?id=dGFWrgEACAAJ&source=kp_book_description&redir_esc=y

Rashid, A., & Chaturvedi, A. (2019). Cloud Computing Characteristics and Services: A Brief Review Proposing an Innovative Approach for Dynamic Resource Scaling Especially in Multi-tenancy Cases On Cloud Networks View project Cloud Computing Characteristics and Services: A Brief Review. *International Journal of Computer Sciences and Engineering.* doi:10.26438/ijcse/v7i2.421426

Riahi, G. (2015). E-learning systems based on cloud computing: A review. *Procedia Computer Science, 62*(Scse), 352–359. doi:10.1016/j.procs.2015.08.415

Sareen, P. (2013). Cloud Computing: Types, Architecture, Applications, Concerns, Virtualization, and Role of IT Governance in Cloud. *International Journal of Advanced Research in Computer Science and Software Engineering, 3.* Retrieved from www.ijarcsse.com

Sehgal, N. K., & Bhatt, P. C. P. (2018). Cloud computing: Concepts and practices. In *Cloud Computing.* Concepts and Practices. doi:10.1007/978-3-319-77839-6_3

Soomro, T. R., & Wahba, H. (2010). Perspectives of cloud computing: An overview. *14th International Business Information Management Association Conference, IBIMA 2010, 2*, 631–637. Retrieved from http://www.scopus.com/inward/record.url?eid=2-s2.0-84905099773&partnerID=40&md5=f69f5d8565b11d01a6c44676249ac1dd

Soomro, T. R., & Sarwar, M. (2012). Green Computing : From Current to Future Trends. *International Journal of Social, Behavioral, Educational, Economic, Business and Industrial Engineering, 6*(3), 326–329. Retrieved from http://waset.org/Publications?p=63

Sullivan, D. (2010). *The Definitive Guide to Cloud Computing* (Vol. 1). Retrieved from http://www.realtimepublishers.com/book?id=157

Systems Kerridge Commercial. (2016). *A History of Cloud Computing Timeline*. Retrieved March 28, 2019, from Industry Insights website: https://blog.kerridgecs.com/a-history-of-cloud-computing-timeline

technavio. (2018). *Top 10 Data Center Companies in the World 2018 | Global Data Center Market Report - Technavio*. Retrieved April 25, 2019, from https://blog.technavio.com/blog/top-10-data-center-companies

The Four Types of Cloud Computing Models. (n.d.). Retrieved April 15, 2019, from https://www.paranet.com/blog/bid/128265/The-Four-Types-of-Cloud-Computing-Models

Types of Cloud Computing Explained | GlobalDots. (n.d.). Retrieved April 15, 2019, from https://www.globaldots.com/cloud-computing-types-of-cloud/

White, C. (2013). *Cloud computing timeline illustrates cloud's past, predicts its future*. Retrieved April 10, 2019, from TechTarget website: https://searchcloudcomputing.techtarget.com/feature/Cloud-computing-timeline-illustrates-clouds-past-predicts-its-future

White, T. (2015). Hadoop: The definitive guide. In *Online* (4th ed.; Vol. 54). Academic Press.

Wittig, M., Wittig, A., & Whaley, B. (2018). *Amazon Web Services in action* (2nd ed.). Retrieved from https://books.google.com.pk/books/about/Amazon_Web_Services_in_Action.html?id=-LRotAEACAAJ&source=kp_book_description&redir_esc=y

Zhan, Z.-H., Liu, X.-F., Gong, Y.-J., Zhang, J., Chung, H. S.-H., & Li, Y. (2015). Cloud Computing Resource Scheduling and a Survey of Its Evolutionary Approaches. *ACM Computing Surveys, 47*(4), 1–33. doi:10.1145/2788397

KEY TERMS AND DEFINITIONS

Application Program Interface (API): Is a tool for building routines, software, and protocols for applications. API helps in software interaction between different components.

Data Analyzer: Is a process of cleaning the data using analytical tools. Collection of data from various sources is gathered and analyzed to make a proper decision. Some methods are business intelligence, data mining, decision support system, and text mining.

Edge Computing: Is referring to the infrastructure that is present close to the original source of data and edge is develop for the solution to an enterprise environment. The edge technique is far away from the centralized cloud structure because of this data lost is very much less in this environment.

Fog Computing: Is created by Cisco company. It is a decentralized architecture between data source and cloud. Fog is similar to Edge computing, but fog gives benefits and power access of cloud to the users.

Green Computing: Refers to the building of computer and resources in such a manner that an eco-friendly environment will be created, which reduces the carbon footprint of computers and resource use by them from the environment.

Internet of Things (IoT): Is a term used to connect different devices through the internet. IoT gives life to electronic devices by embedding sensors, internet connectivity in them. These devices are automatically controlled or remotely operate according to built-in functions.

Middleware: Was introduced in 1968 but get a boost in the 1980s, as software that links/band two applications together. It makes life easier for a developer. For example, newly created application band together with a legacy application. Its services are beyond the capacity of the operating system.

Quality of Services (QoS): Is a technique used for managing the data. It reduces the loss of packet, dormancy, frequency rate, delay, and jitter over the network.

Service-Oriented Architecture (SOA): Is a collection of services provided to communicate with each other.

Ubiquitous: Means it seems to be everywhere. It is a term used in the business world for having the same technology used in all companies.

Virtual Private Network (VPN): Is a programming method that encrypts the public internet connection to a secure private network. VPN gives benefit over the public infrastructure by securing the resource to be used on sharing.

Chapter 2
Cloud Enhances Agile Software Development

Saikat Gochhait

 https://orcid.org/0000-0003-4583-9208

Symbiosis Institute of Digital and Telecom Management, Symbiosis International University, India

Shariq Aziz Butt

 https://orcid.org/0000-0002-5820-4028

University of Lahore, Pakistan

Tauseef Jamal

 https://orcid.org/0000-0003-4965-0322

PIEAS University, Pakistan

Arshad Ali

University of Lahore, Pakistan

ABSTRACT

The software industries follow some patterns (i.e., process model to develop any software product). Agile methodology is the most famous and used process model. It is a trend to develop efficient software products with high client satisfaction. In this chapter, the authors discuss agile methodology and its components, benefits, and drawbacks while using the cloud computing in agile software development, existing frameworks for agile-cloud combination, and some security measures.

DOI: 10.4018/978-1-7998-1294-4.ch002

CLOUD COMPUTING

Introduction

The cloud computing is the most trendy domain for e-Business due to its services that facilitate the customers. These customers include large scale organizations, IT experts, Data Storage, and handling industries and e-commerce businesses. Now cloud computing is emerging with many fields like smart health, mobile e-commerce, online education systems, and social business interactions. Cloud computing is playing an enormous role in software development due to its inimitable features that make the software development efficient. These features include data storage, use of servers, network infrastructures, data security, pay as per use, the data controller and use of hardware and software tools. The pay as per use is the most owing feature that enhances cloud adoption in industries. The second reason is, the user only needs to pay for services that use not for the entire package and it is the main reason for the organization's shift on the cloud (Qureshi, 2015 ; Pandey, 2009). For accessing these services the cloud computing has different infrastructures that include the three types of clouds and three types of services platforms. These three clouds types are public cloud, private cloud, and hybrid cloud and three types of services are IaaS (Infrastructure as a Service), PaaS (Platform as a Service) and SaaS (Software as a Service). The combination of these services and cloud types has a great impact on cloud adoption (Buyya, 2011).

Cloud Services

Figure 1 is explaining the cloud's services with facilities that the cloud provides to organizations. Every service of the cloud has different facility and support for single user and organizations. The **SaaS** provides the user different types of services as like incorporates enterprise services (ERP), digital signature, CRM applications, the board applications (explicit to coordinated associations financial support, increase sales, seek instruments and so on. This service is used when the information is confidential for the organizations. The **PaaS** supports the consumer for development applications, testing applications, and database integrations. The **IaaS** is a model that gives customers the likelihood to store data, data backup & recovery, services management, capacity, organize resources (which might be utilized to run any software product, including working frameworks) and platform hosting (Leaf, 2011).

The approach these services the cloud has 3 types of infrastructure, **Public Cloud**: this infrastructure is publically available and owned by the cloud service provider, **Private Cloud:** this infrastructure is owned for a single organization and managed by organization internal or external. The **Hybrid Cloud:** is the combination of these

Figure 1. Cloud Services to Consumers (Leaf, 2011)

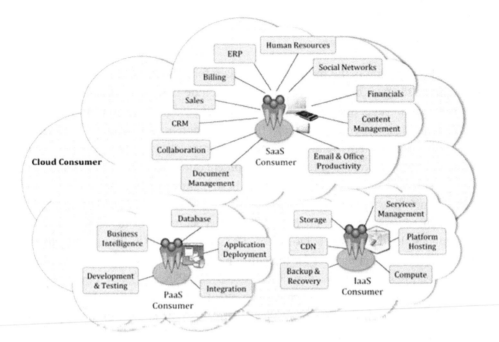

cloud infrastructures. The infrastructure is formed by at least two public networks or on another hand private cloud interconnected to guarantee the transportability of information and applications as shown in Figure 2 (Leaf, 2011 ; Xu, 2012).

PROS AND CONS OF CLOUD

Benefits of The Cloud for e-Commerce Industries

The cloud computing provides different types of benefits that engage the users to use cloud's resources. Some of these benefits are as follows:

1. It's providing the cost and scale benefit to e-commerce and global business industries. The cost benefits directly influence the scale benefit i;e means that when the organization increases the resource scale than the cost increase. But it still facilitates the industries in term of money saving (Zhang, 2014 ; Uscatu, 2014).

Figure 2. Types of cloud networks (Petznick, 2018)

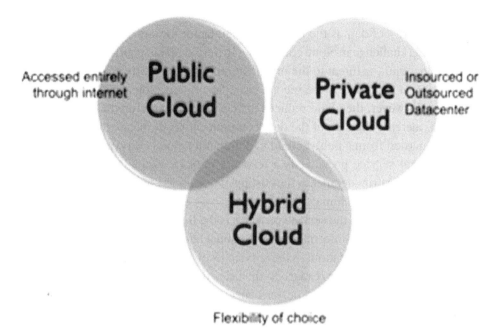

2. Cloud also provides a platform for industries to share there processes, application and organizational integration. It supports within the organization and with other different organizations to integrate the processes that they wish to collaborate (Zhang, 2014).
3. Currently, cloud computing is providing next-generation architectures for storing data, new software to use, network-centric, server-centric, computing speed and virtualization space (Abbadi, 2011).
4. Cloud computing provides different types of service providers with choices for users with agility
5. (Petznick, 2018).
6. The most owing benefit of cloud computing for industries is the adaptation to the market need. It means that when an organization needs to compete with the market competition then the cloud can support to meet these requirements (Jin.Y, 2017).
7. Cloud computing facilitates the business to consolidation i;e helps the organization to do business in a precise way (Johson, 2015).
8. Cloud computing facilitates the e-Commerce business such as Amazon to target the new clients and get knowledge about the client's current requirements (Johson, 2015).

Disadvantages of The Cloud for Ecommerce Industries

1. The security of data is the most important factor for any e-Business and it is still a big challenge in cloud computing. In the cloud the security issues include data loss and the threat to the organization's data and software (Sood, 2012).
2. Costing in the cloud is the second issue for organizations and for individual users. However, the cloud reduces the cost of infrastructure but on the other hand, increase the cost of the data communication. It means the cost of data transmission from a public cloud to community cloud (Buyya, 2017).
3. The cloud service provider is a resource pool i;e virtualization and multi-tenancy. The provider makes the costing of resources complex than the regular data centers (Tsukishima, 2009).
4. Another issue with the service provider is the high-security risk. The service provider can reveal information for personal benefits (Pathak, D, 2016).
5. The issue for organizations is the service level agreement. The cloud users do not have control on the resources; the users do not need to ensure the quality, availability, reliability, and performance of these resources when consumers have migrated their core business functions onto their entrusted cloud. In other words, it is vital for consumers to obtain guarantees from providers on service delivery (Lucredio, D, 2012).
6. The organizations have reliability issue as well, the cloud computing services suffered from few hours' outages (Lucredio, D, 2012).

AGILE SOFTWARE DEVELOPMENT

Introduction

There is a major consensus that the nature of the software process has a great impact either positive or negative on the quality of the software applications. Henceforth, enhancing process's quality helps in developing efficient software applications on time and within the cost with less imperfection. The numerous software industries are directing software process enhancement activities to upgrade their development in creating software. Currently, the agile methodology is using globally in software industries to develop software applications. It is due to agile's unique features like product development within quality, cost, deadline, meet user requirements, client satisfaction and trust in the team(s). The agile methodology is complete with its widely followed components such as Scrum methodology, Extreme Programming (XP) and Test-driven development (TDD) (Butt, S. A, 2016). The agile was introduced to overcome the challenges from the efficient software development. All previous software development life cycles have some issues to meet the client's requirements and to develop qualitative products. However, the agile main features are client satisfaction, meet user requirements and promote the client-developer interaction, frequent delivery of sprints to get feedback from the client and team coordination to produce the qualitative products (Darwish, 2015).

Agile Components

Scrum Methodology

The scrum methodology is the most useful component of agile methodology to manage and develop projects. It delivers the product in different small sprints. The main objective of the project splitting into small iterations is to get feedback from the client frequently, allow change request and promote client-developer communication. The scrum methodology improves the requirement gathering mechanism in agile software development. The elicited requirements by the product owner (stakeholder) are stored in product backlog as user stories. The developers select the user stories from the product backlog and start the sprint planning as shown in Figure 3. The scrum also supports testing during the sprint phase (Jaiswal, 2015; Butt, S. A, 2016).

Issues and solutions [19]

- Un-stability is an issue in distributed and large scale software development for industries. The cloud makes the development stable for the organization by providing a single platform as a service.
- The distributed scrum project development issue is the lack of documentation sharing among teams but the cloud computing facilitates them to share and store a document at single place private cloud.
- The scrum methodology faces communication and coordination issue between teams in distributed project development. Cloud computing facilitates the scrum methodology to overcome this issue with social-cloud services.
- Anytime the developers can get feedback from the client. Additionally, the developers can also get feedback from other developers and teams.

Extreme Programming (XP)

Extreme programming supports the four major values in agile methodology like communications, simplicity, feedback, and courage. The XP performs four basic activities coding, testing, listening and debugging. These all values and factors lead to 12 core practices of agile methodology such as planning game, small sprint

Figure 3. Scrum methodology

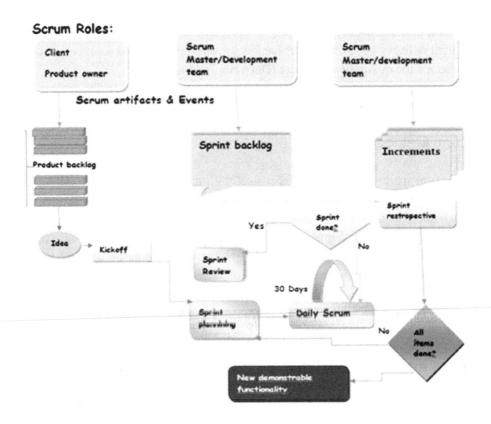

releases, metaphors, product design, testing, refactoring, pair programming, collective ownership, continuous integration, 40-hour weeks, on-site customers, and coding standards. The XP allows developing products in a timely manner (Guha, 2010; Qureshi, 2015).

Issues and Solution

- Cloud computing facilitates Extreme Programming in product designing to make it reusable.
- Cloud computing helps the XP for product planning and development.

Test Driven Development (TDD)

This component of the agile methodology ensures the product quality and makes the final product free from errors and faults. In the TDD short test cases are developed simultaneously with the sprint development according to the user stories in that sprint. These short test cases ensure the completion of user stories in a sprint and make sure that the product is developed according to user requirements. The TDD helps to remove all bugs from the product during iterations delivery to client (Alagarsamy, 2012; Juristo, 2016).

Issues and Solutions

- In the distributed development the testing and integration of sprints is an issue. The cloud computing resolves this issue by facilitating users to store code, test code, and merge sprints at single place.
- Cloud computing also facilitates TDD with different testing tools offered by service providers. The organizations can rent any testing tool according to the application.
- The use of the cloud can reduce software testing cost.

AGLIE-CLOUD BASED DEVELOPMENT

Impact of Cloud on Agile Development

The software development needs efficient processes to develop quality products with less use of resources i.e., tool and hardware. The software industries are interested to get more profit from business with less expenditure. The agile methodology has a great combination with cloud computing to enhance software development at less cost. The main purpose of merging is to remove some issues present in agile software development. The cloud is improving the agile development processes such as testing, run time feedback, data storage, coordination, and communication. As agile always allows the client to give change request and can also give new requirement at any stage of the project therefore over the cloud services it becomes easy to manage the project. The agile-cloud combination is shown in Figure 4 (Butt, S. A, 2016).

Figure 4. Agile-Cloud Combination (Butt, S. A, 2016)

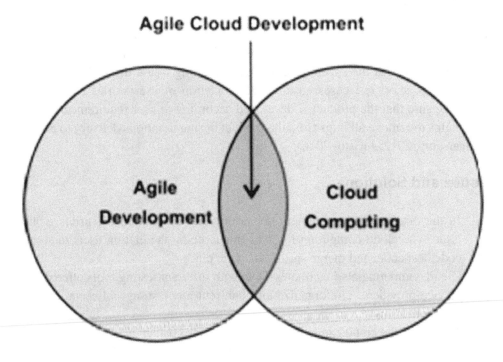

Benefits and Challenges of Agile-Cloud

Agile-Cloud Benefits

The Agile-Cloud Combination has some benefits that increase the adoption of cloud in agile software industries which are as follows (Colmeiro, 2012):

1. The major benefit of cloud computing to software industries is the cost control of software development. As this cost includes the hardware cost, installation cost, effort cost, licensed tool's cost, and product support tool's cost. Cloud computing facilitates agile development to overcome these costs by renting these tools and services. Now the software industries only have to pay as per use of services and tools and not need to buy till the project completion (Colmeiro, 2012).
2. Cloud computing facilitates agile industries in distributed software development. In the distributed development the major issue faced by the teams is communication that cloud computing assists with the cloud-based social technologies. These cloud social technologies include video conference,

knowledge management, and web portals. This cloud service facilitates the scrum methodology in daily basis communication between the developers and teams located in distributed environments (Alagarsamy, 2012).

3. The cloud computing supports the agile software industries to store data on the cloud as much they need to store. The storing capacity can easily be increased on the cloud by only pay extra but still, the storing cost on cloud is less as compared to their own storage cost (Dhar, S, 2012).

4. Cloud computing supports the agile methodology in the iteration's testing. In agile methodology, the iterations are tested with the use of the TDD concept. In the TDD the tests are made according to user stories simultaneously in each iteration. Cloud computing facilitates agile testing with the TaaS (Testing as Service). The TaaS provides different kinds of testing tools as per the need of a product. Hence the organizations do not need to buy a licensed new testing tool for each project; simply the organizations can pay TaaS for testing each project according to test requirement. TaaS improves product quality before product deployment (Khan, M. M, 2016).

5. Cloud computing makes agile development a parallel activity where the tasks can be completed efficiently and effectively (Siau, K, (2005).

6. The cloud computing helps agile methodology in instant delivery of iteration to the client for getting feedback. The client simply uses the public cloud infrastructure to verify the requirement's completion in every iteration (Sato, M, 2010).

7. Cloud computing builds many platforms as external services available for agile development. These services are related to project management issues and automated testing environments. These services for agile development are accessible on the cloud as SaaS (Tanner, M, 2016).

8. Cloud computing also provides a code merging and branching facility to agile development. The code merging and branching include the copy of many versions of build and development stages. The agile industries do not need to buy additional servers for these reasons (Khan, M. F, 2013).

9. The cloud provides different services as tools for agile development teams. These tools include JIRA, Mingle, Rally, Scrum Works, Trac, Version One, and XPlanner. The SaaS provides these tools as services in cloud computing. This cloud service for agile teams facilitates them with 4 benefits; First, these tools are globally accessible by all teams. Second, using the tool team members can easily share information across all teams. Third, these tools are not required to install and deploy internally. Fourth, these tools are scalable i;e agile teams can increase the scale and add new members without degrading the performance of the tool. It also removes team collaboration issue from the Extreme Programming.

10. The cloud-agile combination is improving customer experience in agile development (Krasteva, 2013).
11. Cloud computing provides new infrastructures for agile development (Krasteva, 2013).
12. The cloud helps the agile software industries to target market and find new customers (Butt, S. A, 2017).
13. Cloud computing assists the agile development for productive team utilization with a stable workload (Krasteva, 2013).
14. Time of decision making and to see its consequence is reduced using the cloud-agile combination (Butt, S. A, 2016).
15. The refactoring of an existing application becomes easy with the services of cloud infrastructures in cost-effective ways (Butt, S. A, 2019).

Agile-Cloud Issues

The Agile-Cloud Combination has some drawbacks that influence the less adoption of cloud in agile software industries which are stated below ((Butt, S. A, 2019):

1. The major issue with the agile-cloud combination is the data security of software applications. As some software applications have precious information about the users i.e., banking applications. The banking software application has valuable information of users like credit card, bank account detail and balance information. These applications can't be developed and tested easily with the assistance of cloud services due to security risks that include data loss, threats to data and organization's software (Butt, S. A, 2017).
2. The second major limitation in agile-cloud combination is interoperability during the migration of organizations to cloud computing. It is due to the change in the development environment when migrating to cloud computing. The interoperability issue affects SaaS with other activities. These SaaS activities identify interoperability problems and implement interoperability components. Cloud computing has to provide different services to all organizations to make services compatible for use when they migrate. The migration for the software industries is costly (Cito, 2015).
3. The cloud-agile combination has risk associated with the cloud service provider called a third entity in the cloud computing environment. Cloud computing has many different service providers such as Amazon, Microsoft Azure, and IBM cloud. The service provider can reveal the information for their personal benefits (Hashmi, 2011).

4. The software organizations need 24/7 availability of services, especially when the organizations working are distributed. But they are sometimes not able to provide services due to severe damage. This may lead to a high potential loss for the software industry (Patidar, 2011).

5. The project safety on cloud is difficult because during the development of the team(s) use tools to support project on public cloud, this may lead to disclosing the project code, documentation and configuration data (Singh,S, 2016).

6. The software testing has some issues with cloud computing as different software applications need suitable tools for requirements testing, therefore provide all types of testing tools to organizations is difficult for the cloud. There are some standards for developing any software application. When software organizations merge with the cloud for efficient software development then the cloud does not provide and maintain these standards (Mohagheghi, 2011).

7. While using the cloud the developers face Data Lock-In issue. The data lock-in means that when the developers shift from one cloud to another cloud then the developer face platform flexibility issue. This issue mostly arises when the developer is using the PaaS service of the cloud. The developers face this issue due to service providers in the cloud because every service provider has a different platform, elasticity, flexibility, and type of services to users (Guha, 2010).

FRAMEWORKLS FOR AGILE-CLOUD

In this section, we are explaining the existing frameworks for agile-cloud development. The main objective of these frameworks is to promote the cloud computing adoption in software industries in terms of secure development, reduced development cost, better utilization of the cloud's services and migration to the cloud.

3.3.1 For global distributed agile development, a framework is proposed by authors in (Younas, 2016). The main objective of the framework is to provide developers the software and hardware infrastructure like IDEs to code. The existing framework has four steps to explain the working of the current framework as shown in Figure 5. In the first step, the cloud can facilitate the agile development team by providing different kinds of services and tools such as Axosoft, PlanBox, and Jira. In the second step, the framework guides the organizations to select the platform for development according to the size, business need, and type of application. The third phase of the framework guides the organizations to select the cloud repository. Because in the distributed development a number of developers work on the same project modules, therefore, they need a central tool to merge the code such as GitHub. The fourth

Figure 5. Distributed agile development framework (Younas, 2016)

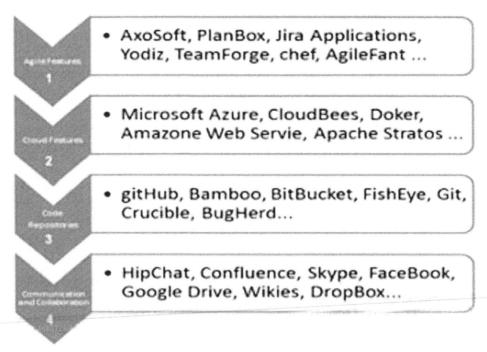

phase of the framework guides the organizations for selection of cloud's platform for efficient developer's communication and collaboration.

2.2.2. In [29], the authors provide a framework with 5 layers to support agile software testing. The framework's first layer includes the testing on a tenant with service contributor layer. The second layer facilitates agile testing to provide test task management support. A tester describes a test scenario. It means that the cloud provides a guest operating system with setting up the facility to test the code. The third layer is a tested resource management layer, which manages the resources for tester from start to end. The fourth layer of the framework provides the test layer with components such as testing service composition, testing service pool, and testing task reduce. The last and fifth layer supports the agile organizations to test the databases as shown in Figure 6.

There are different tools that enhance agile software development with the combination of cloud computing as shown in Table 1.

Figure 6. Five Layers Framework for agile cloud (Banzai, 2010)

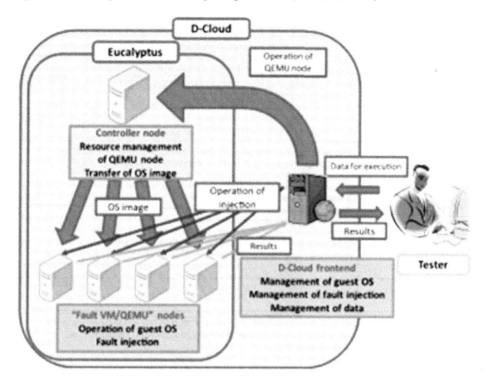

Security Measures:

There are different existing security models to enhance the security of data on the cloud. The objectives of the proposed models are prevention from vulnerable attacks, control data leakage, and modifications, and improving client's and organization's contentment (Sood, 2012).

Un-authorized Server:

In this security endanger an intruder can get access to cloud server as a service provider. As a result of this, an intruder can destroy or modify the data of the user. To prevent the data in this situation, Secure Socket Layer (SSL) certification in this model is used. This certificate secures the data by using the digital signature concept of provider and user to send data on the cloud.

Table 1. Tools for Agile Cloud Development

Tool	Description
Jira software	Project management and issue tracking
Zapier	Connect Axosoft with many other services and tools.
Jenkins	Open source automation server, plug-in to support building, testing, deploying and automation for virtually any project.
Apache Stratos	Provides an environment for developing, test, and run cloud-based applications. PaaS framework to run PHP, MySql, and tomcat.
Salesforce.Com	Enhances the customer and developer relation in agile development by customer relationship management (CRM). It is a platform to control all interactions of client and developer.
Puppet Enterprise	It manages infrastructures patching and configuration of operating systems and devices for agile.
Google App, Engine, Compute Engine	Building scalable web applications, virtual machines, and scalable cloud resources.
Microsoft azure	The integrated tools, pre-built templates, and managed PaaS services.
Amazon Web Service	It facilitates the agile in terms of reliable, scalable, and inexpensive cloud computing services, storage, database, and analytics, application, and deployment services.
Coordination and Communication tools	
HipChat	Provides a private chat infrastructure plus it uses for sharing files.
Confluence	Promotes the teamwork by collaboration, team organizing and discuss work in a team and between teams.
Merge and sharing code tools	
BitBucket	Code collaboration using pull requests and comments. It is used to build and deploy software.
Bamboo	Code Merging.
FishEye	Helps in code finding and tracking of subversions from code repositories.
Crucible	Allows the developer to Peer review the code and improve the code quality.
BugHerd	Supports in the Bug tracking

Brute Force Attack:

Data on the cloud can be attacked by intruders like a brute force attack. It is not difficult to crack using current computers that can crunch huge number combinations rapidly so as to decide each conceivable key in an effort known as a brute force attack. The cloud data can be prevented by using the 128-bit Secure Socket Layer

(SSL) encryption; it makes key size lengthy as compared to the previous size of 40 bits. This lengthy key size is sufficient enough to make the brute force attack useless.

Threat From the Service Provider:

The service provider can also reveal the information for personal benefits. To secure the information from the service provider the best solution is the encryption of data stored on the cloud. Secure Socket Layer (SSL) can secure the communication of data.

Tampering of Data:

In cloud computing un-authorized users can temper data, therefore to secure the data Message Authentication code (MAC) approach can be used. A MAC code is generated by the data owner before sending on a cloud. The receiver verifies the code if the code is same only then the user can integrate data.

CASE STUDY

Netsol Technologies is a Multinational software organization located in Pakistan. The number of employee in the Netsol is more than 1800. Netsol mostly develops smart software technologies for all kinds of industries. It has national as well as international clients ((Butt, S. A, 2017).

Due to economic and technological requirements, the Netsol is also using cloud computing services; in this regard, Netsol has introduced the LeasePak Solution by using the Microsoft Azure cloud. The LeasePak is an end to end portfolio management solution for the US-based finance industry. The LeasePak is used by the Blue Chip auto and equipment finance companies. The LeasePak solution is robust, scalable and highly functional for the automobile leasing industry. The basic objective of the LeasePak solution is to satisfy the client, get new business, meet the client's requirements and make communication easy with the client. The Azure provides a very flexible environment of the cloud for Netsol. The IT persons develop the LeasePak in VB.Net 7.0 and introduce the mAccount solution in LeasePak. The mAccount facilitates the customers to track their project details, contract, payment details, and new project update status. The MAzure facilitates the Netsol clients in terms of scalability, the security of data and a stable environment. The cloud supports Netsol clients to use the technology in a flexible manner. The cloud increases the business value of Netsol in terms of getting new clients. The MAzure reduces the cost of Netsol through this LeasePak solution 90% as stated by the chief founder of the company.

Table 2. Industrial case study of project with agile-cloud combination

Key Attributes	Benefits	Limitation
Customer involvement	√	x
Bandwidth limitations	√	x
Lack of trust	x	√
Project tracking	√	x
Management of change requests from client	√	x
Tools support	√	√
Client Run-time feedback	√	x
Data security	x	x
Cost	√	x

As mentioned in the Table.2 that some benefits and limitations face by the industry while using the cloud-agile combination for development. The major benefits of the software industry is reduction in the cost of development. The cloud has no limitations for the industry related to cost. The cloud also provide support to the team/s to involve the client in the project development. It controls the change of request from the client side and develop project according to client's requirements. The cloud facilitate industry related to bandwidth issue and has no limitation. The major issue that the industry face is the trust on cloud service providers. The cloud do not provide any authentic support to the customers related to security of data. The cloud-agile combination also facilitate the developers to tract project progress, inputs and outputs. The major support of cloud to industry by providing the different tools are in terms of cost, easiness to develop project's contents, easily availability of services, software testing tools and splitting of project in different small iterations. Using the tools on cloud the industry can get run-time feedback from client, which save developers time to complete the project and understand the client requirements.

FUTURE WORK

Cloud-Agile is a great combination to enhance software development. This combination makes software development efficient and facilitates the software industries to make more business. As the agile-cloud has some benefits for development, on the other hand, it also has some challenges that affect cloud adoption in agile industries. Existing work has some frameworks that try to overcome these challenges but still, it is a research domain to introduce new frameworks. The agile-cloud combination has a data security issue that needs to address in new frameworks.

CONCLUSION

The agile software development is getting benefits from cloud services. The major benefit is reduction in cost during the software development and testing. Cloud computing is providing different kind of testing tools to test the software product according to its functionality by TaaS service of cloud. On the other hand the major issue with the cloud adoption in the agile industries is data security. The cloud has less secured environment to protect the customer's data. Existing work include many security frameworks and approaches to secure the data on cloud but have some limitations due to new threats launched by intruders. Therefore there is need to introduce new security approaches to secure the data on cloud.

REFERENCES

Agrawal, D., Das, S., & El Abbadi, A. (2011, March). Big data and cloud computing: current state and future opportunities. In *Proceedings of the 14th International Conference on Extending Database Technology* (pp. 530-533). ACM. 10.1145/1951365.1951432

Almudarra, F., & Qureshi, B. (2015). Issues in adopting agile development principles for mobile cloud computing applications. *Procedia Computer Science, 52,* 1133–1140. doi:10.1016/j.procs.2015.05.131

Almudarra, F., & Qureshi, B. (2015). Issues in adopting agile development principles for mobile cloud computing applications. *Procedia Computer Science, 52,* 1133–1140. doi:10.1016/j.procs.2015.05.131

Banzai, T., Koizumi, H., Kanbayashi, R., Imada, T., Hanawa, T., & Sato, M. (2010, May). D-cloud: Design of a software testing environment for reliable distributed systems using cloud computing technology. In *2010 10th IEEE/ACM International Conference on Cluster, Cloud and Grid Computing* (pp. 631-636). IEEE.

Butt, S. A., Abbas, S. A., & Ahsan, M. (2016). Software development life cycle & software quality measuring types. *Asian Journal of Mathematics and Computer Research*, 112-122.

Butt, S. A. (2016). Study of agile methodology with the cloud. *Pacific Science Review B. Humanities and Social Sciences*, 2(1), 22–28.

Butt, S. A. (2016). Analysis of unfair means cases in computer-based examination systems. *Pacific Science Review B. Humanities and Social Sciences*, 2(2), 75–79.

Butt, S. A., & Jamal, T. (2017). Frequent change request from user to handle cost on project in agile model. *Proc. of Asia Pacific Journal of Multidisciplinary Research*, 5(2), 26–42.

Butt, S. A., Tariq, M. I., Jamal, T., Ali, A., Martinez, J. L. D., & De-La-Hoz-Franco, E. (2019). Predictive Variables for Agile Development Merging Cloud Computing Services. *IEEE Access: Practical Innovations, Open Solutions*, 7, 99273–99282. doi:10.1109/ACCESS.2019.2929169

Buyya, R., Garg, S. K., & Calheiros, R. N. (2011, December). *SLA-oriented resource provisioning for cloud computing: Challenges, architecture, and solutions. In 2011 international conference on cloud and service computing* (pp. 1–10). IEEE.

Cito, J., Leitner, P., Fritz, T., & Gall, H. C. (2015, August). The making of cloud applications: An empirical study on software development for the cloud. In *Proceedings of the 2015 10th Joint Meeting on Foundations of Software Engineering* (pp. 393-403). ACM. 10.1145/2786805.2786826

da Silva, E. A. N., & Lucredio, D. (2012, September). Software engineering for the cloud: A research roadmap. In *2012 26th Brazilian Symposium on Software Engineering* (pp. 71-80). IEEE. 10.1109/SBES.2012.12

Dhar, S. (2012). From outsourcing to Cloud computing: Evolution of IT services. *Management Research Review*, 35(8), 664–675. doi:10.1108/01409171211247677

Erickson, J., Lyytinen, K., & Siau, K. (2005). Agile modeling, agile software development, and extreme programming: The state of research. *Journal of Database Management*, 16(4), 88–100. doi:10.4018/jdm.2005100105

Fucci, D., Erdogmus, H., Turhan, B., Oivo, M., & Juristo, N. (2016). A dissection of the test-driven development process: Does it really matter to test-first or to test-last? *IEEE Transactions on Software Engineering*, 43(7), 597–614. doi:10.1109/TSE.2016.2616877

Ghilic-Micu, B., Stoica, M., & Uscatu, C. R. (2014). Cloud Computing and Agile Organization Development. *Informatica Economica, 18(4).*

Guha, R., & Al-Dabass, D. (2010, December). Impact of web 2.0 and cloud computing platform on software engineering. In *2010 International Symposium on Electronic System Design*(pp. 213-218). IEEE. 10.1109/ISED.2010.48

Guha, R., & Al-Dabass, D. (2010, December). Impact of web 2.0 and cloud computing platform on software engineering. In *2010 International Symposium on Electronic System Design* (pp. 213-218). IEEE. 10.1109/ISED.2010.48

Gupta, G., & Pathak, D. (2016). *Cloud Computing: "Secured Service Provider for data mining*. International Journal Of Engineering And Computer Science.

Haig-Smith, T., & Tanner, M. (2016). Cloud Computing as an Enabler of Agile Global Software Development. *Issues in Informing Science & Information Technology, 13*.

Hashmi, S. I., Clerc, V., Razavian, M., Manteli, C., Tamburri, D. A., Lago, P., ... Richardson, I. (2011, August). Using the cloud to facilitate global software development challenges. In *2011 IEEE Sixth International Conference on Global Software Engineering Workshop* (pp. 70-77). IEEE. 10.1109/ICGSE-W.2011.19

Hentschel, R., Leyh, C., & Petznick, A. (2018). Current cloud challenges in Germany: The perspective of cloud service providers. *Journal of Cloud Computing, 7*(1), 5. doi:10.118613677-018-0107-6

Ibrahim, M. H., & Darwish, N. R. (2015). Investigation of Adherence Degree of Agile Requirements Engineering Practices in Non-Agile Software Development Organizations. *International Journal of Advanced Computer Science and Applications, 6*(1).

Jin, Y., & Wen, Y. (2017). When cloud media meets network function virtualization: Challenges and applications. *IEEE MultiMedia*.

Jinno, M., & Tsukishima, Y. (2009, March). Virtualized optical network (VON) for agile cloud computing environment. In *2009 Conference on Optical Fiber Communication-incudes post-deadline papers* (pp. 1-3). IEEE. 10.1364/OFC.2009. OMG1

Katherine, A. V., & Alagarsamy, K. (2012). Software testing in the cloud platform: A survey. *International Journal of Computers and Applications, 46*(6), 21–25.

Katherine, A. V., & Alagarsamy, K. (2012). Software testing in cloud platform: A survey. *International Journal of Computers and Applications, 46*(6), 21–25.

Krasteva, I., Stavros, S., & Ilieva, S. (2013). Agile model-driven modernization to the service cloud. *The Eighth International Conference on Internet and Web Applications and Services (ICIW 2013)*.

Liu, F., Tong, J., Mao, J., Bohn, R., Messina, J., Badger, L., & Leaf, D. (2011). NIST cloud computing reference architecture. *NIST special publication, 500*(2011), 1-28.

Maciá Pérez, F., Berna-Martinez, J. V., Marcos-Jorquera, D., Lorenzo Fonseca, I., & Ferrándiz Colmeiro, A. (2012). *Cloud agile manufacturing*. Academic Press.

Mansouri, Y., Toosi, A. N., & Buyya, R. (2017). *Cost optimization for dynamic replication and migration of data in cloud data centers*. IEEE Transactions on Cloud Computing.

Mohagheghi, P., & Sæther, T. (2011, July). Software engineering challenges for migration to the service cloud paradigm: Ongoing work in the remics project. In *2011 IEEE World Congress on Services* (pp. 507-514). IEEE. 10.1109/SERVICES.2011.26

Nazir, A., Raana, A., & Khan, M. F. (2013). Cloud Computing ensembles Agile Development Methodologies for Successful Project Development. *International Journal of Modern Education and Computer Science*, 5(11), 28–35. doi:10.5815/ijmecs.2013.11.04

Padilla, R. S., Milton, S. K., & Johnson, L. W. (2015). Components of service value in business to business Cloud Computing. *Journal of Cloud Computing*, 4(1), 15. doi:10.118613677-015-0040-x

Patidar, S., Rane, D., & Jain, P. (2011, December). Challenges of software development on cloud platform. In *2011 World Congress on Information and Communication Technologies* (pp. 1009-1013). IEEE. 10.1109/WICT.2011.6141386

Raj, G., Yadav, K., & Jaiswal, A. (2015, February). Emphasis on testing assimilation using cloud computing for improvised agile SCRUM framework. In *2015 International Conference on Futuristic Trends on Computational Analysis and Knowledge Management (ABLAZE)* (pp. 219-225). IEEE. 10.1109/ABLAZE.2015.7154995

Singh, S., & Chana, I. (2016). A survey on resource scheduling in cloud computing: Issues and challenges. *Journal of Grid Computing*, 14(2), 217–264. doi:10.100710723-015-9359-2

Sood, S. K. (2012). A combined approach to ensure data security in cloud computing. *Journal of Network and Computer Applications*, 35(6), 1831–1838. doi:10.1016/j.jnca.2012.07.007

Vecchiola, C., Pandey, S., & Buyya, R. (2009, December). High-performance cloud computing: A view of scientific applications. In *2009 10th International Symposium on Pervasive Systems, Algorithms, and Networks* (pp. 4-16). IEEE. 10.1109/I-SPAN.2009.150

Xu, X. (2012). From cloud computing to cloud manufacturing. *Robotics and Computer-integrated Manufacturing, 28*(1), 75–86. doi:10.1016/j.rcim.2011.07.002

Younas, M., Ghani, I., Jawawi, D. N., & Khan, M. M. (2016). A Framework for agile development in cloud computing environment. *Journal of Internet Computing and Services 2016.*

Zhang, L., Luo, Y., Tao, F., Li, B. H., Ren, L., Zhang, X., ... Liu, Y. (2014). Cloud manufacturing: A new manufacturing paradigm. *Enterprise Information Systems, 8*(2), 167–187. doi:10.1080/17517575.2012.683812

Chapter 3
Cloud Security in E-Commerce Applications

Shah Rukh Malik
Government College University, Pakistan

Mujahid Rafiq
The Superior University (Defence Road Campus), Lahore, Pakistan

Muhammad Ahmad Kahloon
The Superior College (University Campus), Lahore, Pakistan

ABSTRACT

In this chapter, the authors focus on the most fundamental barrier in the e-commerce application's adoption: security. The most significant or important aspect to explore in cloud computing is how to keep the data secure in the most efficient way with cutting-edge technologies. Cloud computing has taken its place by providing its convenient services like on-demand service, pay-per-use, rapid elasticity, resource pooling, and other lucrative facilities. In this chapter, the authors will firstly describe the introduction related to cloud computing, major characteristics, types, and a few security concerns and issues in cloud computing. Furthermore, they discuss the introduction of e-commerce applications, how it is interlinked with cloud computing, and what the possible threats are. Moreover, what the possible solutions could be are discussed, so that we can secure data on both user side as well as on the server side. The authors suggest some existing solutions at the end of the chapter.

DOI: 10.4018/978-1-7998-1294-4.ch003

INTRODUCTION

E-Commerce has become an essential part of the user's daily life activities. Detailed discussions on E-commerce applications are already available in previous chapters of this book. Just to show the importance of E-commerce applications once the CEO of the famous Company (Amazon.com™), Jeff Bezos said, "I should have 3 million stores on the Web if I have 3 million customers" (Schafer, Konstan, & Riedl, 2001). The understanding related to consumer trust is very much essential for the growth and development of e-commerce but it involves the number of technical issues and challenges including security and privacy (Ahuja, 2000; Feldman, 2000). In the Information Technology domain, cloud computing has become one of the booming technology. Due to elasticity, availability, vast infrastructure and better support for software, cloud technology attracts the developers of e-commerce applications towards it. The main advantages of cloud computing include low-cost infrastructure (Software, Hardware and their license) and some big companies like Microsoft and Google also offer cloud services for free or on very less cost. Despite all benefits, the major concern for the cloud's implementation in the e-commerce domain is the security issue. Security in the cloud includes data security and confidentiality related to privacy(Saleh, 2012). In this chapter, our main focus area is the Security of E-commerce related to the cloud. Transporting sensitive and important data to the cloud data centers and then to maintain its security is the most important concern nowadays. The cloud service provider (CSP) must ensure and responsible to secure and protect data traffic that travels between the application to the cloud data centers. CSP's signs a Service Level Agreement (SLA) with the service user of cloud to certify and ensure the level of security, privacy, and also facilities the user wants.

For a detailed overview of the topic and discussion, this chapter is further divided into different small sub-sections. Section 1 includes details on Cloud Computing, (a) its characteristics, (b) major service providers of cloud, (c) Deployment Models of cloud (d) Service Models of cloud (e) Security Concerns and Issues in Cloud Computing. Section 2 discusses, the Introduction of E-commerce Application and further subdivides into 2 sections (a) E-Commerce application and its relation with cloud and (b) include the Security Concerns in E-Commerce applications. Section 3 is the last section of the chapter that is based on the Solutions of Cloud Security in an E-commerce application.

CLOUD COMPUTING

Cloud computing model enables the network to access shared resources that can be provided on-demand and user can access it anywhere. This shared pool of resources is used by cloud service. Users can use this by signing an SLA with a CSP (Dikaiakos, Katsaros, Mehra, Pallis, & Vakali, 2009). Detailed characteristics and techniques are given below.

a.   **Cloud computing characteristics**

Cloud have different characteristics related to their usage, In this section, we will summarize the most common characteristics defined by some famous researchers (Mell & Grance, 2011)

i.   Scalability

As we know that the world's most famous giants in cloud services are Google, Amazon, Yahoo, and others, Millions of servers are located all around the world by the CSP's. They can easily add or remove nodes and servers with little modification to cloud server and infrastructure due to the scalable property of cloud.

ii.   Virtualization and Broad Network Access

The client can access all the services by using any medium like mobiles, laptops, tablets, and workstations. Cloud has a built-in capacity to handle and virtualize all the physical resources used by the client

iii.   Self-Service On-demand

A user or consumer can easily demand any service related to cloud i-e provisioning of computing resources like storage, server time, etc. without any human intervention. You just have to sign a contract of services by any of CSP's and simply you have to pay charges mentioned in your contract to use all existing services.

iv.   Shared Resource Pooling

Table 1. Cloud Services by Amazon ("Amazon Web Services," 2019)

Name of Cloud	Services
EC2(Elastic compute cloud) by Amazon	Provide elastic computing capacity on the cloud
RDS(Rational Database Service) by Amazon	Provide tools for managing DB
Simple DB by Amazon	Provide database functionalities
Scalable DNS by Amazon	Provide secure routing server over the internet
Elastic Map Reduce by Amazon	Provide a vast amount of data on the cloud

Table 2. Cloud Service by Google ("Google Cloud,")

Name of Cloud	Services
Compute Engine by Google	An IaaS, where customer can divide workload in virtual server
App Engine by Google	A PaaS, where customer can develop an application
Cloud storage by Google	It is used for storage of any type, capacity
Cloud SQL by Google	Deal with relational DBMS
Cloud data store by Google	Deal with unstructured DB
Big query by Google	Used for a large amount of data

Cloud is considered as a shared pool of infinite resources. CSPs resources related to computing are arranged/pooled to serve multiple consumers request using the multi-talented model that can be easily added or released resource according to the user's virtual and physical demand. Some example resources include storage, processing, network bandwidth, and memory.

v.   Minimum Cost & Availability:

Cloud services basically reduce the manpower you need to maintain the setup and to maintain the servers, you can easily maintain a complete virtual office and you don't need to rent an office hire the staff to run your setup. All these costs are reduced by using cloud services. Cloud services are quite available anywhere at any time. You just need an active internet connection and a device that have OS and Browser. It can either be mobile, laptop, tablet or another similar device.

Table 3. Cloud Services by Microsoft ("Microsoft Azure," 2019)

Name of cloud	Services
Infrastructure	On-demand infrastructure with full support
Media	This cloud is dedicating for all type of media
Web development	Platform to build and develop web apps
Mobile development	Platform to build and develop mobile apps
Storage	A large cloud storage

vi.   Easy to Measure and Manage

Applications that are used to access the cloud environment are quite easy to use as compared to other related environments. At the user's end, they just need a browser on a computing device and have an active internet to connect with CSP. Cloud Systems can automatically optimize and control the resources by measuring capability related to services (e.g., processing, storage, active user accounts, and bandwidth).

b.   Major Service Providers of Cloud

These days there are many companies that are providing cloud services. Below Tables 1- summarize few major stakeholders in Cloud-related services.

c.   Deployment Models

Four Deployment Models are commonly considered for the cloud that the CSP's can provide to the user (Mell & Grance, 2011; Zissis & Lekkas, 2012), are:

i.   **Private Cloud:** CSP's provide exclusive access to a single organization. The organization may comprise of multiple consumers. It may be owned, managed, and operated by a third party itself.
ii.   **Public Cloud:** Infrastructure of the cloud may be provisioned for an open-access usage for the general public. It may be owned, managed and operated by an academic, business, or some kind of non-government/private or government organization, or maybe the mixture of them.
iii. **Hybrid Cloud:** Infrastructure commonly used in the cloud that is composed of two or more different cloud infrastructures (private, community or public). Hybrid cloud bonds together standardized technologies that enable application and data portability

Table 4. Summarize the previously explained services of cloud w.r.t to Application Software & OS

Services	Application software	Operating system
IaaS	Customer	Customer
PaaS	Customer	CSP
SaaS	CSP	CSP

iv. **Community Cloud:** This type of infrastructure is for exclusively used by a community of consumers from different organizations that may have bilateral concerns, For example, they may have a similar compliance consideration, security, and privacy policies. Community cloud may be operated, managed and owned by one or more than one organization.

d. Service Models of cloud

There are three main Service Models of cloud that the CSP's provide to the user (Mell & Grance, 2011; Takabi, Joshi, & Ahn, 2010; Vaquero, Rodero-Merino, Caceres, & Lindner, 2008; Zissis & Lekkas, 2012), they are:

i. Infrastructure as a Service (IaaS)

IaaS provides customer or user provision to use any resource like storage, network, processing, and other fundamental resources virtually. This is also working as a "virtual data center" in which the user can use any resource from any place virtually by just connecting with the cloud. The consumer can also deploy any arbitrary software on the cloud which may include any software application or operating system.

ii. Platform as a service (PaaS)

PaaS delivers an environment to the consumer where the consumer can organize and deploy his own created business application on cloud. These applications may be built with any programming language, tools, and libraries supported by service providers. In PaaS, consumers don't control over the operating system and other core components of cloud but they can manage or use only its own application.

Table 5. Summary of the previously explained models of cloud w.r.t to Security

Models	Owned by	Managed by	Security level
Private	Single organization	Single organization/ CSP	Very high
Public	CSP	CSP	Low
Hybrid	Organization/CSP	Organization/CSP	Medium
Community	Several organizations	Several organizations/ CSP	High

iii.   Software as a service (SaaS)

SaaS offers consumers access to software that already installed on the cloud by providers. SaaS will be the most useable server of the cloud as the usage of cloud increases with the passage of time. The consumers haven't need to install software on their own machine. They just need a browser with a good internet connection to use this service. The software uses the computation power of the server. Figure 2 categorizes security architecture with respect to Cloud Services.

e.   Security Issues in Cloud Computing

If we talk about cloud computing there are some concerns and challenges also exists. (Popović & Hocenski, 2010) discuss some major concerns related to cloud security. (i) If you are using the cloud computing model the physical security related to data and information will lose immediately because you are sharing your computational resources with other companies. You have no knowledge about where data is placed on cloud and resources are running. (ii) Storage services provided by one CSP may be mismatched or incompatible with other vendor or service provider. So in future, if you want to migrate or shift your data from one to the other. It might be possible you face issues like Microsoft cloud is irreconcilable/incompatible with cloud services by Google (Mont, Pearson, & Bramhall, 2003). (iii) Who controls the keys for Encryption/Decryption? If keys go in some wrong hands then there are chances to harm or misuse of your important data. (iv) Ensuring the integrity of data is also a big challenge. For example, if you want to move, transfer, store and retrieve your data which authorized channel or standard you will use? A common standard yet doesn't exist. (v) Almost all E-commerce applications use payments gateways. In case of Payment Card Industry Data Security Standard (PCI DSS), your records and logs related to data must be provided to security managers and regulators (Salmon, 2008), which is also the big concern for a customer using cloud services. (vi) Some countries strictly restrict on their citizen's data that it can be

Figure 1. Security Architecture of Cloud Computing w.r.t Services (Chen & Zhao, 2012)

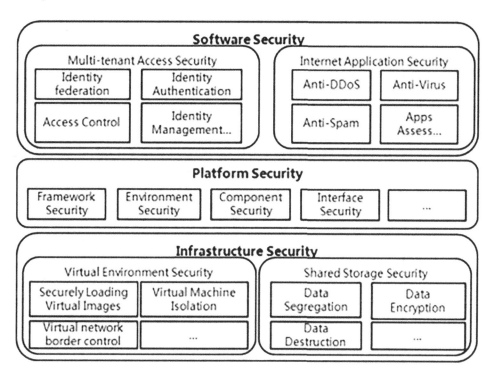

stored for a specific period of time and some countries restrict to place financial data of their citizens outside so E-Commerce using cloud must manage this issue. The fluid and dynamic nature of virtual machines make it problematic to maintain core issues like security and auditability of data.

User can hold key to encrypt or decrypt data but it is less secure on user side because there is a chance that he might take this as ordinary key and might forget the key or it may be stolen or misused by someone else without the owner's information. So it is not secure at all on the user end. The popular cloud services including Mega and SpiderOak are a few cloud service providers that allow the user to use specific client service applications that include encryption function during data/file uploading and decryption while data/file downloading. But this platform allows the user to keep the keys by themselves but as mentioned earlier, It is not secure at all to keep key on the user end. According to the survey ("Top 10 Security Concerns for Cloud-Based Services," 2015), the top concerns are Data Breaches, Insider Threats, Malware Injection, Abuse of Cloud Services, Insecure APIs, Shared vulnerabilities, Denial of Service Attacks, Hijacking of Accounts, Insufficient Due Diligence, and Data Loss.

Figure 1 is categorizing the security-related issues in the cloud depends upon the services that clouds are providing to its customer's i-e Software, Platform and Infrastructure as mentioned in detail earlier

MAIN FOCUS OF THE CHAPTER

E-commerce Applications- check

E-commerce is growing and popular web application that enables the partners, employees, and customers to achieve a variety of services and purposes. E-commerce Association defines "E-commerce covers any form of administrative transaction or business or information exchange that is executed by using any Information and Communication Technology (ICT)" (Saleh, 2012), There are different types of e-commerce applications such as business-to-consumer (B2C), consumer-to-business (C2B), business-to-business (B2B), and consumer-to-consumer (C2C) There are several organizations like government agencies or academic institutions that use E-commerce to improve services or reduce expenses, (King, Chung, Lee, & Turban, 1999)

E-commerce Application & Cloud Computing

E-commerce applications can take benefits from the cloud in multiple ways. The most common benefits include Usage of Infrastructure, Platform, and Services. Cloud gives ease to E-commerce developers in multiple ways. For example low cost, Flexibility, Accessibility, No or minimal hardware requirement, no need to install specific software. In addition to these benefits cloud computing have some disadvantages also like Internet speed may affect overall performances of E-commerce application. If application developer takes long term subscription of cloud then subscription cost will be more than buying actual hardware by own. And the most costly disadvantage of the cloud is data security regarding applications and their Users. Cloud security issues related to E-commerce Application is discussed in detail later in this chapter

Figure 2. Compares the Benefits and Disadvantage of Using Cloud in E-Commerce Application (Kumar & Charu, 2015)

Advantages	Disadvantages
Shared Resources	Internet Required
Automatic Software Integration	Dependency and vendor lock-in
Cost Efficient	Non-Interoperability
Easy Access to Information	Less Reliability
Quick Deployment	Technical Issues
Almost Unlimited Storage	Security in the Cloud
Backup and Recovery	Prone to Attack
Better Hardware Management	Increased Vulnerability
Mobility	Less Control
Versatile Compatibility	No always many room

ISSUES, CONTROVERSIES, PROBLEMS

Security Issues in E-Commerce

With the increase in the usage of e-commerce applications, the concerns about users security also increase. CSPs are responsible for the security of client personal data but they always claim that their data must secure and safe on E-commerce applications. But still, cloud service worries about their personal data and information because their data is totally in the cloud service providers hands. Many customers are using the cloud services for the first time so they are not familiar with the cloud security concerns that is why they hesitate to use it because they don't want to lose the control on their private data. As the big organization is storing a large amount of their personal and business data on the cloud, this data further processed and then transmitted. If any problem occurs during any of the processes then there are chances that whole data might be corrupted or harmed completely. Some security-related issues are discussed below

i.   Issues during data storage

These days, mostly E-commerce sites are using cloud computing services for data storage and other important purposes. In cloud computing a data center stores a large amount of data. All the private information stored on the cloud side. E-commerce companies are also concerned about how the client's personal data stored on cloud data centers. In cloud computing, users store all the private data on a virtual data center which may be located anywhere in this world. E-commerce application data can be stored on any virtual data center. The application is mostly unaware of its location of data. They are not clear about where the data is to store and in which country their data is placed by CSP's. As millions of user are using a single application at the same time and store their personal data on applications. The main concerns here are (i) Data is encrypted or not? (ii) Is the data stored on a single data center (location) or in a different position? The similar storage concerns thus lead towards the data security issue which is one of the major issues in E-commerce applications using cloud services.

ii.   Data transmission issue

In the cloud computing model, the business data is transmitted to the cloud side over the internet because the E-commerce companies are also concerned about the client data. So they want to be treated as confidential and should be encrypted before transmission so that it is not misused or captured by an unauthorized person. Keep it

Table 6. Comparison of CSP's according to different parameters

Application Name	Price plan	Free storage	Max storage	Mobile Support Device	Security	SLA	API
DropBox	9.99$/ month	2GB	10GB	Android, IPad, iPhone, Blackberry	SSL, AES-256, Encryption	Yes	SDK for Major Platform
Google Drive	1.99$/ month	15GB	30TB	Android systems, iPhone, IPad	SSL	Yes	Java, Php, JS,. Net
OneDrive	25$/ year	7GB	100GB	Android,iPhone, Windows phone	SSL, No built-in, Encryption	Yes	REST API
ICloud	20$/ year	5GB	50GB	iPhone. IPad, iPod Touch	SSL	Yes	Yes

as strictly confidential. by using some security measures. But as data is transmitted on the internet so there are chances of corruption and miss utilization of data.

iii.   Data Audit issue

If an organization manages its internal data, then in order to check the accuracy of the data, the organization needs to involve a third party that ensures the correctness of the data. You can take this as an example that if the data is transmitted from user A to user B some measures need to be checked whether the correct data is transmitted to another end. In the middle of the transmission the data is changed or not? Or due to any attack, the complete data reached on other end or not? Is it completely reached on other end or not? In a cloud computing environment, it is the CSP's responsibility to ensure the correctness of the data.

iv.   Viruses and hackers attack issues:

As virtualization is used on large scale in a cloud environment, a hacker can take advantage from this technology by writing a virtual machine in form of malicious software that will be more difficult for the user to detect and remove viruses from their data. As they are unaware of hackers. So in this situation, e-commerce applications data will be harmed very badly. So more security techniques should be adopted to prevent such hackers and viruses. Hackers can take access to your data by using different means, so if your data is on some remote place i-e on Cloud it has more chances to effect with system intrusion and social engineering attacks by hackers. They can misuse this data by taking control over the data blackmail the clients and e-commerce application owners. They can also destroy your data by taking monetary benefits from your competitor.

SOLUTIONS AND RECOMMENDATIONS

Solutions of Security in E-commerce Related to Cloud

As discussed earlier Security is our main concern when we talk about e-commerce. Different researchers have provided us with various solutions. Few of them are discussed here in this chapter.

(Zhang, Zhang, & Sun, 2010), worked on trust and try to solve the issues related to transaction security. A model was proposed which based on cloud model theory and the experiments in their work shows that this model is practical and valid for the merger of trust cloud. But this model was only applied to the customer to customer (C2C) E-commerce. (Pawar, Sajjad, Dimitrakos, & Chadwick, 2015) proposed a host and application-level framework that provide more security to the user's data by using resources in a cloud federated environment. It performs encryption on file level so it allows the user to monitor at the host or on the application level. (Rizvi, Ryoo, Kissell, Aiken, & Liu, 2018) proposed a framework to evaluate the security strength by necessary quantitative matrices. The core factors included in the matrix are interoperability, transparency, and portability. *(Huwedi, Talhi, & Boucheneb, 2018)* proposed a security service detection system by using intrusion for public cloud systems. In their work researchers used an algorithm that fills the gaps in an existing security system that provides more security to cloud service user which also help the CSPs to maintain security in an existing system. (Sharma, Dhote, & Potey, 2016) proposed an identity and access management system (IAMaaS). It was an on-demand portable available pay-per-use cost model. A similar Identity and Access Management architecture was also purposed by (Yang, Chen, Wang, & Cao, 2014) to achieve similar security requirements like Data Loss Prevention, Strong Authentication, and Security as a Service. The main benefit of their work was standardized architecture, comprehensive identity management, and scalable system design.

In another work by (Samlinson & Usha, 2013) authors proposed user-centric trust identity service that was aimed to create trust among CSP's. The model proposed in their work had Authorization, Authentication, Provisioning and an Audit module along with Trust agent. When user move from one CSP to other their credentials follow in the federated environment. The trust agent in the Identity module sends trust token with the user's attribute which creates trust among CSP's. (Zissis & Lekkas, 2012) gave the concept of a unique security system that helps to eliminate the threats. They introduced a concept that the use of a trusted third party to ensure the use of Public Key Infrastructure (PKI). This solution provided security, integrity, authentication, and confidentiality of user data because of the use of public key infrastructure.

(Costa et al., 2005) Purposed a collaborative end to end approach for prevention and detection of the worms. Authors called this approach as Vigilante. Some specific software is needed to run on each host that captures information about the worm exploitation and spread or distribute a Self-Certifying Alert (SCA) to warn other hosts regarding the worm spreading. Then end host used that information in SCA to check that if the message or coming information vulnerable to worm then apply a host-based filter to protect from the worm. (Egele, Kruegel, Kirda, Yin, & Song, 2007) Proposed a spyware analysis tool that monitors the flow of important and sensitive data. The tool is proposed for the web browser and browser helps objects. This tool analyzed the suspicious behavior and then generate a report about data being sent and the location where this data was sent. (Elbadawi & Al-Shaer, 2009) Proposed to the use of Timm, that replay with log to achieve availability of few important services like FTP, HTTP, and SMTP. The traffic of every server is replayed and recorded to clone the virtual machines at some random time intervals. If some attack happened on any virtual machine it can be detected on time and then it automatically excludes the traffic under attack and high-performance reply to all virtual machines for fast recovery on their services.

Recently (Hawedi et al., 2018) purposed a security architecture that offered an elastic and efficient paradigm for security as a service for cloud tenants. The third parties could offer a purposed solution of security to their tenants or tenants could monitor their VM's. It was designed for the deployment on the top of the hybrid cloud. This also used anomaly detection and signature-based techniques. In past similar architecture also purposed by (Tupakula, Varadharajan, & Akku, 2011) that was deployed on IaaS against the cloud's attack. That monitored the traffic and ensured that neither traffic belongs to an intrusion or nor contain any malicious content.

(Juncai & Shao, 2011) suggested some basic tips related to safety and security which are, (a) the data that is stored in the cloud should be backed up frequently so in case of attack, theft or any other loss it can easily recover our data. (b) Your files on Cloud must be in Encrypted form and this encryption is also protected by a strong password. Encryption will protect your data if you want to move or shift from one cloud server r data center to another. (c) Hacker, data criminal or another person who wants to destroy your data on the cloud can enter into your network through Email. So the suggested method is to use a secure or encrypted email service for this author suggested using M Ute email or Hush mail for email related services. (d) Always use credible cloud services from a well-reputed organization and always read their privacy statement related to data security first before any kind of contract and agreement. (e) Always use Filters for data security. The author suggested taking services from companies like Web sense, vent, and VeriTest offers data monitoring and prevents sensitive data. Some other general tips were Enhance security-related awareness in clients and developers.

FUTURE RESEARCH DIRECTIONS

For Further studies on Security Solutions presented in past you can read the mentioned work of researchers (Mather, Kumaraswamy, & Latif, 2009), (Alharkan & Martin, 2012), (Dunlap, King, Cinar, Basrai, & Chen, 2002; Garfinkel & Rosenblum, 2003),

REFERENCES

Ahuja, V. (2000). Building trust in electronic commerce. *IT Professional, 2*(3), 61–63. doi:10.1109/6294.846215

Alharkan, T., & Martin, P. (2012). Idsaas: Intrusion detection system as a service in public clouds. *Proceedings of the 2012 12th IEEE/ACM International Symposium on Cluster, Cloud and Grid Computing (ccgrid 2012)*. 10.1109/CCGrid.2012.81

Amazon Web Services. (2019). Retrieved from https://aws.amazon.com/

Chen, D., & Zhao, H. (2012). *Data security and privacy protection issues in cloud computing*. Paper presented at the 2012 International Conference on Computer Science and Electronics Engineering. 10.1109/ICCSEE.2012.193

Costa, M., Crowcroft, J., Castro, M., Rowstron, A., Zhou, L., Zhang, L., & Barham, P. (2005). *Vigilante: End-to-end containment of internet worms*. Paper presented at the ACM SIGOPS Operating Systems Review. 10.1145/1095810.1095824

Dikaiakos, M. D., Katsaros, D., Mehra, P., Pallis, G., & Vakali, A. (2009). Cloud computing: Distributed internet computing for IT and scientific research. *IEEE Internet Computing, 13*(5), 10–13. doi:10.1109/MIC.2009.103

Dunlap, G. W., King, S. T., Cinar, S., Basrai, M. A., & Chen, P. M. (2002). ReVirt: Enabling intrusion analysis through virtual-machine logging and replay. *ACM SIGOPS Operating Systems Review, 36*(SI), 211-224.

Egele, M., Kruegel, C., Kirda, E., Yin, H., & Song, D. (2007). *Dynamic spyware analysis*. Academic Press.

Elbadawi, K., & Al-Shaer, E. (2009). TimeVM: A Framework for online intrusion mitigation and fast recovery using multi-time-lag traffic replay. *Proceedings of the 4th International Symposium on Information, Computer, and Communications Security*. 10.1145/1533057.1533077

Feldman, S. (2000). The changing face of e-commerce: Extending the boundaries of the possible. *IEEE Internet Computing, 4*(3), 82–83. doi:10.1109/MIC.2000.845395

Garfinkel, T., & Rosenblum, M. (2003). *A Virtual Machine Introspection Based Architecture for Intrusion Detection.* Paper presented at the Ndss. Google Cloud. Retrieved from https://cloud.google.com/

Hawedi, M., Talhi, C., & Boucheneb, H. (2018). Security as a service for public cloud tenants (SaaS). *Procedia Computer Science, 130*, 1025–1030. doi:10.1016/j.procs.2018.04.143

Juncai, S., & Shao, Q. (2011). Based on Cloud Computing E-commerce Models and ItsSecurity. *International Journal of e-Education, e-Business, e- Management Learning, 1*(2), 175.

King, D., Chung, H. M., Lee, J. K., & Turban, E. (1999). *Electronic commerce: A managerial perspective.* Prentice Hall PTR.

Kumar, R., & Charu, S. (2015). Comparison between cloud computing, grid computing, cluster computing and virtualization. *International Journal of Modern Computer Science and Applications, 3*(1), 42–47.

Mather, T., Kumaraswamy, S., & Latif, S. (2009). *Cloud security and privacy: an enterprise perspective on risks and compliance.* O'Reilly Media, Inc.

Mell, P., & Grance, T. (2011). *The NIST definition of cloud computing.* Academic Press.

Microsoft Azure. (2019). Retrieved from https://azure.microsoft.com/en-us/

Mont, M. C., Pearson, S., & Bramhall, P. (2003). *Towards accountable management of identity and privacy: Sticky policies and enforceable tracing services.* Paper presented at the 14th International Workshop on Database and Expert Systems Applications. 10.1109/DEXA.2003.1232051

Pawar, P. S., Sajjad, A., Dimitrakos, T., & Chadwick, D. W. (2015). *Security-as-a-service in multi-cloud and federated cloud environments.* Paper presented at the IFIP international conference on trust management. 10.1007/978-3-319-18491-3_21

Popović, K., & Hocenski, Ž. (2010). *Cloud computing security issues and challenges.* Paper presented at the The 33rd International Convention MIPRO.

Rizvi, S., Ryoo, J., Kissell, J., Aiken, W., & Liu, Y. (2018). A security evaluation framework for cloud security auditing. *The Journal of Supercomputing, 74*(11), 5774–5796. doi:10.100711227-017-2055-1

Saleh, A. A. E. (2012). A proposed framework based on cloud computing for enhancing e-commerce applications. *International Journal of Computers and Applications, 59*(5).

Salmon, J. (2008). Clouded in uncertainty–the legal pitfalls of cloud computing. *Computing,* 24.

Samlinson, E., & Usha, M. (2013). *User-centric trust based identity as a service for federated cloud environment.* Paper presented at the 2013 Fourth International Conference on Computing, Communications and Networking Technologies (ICCCNT). 10.1109/ICCCNT.2013.6726636

Schafer, J. B., Konstan, J. A., & Riedl, J. (2001). E-commerce recommendation applications. *Data Mining and Knowledge Discovery, 5*(1-2), 115–153. doi:10.1023/A:1009804230409

Sharma, D. H., Dhote, C., & Potey, M. M. (2016). Identity and access management as security-as-a-service from clouds. *Procedia Computer Science, 79,* 170–174. doi:10.1016/j.procs.2016.03.117

Takabi, H., Joshi, J. B., & Ahn, G.-J. (2010). Security and privacy challenges in cloud computing environments. *IEEE Security and Privacy*, *8*(6), 24–31. doi:10.1109/MSP.2010.186

Top 10 Security Concerns for Cloud-Based Services. (2015). Retrieved from https://www.imperva.com/blog/top-10-cloud-security-concerns/

Tupakula, U., Varadharajan, V., & Akku, N. (2011). *Intrusion detection techniques for infrastructure as a service cloud.* Paper presented at the 2011 IEEE Ninth International Conference on Dependable, Autonomic and Secure Computing. 10.1109/DASC.2011.128

Vaquero, L. M., Rodero-Merino, L., Caceres, J., & Lindner, M. (2008). A break in the clouds: Towards a cloud definition. *Computer Communication Review*, *39*(1), 50–55. doi:10.1145/1496091.1496100

Yang, Y., Chen, X., Wang, G., & Cao, L. (2014). *An identity and access management architecture in cloud.* Paper presented at the 2014 Seventh International Symposium on Computational Intelligence and Design. 10.1109/ISCID.2014.221

Zhang, J., Zhang, J.-A., & Sun, P. (2010). Trust evaluation model based on cloud model for C2C electronic commerce. *Comput. Syst. Appl*, *19*(11), 83–87.

Zissis, D., & Lekkas, D. (2012). Addressing cloud computing security issues. *Future Generation Computer Systems*, *28*(3), 583–592. doi:10.1016/j.future.2010.12.006

Chapter 4
Security for the Cloud

Shweta Kaushik
ABES Engineering College, Ghaziabad, India

Charu Gandhi
Jaypee Institute of Information Technology, Noida, India

ABSTRACT

Today's people are moving towards the internet services through cloud computing to acquire their required service, but they have less confidence about cloud computing because all the tasks are handled by the service provider. Cloud system provides features to the owner to store their data on some remote locations and allow only authorized users to access their data according to their access capability. Data security becomes particularly serious in the cloud computing environment because data are scattered in different machines and storage devices including servers, PCs, and various mobile devices such as smart phones. To make the cloud computing be adopted by enterprise, the security concerns of users should be rectified first to make cloud environment trustworthy. The trustworthy environment is the basic prerequisite to win the confidence of users to adopt this technology. However, there are various security concerns that need to be taken care of regarding the trust maintenance between various parties, authorized access of confidential data, data storage privacy, and integrity.

INTRODUCTION

Security of user's data in a cloud environment is a most challenging concern. Although service provider always says that the information of the users is stored securely on the cloud environment, still e-commerce companies and cloud end-users

DOI: 10.4018/978-1-7998-1294-4.ch004

worry about the security of the data as their sensitive information are in the hands of other party. These security concerns make customers hesitate to implement Cloud E-commerce. Since most of the customers don't have prior experience of using cloud, they fear for their sensitive data leakage. Due to the storage of large amount of data related to business on the cloud system, and further this data is transmitted and processed by the third party, the risk involved will be much higher in the cloud computing-based E-commerce model than traditional E-commerce model. As the cloud computing model is based on E-commerce platforms where all data is stored in the cloud, the e-commerce companies are worried about the cloud computing security of the data as they are unable to supervise the sensitive information of the business. While considering the data security, the three primary major concerns are-

- **Trust: -** Trust means a confidence of doing a job as expected without introducing any vulnerability while performing any task. Trust can incorporate security while performing, validity of its loyalty, encoding and user-friendliness to attract other towards it. In cloud-based E-commerce application the organization data is stored at third party, cloud service provider and user will get their required their data from third party also. There is a need arise for a mutual trust between various communicating parties to ensure that data stored and retrieved from third party is intact without any malicious attack. Data owner requires that service provider should be trustworthy to store its confidential data without any exposure to unauthorized user and other service provider. On the other hand, users who will retrieve its data from the service provider also require that provider is trustworthy, who deliver the exact correct data without any loss of integrity and damage of data.
- **Privacy: -** Privacy means to kept data secret and hide from its unauthorized access. Privacy of data requires encoding, encryption, translations etc. which transform your confidential data into some other form without letting know the way of doing it to others. It generally includes protection of data from any malicious activity. Users can access the data according to their defined role, access criteria, attribute they have while rest of the data is kept safe. Data owner requires that service provider will deliver its data according to access criteria defined by it in order to protect its data from unauthorized access.
- **Security Issues: -** Apart from privacy and trust maintenance between different parties there are another security issue need to manage such as authorization and access control, integrity, non- repudiation, network security, confidentiality etc. To provide the authorization and access control data owner can decide one of the mechanism forms role-based access control, user-based access control or attribute-based access control to allow the users to get their required data according to this. Owner also needs to update service provider

Table 1. User specific Security Requirements and threats

Service Level	Type of Service	User involved	Security requirements	Threats
Physical Level	Data centre	An owner- it may be an organization or a person who have some infrastructure upon which cloud environment can be deployed.	• Use of cloud computing legally • Hardware security and reliability • Network and its resources protection	• Natural disasters • Hardware modification, interruption or theft • Infrastructure misuse
Virtual Level	• Infrastructure as a Service (IaaS) • Platform as a Service (PaaS)	A moderator or developer- it may be an organization or a person who deploys the software on cloud environment.	• Application and Data Security • Users access control • Virtual cloud protection • Data communication security	• Software modification or interruption • Impersonation • Connection flooding and traffic flow analysis • Flaws in programming
Application Level	Software as a Service (SaaS)	A user- it may be an organization or a person who actually uses the services provided by the cloud environment.	• Data or service availability and protection against malicious attack • Security and privacy of software in multitenant environment • Data communication security	• Data interruption or modification while data at rest or transit • Impersonation • Connection flooding and traffic flow analysis • Privacy breach

about this access criteria for verification purpose before transferring the data to users. To prove that data integrity is maintained without any vulnerability's owner can encrypt the data and digitally sign this. Only the authorized users have verification key to check the integrity of received data from the service provider to ensure that retrieved data is intact.

Based on the user security requirements at different service level of the usage of Cloud Computing along with its threats can be described as shown in Table 1.

Table 2. Security Requirements

Security Principles	Description with solution
Authentication and access control	To provide the owner's data to authorized user according to their access criteria, there is a need of identification system. This system will be able to differentiate between the authorized and unauthorized users and allow to authorized users to access their required data according to their role, capability, identification etc.
Confidentiality & Privacy	To guarantee the confidentiality of data, it should be encrypted first before outsource and only the authorized user have the decryption key for that. Service provider is unaware of this security key.
Auditing	It will help to maintain the interoperability feature in cloud based system. Any malicious activity will be monitored by this and report sent back to owner to alert him. Owner will take necessary action to handle this problem.
Integrity	Data owner need to sign its data and only the authorized users has its verification key to check whether they got the exact or malicious data.
Relevance	Users will be able to get the data according to their access criteria only. For Example-A doctor can read the prescription details of his patient not the pharmacy person. To guarantee that only the person meeting accessibility criteria will be able to get that much information assigned to it not more than it.
Trust	This is required to belief that data is stored at right place and also retrieved correctly without introducing any vulnerability. It can be achieved by a contract signed between the different communicating parties such as service level agreement.

SECURITY PRINCIPLES IN CLOUD ENVIRONMENT

While accessing the data from cloud environment different security principles needs to be follow as shown in Table 2.

SECURITY ISSUES AT DIFFERENT SERVICE LEVEL

Under the cloud environment it is required to analyse the various possible attack and vulnerability before actually utilize the cloud environment. The various security issues can be classified under the category of host level, application level and network level as shown in figure 1-

Figure 1. Security issues at different service level

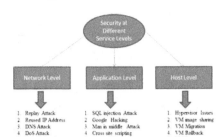

- **Network level security issues-** At the network level the different security issues are classified to ensure the data availability, integrity and confidentiality etc. These can be classified as-replay attack, reused IP address, DNS attack, DoS attack and in sybil attack etc.
- **Application level security issues-** Many organizations are providing their users with various services which are available online over the internet 24*7. Many users are using the services without considering that by whom, whose and where the services actually exist and what security consideration are utilized behind its management. Therefore, service provider always needs to be careful about the services by employing the various security issues as- SQL injection attack, Google hacking, Man in the Middle attack, Cross site scripting and cookie poisoning etc.
- **Host level security issues-** While providing any service to the user, service provider will not reveal any information related to the host operating system, processes and host platform which are utilized to provide the security at host level. These host level services need to be secure to minimize the possibility of any intruder or malicious attacker. The various security issues solved at this level are as as- Hypervisor issues, VM image sharing, VM migration, VM rollback and VM escape etc.

RISK IN CLOUD SECURITY

There are the possibilities of many risk occurrences which needs to be solved by the cloud security strategies. Some possible risks in cloud environment can be classified as shown in figure 2-

- **Absence of Control** - Usage of a public cloud administration implies that an association is viably "leasing" IT resources. They never again have responsibility and ownership for hardware and software resources, applications, or programming on which the cloud administrations run — rather they are renting IT administrations. Encompassing cloud security approach will guarantee that there are proper strides set up to comprehend the cloud merchant's way to deal with these benefits.

- **Absence of Visibility** - Cloud processing makes it simple for anybody to subscribe for SaaS application or even to turn up new examples and conditions. These kinds of shadow IT might happen outside the view and control of your security arrangement. You need a solid satisfactory use arrangement that guarantees that clients pursue best practices in acquiring approval for, and for buying in to, new administrations or making new cases.

- **Transmitting and Receiving Data** - Cloud applications frequently incorporate and interface with different administrations, databases, and applications. This is normally accomplished through an application programming interface (API). It's indispensable to comprehend the applications and individuals who approach API information and to encode any touchy data.

- **Identity Management and Access Control** - Only approved clients ought to approach the cloud condition, applications, and information. This implies your association needs strong personality the board and validation forms, which could incorporate multifaceted verification, single sign on, as well as different innovations. Also, clients should just approach the information and applications they require to satisfy their job, and nothing more.

- **Malware -** Cloud conditions ordinarily have solid enemy of malware insurances and other safety efforts, yet that doesn't mean they fulfil the adequate hazard profile criteria for your association. Distinguish any holes and guarantee you have the best possible cyber security arrangements set up.

- **Outside Attackers** - Hackers and other awful on-screen characters represent a consistent risk to associations. Watchfulness, early identification, and a multi-layered security approach (firewalls, information encryption, powerlessness the executives, risk examination, and so on.) help keep programmers out of your condition, and empower you to quickly respond with accuracy if a break occasion ought to happen.

- **Insider Threats** – benefits: Whether it's through malignance or basic carelessness, for example, accidentally making a security gap through a misconfiguration or the imprudent sharing or reusing of certifications—insider-related dangers for the most part take the longest to distinguish and resolve, and can possibly result in the most disastrous harm. Once more, having a solid IAM system and the correct benefit the board instruments set

Figure 2. Risk in Cloud Security

up to implement least benefit and best practice special qualification the board is fundamental to restricting the harm from these dangers and keeping them from picking up a toehold in any case.

SECURITY PRACTICE IN CLOUD COMPUTING ENVIRONMENT

Usage of cloud computing environment also requires the various security practices, as shown in figure 3, for effective and efficient processing of data -

- **Early Detection**- This service responsible for detecting and reporting about any vulnerabilities if appear. A report is generally issued to the customer which contain the information related to the threats or vulnerability that may arise and how they can affect the system performance or any particular software or application. In general, this report informs the user that specific action should be taken by the user in order to minimize the effect f any vulnerability.
- **Vulnerability detection and Management**- It enable to verify and manage the security of any information system automatically. It periodically performs an automated test service whose aim is to identify the possible weakness of any service that may expose on internet such as- information regarding the various services which are not updated, vulnerability detection such as phishing, access of any service by un authorized user etc. This service also performs a task periodically in collaboration of security professional to manage the system security and prepare a report which can be utilized further for the improvement in system security.

Figure 3. Security Practice in Cloud Computing Environment

- **Protection from Internal & External Attack**- Security observing administration help to improve the viability of the security foundation of a client by effectively examining the logs and cautions from framework gadgets progressively and non- stop. Checking the group's associate data from different security devices to furnish security analyst with the information they require to wipe out false positives and react to genuine threats against the endeavour. Generally, the skill required to keep up the dimensions of administration of an association is high. The data security group can evaluate framework execution on an occasionally repeating premise and give proposals to progress as required.

- **Service Monitoring & Control**- In order to monitor the operational states of any platform at any time it is feasible to use dashboard interface implemented with the usage of service monitoring platform and control. It will help in access the data remotely using the web interface. This indicator will help in knowing the operational status of each and every element along with its impact on an organization. With the help of this it is easier to determine that which element is utilized nearby and how many resources are utilized beyond their limits. These all measurement will help the organization to take possible prevention to avoid the loss of any service after identifying the problem.

- **Continuous system up gradation**- Security act is improved with ceaseless framework fixing and up gradation of frameworks and applications programming. New fixes, update and service packs for security levels and bolster new form of introduced items. Staying up to date with every one of the progressions to all the product and equipment requires a submitted exertion to remain educated and to convey holes in security that can show up in introduced framework and applications.

- **Log analysis and centralization**- Log centralization and examination is a checking arrangement dependent on the relationship coordinating of log passages. Such investigation builds up a benchmark of operational execution and gives a list of security danger. Alerts can be brought up in the occasion an occurrence moves the built-up benchmark parameters past a stipulated edge. These sorts of modern apparatuses are utilized by a group of security specialists who are in charge of occurrence reaction once such an edge has been crossed and the danger has created an alert or cautioning got by security experts observing the frameworks.

DATA SECURITY AND PRIVACY TECHNOLOGIES

In order to ensure the data security and privacy technologies various approaches are utilized as shown in Figure 4.

- **Cloud information assurance**- Encrypting the sensitive information before it goes to the cloud with the venture (not the cloud supplier) keeping up the keys. Protection against unwelcomed government observation and helps banish the absolute greatest obstacles to cloud selection—security, consistence, and protection concerns.
- **Tokenization**- Substituting an arbitrarily created value—the token—for sensitive information, for example, credit/ debit card numbers, financial balance numbers, and government managed savings numbers. After tokenization, the mapping of the token to its unique information is put away in a solidified database. In contrast to encryption, there is no numerical connection between the token and its unique information; to switch the tokenization, a programmer must approach the mapping database.
- **Big information encryption**- Using encryption and other jumbling procedures to cloud information in social databases just as information put away in the dispersed processing structures of huge information stages, to secure individual protection, accomplish consistence, and decrease the effect of digital assaults and inadvertent information spills.
- **Data access administration**- Providing visibility into what and where delicate information exists, and information get to authorizations and exercises, enabling associations to oversee information get to consents and distinguish sensitive stale information. These devices help computerize, at scale, the test of tending to the low-balancing product of information insurance—sensitive

Figure 4. Data security & privacy technologies

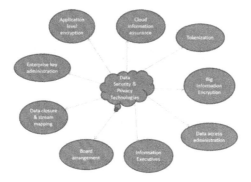

information revelation and tidying up information get to authorizations to uphold least benefit—as information volumes soar.

- **Consent/information subject rights the executives**- Managing assent of clients and workers, just as authorizing their rights over the individual information that they share, enabling associations to look, recognize, fragment, and change individual information as essential.

- **Data protection the board arrangements**- Platforms that help to operate the security procedures and works on, supporting protection by plan and meeting consistence prerequisites and starting auditable work processes.

- **Data disclosure and stream mapping**- Scanning information storehouses and assets to distinguish existing sensitive information, characterizing it suitably so as to recognize consistence issues, apply the correct security controls, or settle on choices about capacity advancement, cancellation, chronicling, and other information administration matters. Information stream mapping capacities help to see how information is utilized and travels through the business.

- **Enterprise key administration**- Unifying the unique encryption key life-cycle forms crosswise over heterogeneous items. Key administration arrangements store, appropriate, updated, and resign keys on an enormous scale crosswise over numerous sorts of encryption items.

- **Application-level encryption**- Encrypting information inside the application itself as it's produced or prepared and before it's submitted and put away at the database level. It empowers fine-grained encryption arrangements and ensures sensitive information at each level in the figuring and capacity stack and wherever information is replicated or transmitted.

FUTURE REQUIREMENTS FOR SECURITY & PRIVACY

Cloud computing is based on multi domain technology in which each domain can have its policy for security, trust for privacy management. It is important to leverage existing research on multi domain policy integration and the secure service composition to build a comprehensive policy-based management framework in cloud computing environments (Takabi et al., 2010). As shown in figure 5, we identify some major security and privacy requirements which requires high consideration-

- **Authentication and identity management-** By using cloud services, user can easily access their personal information and make it available to various services across the Internet (Sen, 2015). The best approach for this identity management which help to identify any user based on its credential and identity. Existing approach for the identity management have their own limitation which increase the risk of secure data leakage. While clients associate with a front-end administration, this administration may need to guarantee that their identity is protected from different administrations with which it associates (Bertino et al., 2009). In multi-domain cloud environment, suppliers must isolate client personality and confirmation data. Validation and identity management segments ought to likewise be effectively incorporated with other security segments. Structure and improvement of dynamic confirmation and character the board conventions is a basic prerequisite for cloud computing.

- **Access control and accounting-** Heterogeneity and decent variety of administrations, just as the areas' differing access prerequisites in distributed computing conditions, request fine-grained get to control approaches. Specifically, get to control administrations should be sufficiently adaptable to catch dynamic, setting, or quality or certification-based access necessities and to authorize the guideline of least benefit. Such access control administrations may need to incorporate security assurance prerequisites communicated through complex guidelines. It ought to likewise be guaranteed that the cloud conveyance models give nonexclusive access control interfaces to appropriate interoperability. Using a protection mindful structure for access control and bookkeeping administrations that is effectively agreeable to consistence checking is in this way a significant prerequisite which needs prompt consideration from the

- **Trust Management framework-** To encourage agreement combination between different entities in cloud conditions, a trust-based structure that encourages computerized trust-based approach incorporation is fundamental. In doing as such, we should respond to a few inquiries: How would we set

Figure 5. Future requirements for security & Privacy

up trust and decide get to mapping to fulfil inter domain get to necessities, what's more, how would we oversee and keep up progressively changing trust esteems and adjust get to necessities as trust develops? One conceivable methodology is to build up an exhaustive trust-based approach coordination system that encourages approach combination and advancement dependent on inter domain-and administration get to necessities. Existing work identified with designation, including job based assignment, has concentrated on issues identified with designation of benefits among subjects and different dimensions of controls with respect to benefit engendering and renouncement. Effective cryptographic instruments for trust assignment include complex trust-chain confirmation and renouncement issues, raising noteworthy key administration issues. These methodologies must be joined in administration organization structures investigate.

- **Secure service integration**- In distributed cloud computing environment, cloud service provider and administration integrators form administrations for their clients. The administration integrator gives a stage that lets autonomous specialist organizations arrange and interwork administrations and agreeably give extra administrations that meet clients' insurance necessities. Albeit many cloud specialist co-ops utilize the Web Services Description Language (WSDL), the conventional WSDL can't completely meet the prerequisites of distributed computing administrations depiction. In mists, issues, for example, nature of administration, cost, and SLAs are basic in administration pursuit and synthesis. Basically, a programmed and efficient administration provisioning and synthesis system that considers security and protection issues is vital and needs dire consideration.

- **Improvement in hardware capabilities**- The unavoidable enhancements in processor speed and expanded memory limits crosswise over IT framework

Figure 6. Trust Mechanism in Cloud Environment

will imply that the cloud will almost certainly bolster progressively mind-boggling conditions with improved execution capacities as standard.

TRUST MECHANISM IN CLOUD ENVIRONMENT

In order to define the trust among different communicating parties in cloud environment, there are various mechanisms as shown in figure 6. These all trust mechanism can be summarized as-

- **Reputation based trust-** Whenever an entity does not have direct interaction with other entity, the only way to maintain the trust is reputation (also known as feedback), provided by some other entity. In this way, trust and reputation are related to each other. In e-commerce technology the reputation-based trust mechanism is widely utilized. The reputation of any web service is calculated using the feedback provided by the other users of the same service in different aspect of the service performance. Any e-commerce application which has high reputation is widely utilized by various users. At the first glance, any user is attracted towards any e-commerce organization only after reviewing its reputation and than trust is maintained afterward based on its performance.
- **SLA verification based-** The communication among different parties in cloud environment is legally based on a signed agreement in between them. This legal contract is known as Service Level Agreement (SLA). In this record the complete description related to security and QoS maintenance is maintained properly and checked on regular basis by different parties. But the major issue with SLA is that through this user can focus only on the visible

component of service provider, such as GUI, speed, performance etc. not on invisible component such as security and privacy control.

- **Transparency based trust-** The future of transparency will help in maintaining the trust among different parties without any discrepancy. To maintain the transparency of different services given by user Cloud Security Alliance (CSA) also introduces the "Security, Trust & Assurance Registry (STAR) program (CSA, 2011). Under this program, the service provider circulates its security control measure for self impression in a matrix form or in a form of questionnaire. This questionnaire has multiple questions which can be asked by the user to verify the transparency of any service.

- **Policy based trust-**All the previously defined approach have a formal way to describe the trust among different parties. In policy based trust mechanism an access criterion is defined for each user along with key. Only the user who have valid set of attribute and key will be able to access the required data.

- **Attribute based trust-**Like policy passed trust mechanism, attribute-based trust mechanism is also an important way for maintaining the trust among different communicating parties. In this case, all the users are initially provided with a set of attributes. Whenever any user wants to access a particular service first they need to show its respective attribute and only after verification of these attribute user is provided with its required service or data.

SECURITY ISSUES FACED BY E-COMMERCE IN CLOUD

- Data Storage Risk- E-commerce companies who are using cloud computing services are not clear about where their data is actually stored, which country their data is located. As the data in cloud computing environment is shared by multiple users so the e-commerce companies are concerned about whether their own data and other user's data are creating confusion? And also, whether their data is encrypted or used in raw format?

- Data Transmission security- In the cloud computing environment, as the Business data is transmitted to the cloud side over the internet, the ecommerce companies are often concerned about the fact that data in the network transmission should be encrypted, strictly confidential without being misused and delivered to authorized user only.

- Data Audit security

- Relevant Laws and Regulations are not perfect

ADVANTAGES OF CLOUD BASED E-COMMERCE

Switching to a cloud-based e-commerce method is highly beneficial for organization in terms of higher profit gains. In fact, it's representative of where e-commerce is going in the future.

- **Enhanced security-** Whenever any organization platform manages valuable information, it's best to prepare itself with updated security measures. Leveraging a cloud-based platform leaves this to the professionals and ensures the website's security. Most importantly, it ensures the security of any organization's customers.
- **Reduced cost-** A lot of the companies offering hosting services do so at a price. While this is a recurring cost, it is much lower than the potential costs of maintaining the platform internally.
- **Care-free reliability-** Of course, for these companies to charge you a rate at all implies something powerful. They are taking on the responsibility of effectively and carefully managing your website's hosting, ensuring its success into the future. This gives you the peace of mind needed to focus on sales and other aspects of your business.

STRATEGIC APPROVAL FOR CLOUD-BASED SECURITY

- Understand the user's information sensitivity and its importance before moving towards cloud computing.
- Decision about which information required more security and what should be the access criteria for this.
- Explore different cloud models according to the information storage and find out the best one among them
- for workload.
- Develop a complete Owner's file and store it over the cloud system in encrypted form as cloud is not trusted. With this also update the service provider about the access criteria also.
- Users will acquire their requisite data from cloud system and also verify it to ensure its correctness.
- Scalability of data is prime concern as most owner's data can be feed into the system according to its popularity.
- Auditing of data is required to ensure the data is intact and deliver to the users as specified in access criteria without any modification, alteration in it.

- Portability of data is required to allow the authorized users to get the information at any place without struggling so hard.

CONCLUSION

With the introduction of cloud computing in the field e-commerce, a new direction is given to various user to communicate their required data from anywhere at any time and improve organization work. But it also faces the various security concerns which need to deal carefully. In this chapter, we are dealing with the trust, privacy and various security issues in cloud-based e-commerce services and also provide the various solutions to deal with any of these problems. In saying this, there are multiple security strategies which any e-commerce provider can instigate to reduce the risk of attack and compromise significantly. Awareness of the risks and the implementation of multi-layered security protocols, privacy policies and strong authentication and encryption measures will go a long way to assure the consumer and insure the risk of compromise is kept minimal. In future, we provide a complete secure framework which will handle all these security concern wisely and maturity will be improved.

REFERENCES

Bertion, E., Paci, F., & Ferrini, R. (2009). Privacy-Preserving Digital Identity Management for Cloud Computing. IEEE Computer Society Data Engineering Bulletin, 1-4.

CSA. (2011). STAR (security, trust and assurance registry) program. *Cloud Security Alliance*. Accessed on 16 Oct. 2012 https://cloudsecurityalliance.org/star/

Sen, J. (2015). Security and privacy issues in cloud computing. In Cloud Technology: Concepts, Methodologies, Tools, and Applications (pp. 1585-1630). IGI Global.

Takabi, H., Joshi, J. B. D., & Ahn, G.-J. (2010, November-December). Security and Privacy Challenges in Cloud Computing Environments. *IEEE Security and Privacy*, *8*(6), 24–31. doi:10.1109/MSP.2010.186

Chapter 5
Auto–Scaling in the Cloud Environment

Ravindra Kumar Singh Rajput
Suresh Gyan Vihar University, India

Dinesh Goyal
Poornima Institute of Engineering and Technology, India

ABSTRACT

Every software application has its own minimum set of requirements like CPU, storage, memory, networking, and power. These have to be integrated into a specific configuration to allow the smooth functioning of the software application. When data traffic becomes higher than expected, higher resources are required. There may not be enough time to provision new resources manually; in such cases, an auto-scaling system is required for managing these situations. Cloud computing means using data, programs, and other resources pooled in the data center and accessed through the internet instead of the user's computer. In the chapter, the authors discussed some aspects related to cloud computing like cloud workload, load balancing, load balancing algorithms, scaling techniques, and auto-scaling to fulfill cloud workload balancing requirements.

INTRODUCTION

Cloud computing is a sophisticated computing environment based on the polling of computing resources, and resources can be used anytime, anywhere on-demand via the internet with pay-as-you-go pricing (R. S. Rajput, and Anjali Pant, 2018). According to Katyal M., and Mishra A. (2013), there are three principal stakeholders of cloud

DOI: 10.4018/978-1-7998-1294-4.ch005

Table 1. Stakeholders of Cloud environment

Stakeholders	Requirement
End-User	Security, Privacy, Provenance, High Availability, Reduced Cost, Ease-of-use
Cloud Provider	Managing Resources, Resource Utilization, Outsourcing, Energy Efficiency, Metering, Providing Resources, Cost Efficiency, Utility Computing, Meet end-user requirements,
Cloud Developer	Elasticity/ Scalability, Virtualization, Agility and Adaptability, Data Management, Availability, Reliability, Programmability

environment viz. end-users, cloud providers, and cloud developers. The end-users are the clients or consumers of cloud resources, use the various cloud resources (Infrastructure/Software/Platform) provided by the cloud provider. Before using the cloud resources, the end-users of the cloud must agree to the specified Service Level Agreement (SLA). They can use cloud resources anytime, anywhere as on-demand, pay as use services. Cloud providers are responsible for the building of the cloud environment using computing resources pooling and provision techniques. Cloud providers are managing the huge bundle of resources that make up the cloud and providing these resources to the end-users. Cloud developer is a significant entity that lies between the end-user and cloud provider. Cloud developers are responsible for adhering to all the technical particulars for cloud, essential to assemble the requirements of cloud users as well as cloud providers.

The workload of the cloud data center does not remain the same all the time. When data traffic for a particular resource becomes higher than expected, such cases, higher resources are required. There may not be enough time to provision new resources manually; in such cases, an auto-scaling system is necessary for managing these situations.

Load-balancing is a procedure to redistribute the workload across computing resources. The decision to balance load is made locally by computing resources, based on its current utilization. Each computing resource continuously measures its resource utilization of CPU, memory, network consumption, and disk space. The auto-scaling technique provides on-demand resources available based on specific workloads in cloud computing systems. The auto-scaling service allows the arrangement of capacity management policies applied to dynamically decide on acquiring or releasing resource instances for a given application. Auto-scaling also make sure that new instances are seamlessly increased during demand spikes and decreased during demand drops, enabling consistent performance for lower expenses. Auto-scaling defines the scaling policies to acclimatize to the application's needs instantly, scales the resources, and examines the history of scaling events.

THE CLOUD WORKLOAD

Cloud computing technologies are being strongly recommended and deployed now in the many trades and scientific fields, such as e-government, e-commerce, finance, engineering, design and analysis, healthcare, web hosting, and social networks. It is remarkable, and these technologies implement cost-effective, scalable, flexible, and elasticity solutions. Cloud computing is a resource provisioning with the use of advanced virtualization and scheduling mechanisms. The term workload refers to any input (e.g., applications, services, transactions, or data transfers) submitted to the cloud data center and requests for the process for e-infrastructure or service.

Workload management is a method for arranging the workload distributions in order to optimize performance for users' applications. Workload monitoring is a process to monitor cloud workload. Workload monitoring focuses on three bask entity workload forecasting, workload scheduling, and maximum capacity behavior. Workload forecasting is a technique to analyzes history for a specified load metric with a particular period and forecasts the future demand for the next timestamp. Workload scheduling: is the technique to forecast workload at the scheduled timestamp. Maximum capacity behavior is the forecast load capacity in the term of the maximum workload.

Maria Carla Calzarossa et al. (2016) describe that workload can be considered as various types of inputs, e.g., applications, services, transactions, and data transfers in the cloud environment that processed by an e-infrastructure. To analyze the behavioral characteristics of cloud workloads, some import dimensions of study are processing model, architectural structure, resource requirements, and non-functional requirements.

According to the dimension of the processing model, there are two types of workload online (interactive) and offline (batch or background). An interactive workload typically consists of short-time processing. However, a batch workload consists of longtime tasks. The architectural structure is expressed as the form of the processing, numbers, and types of services, dependencies, and impact on the scheduling policies. The resource requirements deal with provisioning of resources, e.g., CPU, memory, I/O, network, and non-functional requirements related to SLA constraints, e.g., performance, dependability, security.

There are two board categories of behavioral characteristics qualitative attributes, e.g., priority, termination status, and quantitative attributes, e.g., workload intensity, demands, and usage patterns of cloud resources.

Lorido-Botran et al. (2012) described the term workload as a sequence of users' job requests with arrival timestamp. Abawajy J. (2018), explained that workload has some features like it has arrival rate, execution time, memory usages, Input/output operations, communication, and numbers of processors (VMs) required. Rajput R.S.

et al. (2019), categorize the workload of the cloud into two board categories, static workload, and dynamic workload. A static workload in which a certain amount of workload is given one time and, in the dynamic workload, arrives all the time. Based on the workload execution platform, further separated into two groups, server-centric and client-centric. Websites, web applications, scientific computations, enterprise software applications, database query, e-commerce, and storage, are some examples of server-centric workload. Computer graphics, mobile apps, e-mail, word processing are some examples of client-centric workload.

The workload-based job request is a subset of workload, and its arrival follows Poisson pattern.workload-based job requests can be defined as

$$J = \left\{ j_1, j_2, \ldots\ldots\ldots j_n \right\} \tag{1}$$

The request can be defined as a collection of the sequential task and defined as

$$j_l = \left\{ T_1, T_2, \ldots\ldots\ldots T_m \right\} \tag{2}$$

The task is the smallest entity of work. Further, it cannot be divided. For example, an embedded SQL query in a web application is a task. Execution of VBScript or JavaScript page with references can be a job request. The integrated approach of dynamic web pages to fulfill a specific purpose; those are used by end-users anytime, anywhere can be defined as workload. The utilization of CPU, memory, network, and Input/output operations in a cloud data center is evidence of workload.

Maria Carla. Calzarossa et al. (2016) suggested that virtual machines, physical machines, and client machines are three primary cloud workload monitoring targets and resource usages, and workload intensity are monitoring attributes.

LOAD-BALANCING

Load-balancing is a technique for the distribution of workload cloud over the cloud resources, and ensure smooth working of the schedulers, and minimization of response time via a proper matching of the workload with the available computing resources. Load-balancing is one of the primary problems in cloud computing. The load can be CPU load, memory required, delay, or network traffic load. Load-balancing is used to improve the performance and reliability of web sites, server-centric software applications, server-based databases, and other cloud services that are distributing the workload across multiple computing resources, i.e., server.

Load-balancing is the mechanism of sharing the load among various computing nodes to improve resource utilization, and job response time also ensures any node is not overloaded. The selection of the load-balancing algorithm is not natural because it involves additional constraints like reliability, security, and throughput (Jyoti Rathore et al., 2017).

Arpita Sharma et al. (2018) explained the objectives of load-balancing, i.e., proper resource utilization, cost-effectiveness, less response time, and prioritization. Information policy, resource policy, location policy, and selection policy are some fundamental policies of load balancing. Information policy defines the type of information and how information is collected for execution. The information policy is used to maintain a record of all the nodes of the system.

Resource policy describes all types of available resources. Location policy is used to find a companion for a server as a receiver node. The location policy is accountable for selecting a destination node for the transfer. The selection policy identified which task is located from the overloaded node to the free node.

Steps for Load-Balancing

1. The load balancing process is triggered or stopped in any node x_i; Total available node is N.
2. A new task T_j arrives at a node x_i.
3. Node x_i receives a task T_j, Reevaluate local workload Q_i for x_i.
4. If x_i is already overloaded ($|Q_i| > \alpha_i$), then x_i triggers the load balancing process to go to step 5; otherwise, the task is inserted into the waiting queue of x_i. Here α_i is the threshold value of workload for node x_i.
5. Apply information policy, collect information on the task to be executed, i.e., T_j.
6. Apply resource policy, identify available resources in the cloud system.
7. Location policy is used to find a companion for T_j with x.
8. The selection policy identified a free node for the execution of T_j.

The metrics for load-balancing are throughput, resource utilization, scalability, response time, fault tolerance, and migration time. Swarnkar N. et al. (2013) indicated some challenges in load-balancing, i.e., Overhead associated, Throughput, Performance, Resource utilization, Scalability, Response time, Fault tolerance, and Point of failure. Overhead associated is grown with overhead due to the movement of the task, interprocessor, and interprocess communication. The aim of Load-balancing techniques it should be minimized. Throughput is the measure for completed tasks. Performance is used to examine the efficiency of the system. The utilization of resources should be optimized. Scalability is the capability of an algorithm to

Figure 1. Challenges in the cloud environment

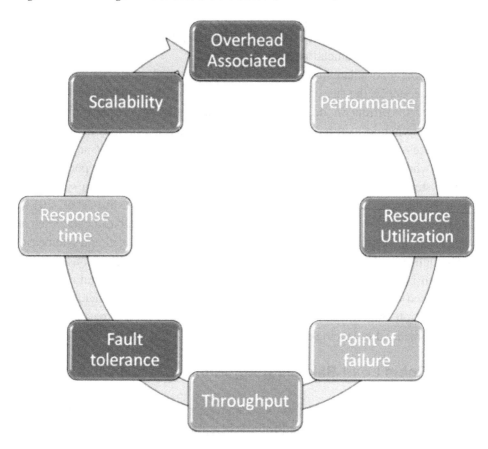

implement load-balancing for a system with any finite number of nodes. Response time is the quantity of time taken to respond by a particular load-balancing algorithm. Fault Tolerance is the capacity of an algorithm to perform uniform load balancing despite an arbitrary node. The load balancing technique should be fault-tolerant and avoids the point of failure.

LOAD-BALANCING ALGORITHMS

The load-balancing algorithms are algorithms for distributing workload among the computing resources for the effective working of the cloud environment. Load-balancing algorithms are divided into two primary categories static load-balancing algorithms and dynamic load-balancing algorithms. In static load-balancing, no dynamic information is used, and the performance of the processor is determined at the beginning of the execution. A static load-balancing algorithm does not consider any account of the previous state of computing resources. The goal of static load balancing algorithms is to reduce the overall execution time of a concurrent program and to minimize communication delays.

In dynamic load-balancing, the workload is distributed among the processor at the run time, unlike the static algorithm dynamic algorithm buffers the process in the queue on the primary node and allocated dynamically upon request from clients nodes. The dynamic load-balancing algorithm checks the previous load status of the resources. The advantage of dynamic load-balancing is that if any resource fails, the whole system will not stop; however, it will only affect the performance of the system. The dynamic load-balancing algorithm can provide a significant improvement in performance over the static algorithm (Jyoti Vashista et al., 2013). Sandeep Bhargava et al. (2013) expressed that there are three basic categories of dynamic load balancing algorithms render-initiated, receiver-initiated, and symmetric.

Throughput and response time are primary criteria for comparing or assessment of the load-balancing algorithms. Throughput is described as the total number of jobs executed within a fixed period without considering the virtual machine creation and destruction time. Response Time is the time taken for completing a job request. Brief of some load-balancing algorithms as:

Round-Robin Load-Balancing Algorithm

This algorithm is not used any previous data related to the load of any node at the time of assigning jobs. It uses round-robin scheduling techniques for assigning jobs. It selects the first node randomly and then assigns jobs to all other nodes in a round-robin manner. This algorithm is not for cloud computing because some nodes will be deeply loaded, and some are not.

Min-Min Load-Balancing Algorithm

The min-min algorithm starts with a set of all unallocated jobs. First, the minimum completion time for all jobs is calculated and prepared a chart. After that, jobs are assigned as per the chart as the preference for the shortest completion time. This process is repeated up to all the unassigned jobs are assigned.

Opportunistic Load-Balancing Algorithm

The goal of these algorithms is to keep busy each node. It is not calculated the execution time of any node.

Max-Min-Max Load-Balancing Algorithm

It is a two-phase scheduling algorithm that combines the opportunistic load balancing algorithm and the min-min load balancing algorithm. An opportunistic load-balancing algorithm keeps every node in the working state, and the min-min load-balancing algorithm is minimized the execution time of each task on the node. This combined approach helps in the efficient utilization of resources.

Central Load Balancing Decision Algorithm

It is based on a session switching technique on the application layer. It is calculated and use the connection time between the client and the node, and if that connection time beyond a threshold value, then the current connection will be terminated, and the task will be forwarded to another computing node. It is generally used the regular round-robin rules for forwarding one node to another.

MapReduce-Based Entity Algorithm

Map and reduce two primary tasks in this algorithm, Map acquires an input pair and produces a set of parallel intermediate pairs of process, and Reduce task accepts standard keys and merges these values as a smaller set of values.

Ant colony Optimization Algorithm

The ant colony optimization algorithm initiated from the movement of Ant. In this algorithm, two types of movements forward and backward. Forward movement means continuously moving from one overloaded node to another node to find a suitable node. If it finds an overloaded node, it will continue moving in the forward direction and check another node. If any node found overloaded check also the previous node, it may be free.

Load Balancing Algorithms Of Virtual Machine Resources

In this algorithm, use current state data and historical data of the workload of the cloud system. The genetic algorithm methods use to find the best strategy for resource utilization.

Index Name Server Load-Balancing Algorithm

The goal of this algorithm is to minimize data redundancy. The index name server algorithm uses some data, i.e., the position of the server, the transition quality, the maximum bandwidth, the data block, and calculate some parameters with help the excellent selection.

Dual Direction Downloading Algorithm

It uses for transferring the files from one server to another using two different directions, one from block 0 and another from block m. This algorithm reduces the network communication between the client and nodes and network overhead.

Exponential Smooth Forecast-Based On Weighted Least Connection

These algorithms firstly analyzed CPU power, memory, number of connections, and currently available disk space after that determine a node for specific tasks based on exponential smoothing.

Honeybee Foraging Behavior Algorithm

It is based on honeybee foraging behavior. In this algorithm, the first operation finds the suitable node and second operation assign node for the specific task.

Throttled Load-Balancing Algorithm

In this algorithm, the client requests to load-balancer for a suitable virtual machine to perform the required task. A load balancer assigns a particular node based on virtual machine data.

The Biased Random Sampling Load-Balancing Algorithm

In this algorithm, a virtual graph is constructed with the connectivity of each node representing the load on the server. Each node is represented as a vertex in a directed graph, and each in-degree represents the free resources of that node. The process of random sampling does the addition and deletion of processes.

Active Clustering Load-Balancing Algorithm

Several load-balancing algorithms are available for cloud computing; each load balancing algorithm has its advantages and drawbacks. The clustering approach is introduced here for a selection of algorithms.

Join-Idle Queue Algorithm

The join-idle queue is used for large-scale systems to use distributed dispatchers. Dispatchers are assigning jobs to processors as a manner to reduce average queue length at each processor.

SCALING POLICIES

Scaling means keeping the behavior of an application will be constant when the workload changes by the alteration with computing resources. There are two threshold values can be defined for any scaling policies lower bound and upper bound. An alarm type system monitors the metric values of the workload load on computing resources. When the metric value breaks the threshold values, the scaling function will be triggered by to alter computing resources as per the policy. The scaling policy is a basic plan that is relevant to the scaling algorithm.

Alexandros Evangelidis et al. (2018) described rule-based auto-scaling policies, In that policy application developers specify an upper and lower bound on a performance metric (e.g., CPU utilization) along with the desired change in capacity for this situation. CPU utilization, Memory utilization, Custom monitoring metrics, e.g., Load average, queue length, connections, HTTP load, are some metrics for rule builders. Generally, each scaling policy has three primary components threshold values, performance metrics, and triggered functions. Some scaling policies as under:

Dynamic Scaling Policy

Dynamic scaling is a goal tracking scaling policy of computing resources. In the dynamic scaling policies, the computing resources will be scaled as per live changes in resource utilization. It is very similar to the thermostat of air-conditioned that maintains the temperature.

Predictive Scaling

Predictive scaling forecasts the future workload using machine learning techniques, firstly that analyzed the historical workload of computing resources then prepare the scaling schedule for future use.

Horizontal Scaling Policy

The horizontal scaling policy is the ability to increase capacity by connecting several new computing resources, and all computing resources considered as a single logical computing unit.

Vertical Scaling Policy

The vertical scaling policy is the ability to upgrade computing resources with a higher capacity resource. Vertical scaling means that scale by the capacity of components (CPU, RAM) to existing computing resources.

Scheduled Scaling Policy

Schedule-based auto-scaling can be used to scale computing resources at a specific period of the day.

AUTO-SCALING

The cloud computing systems are managing cloud workload by distributing the workload among several nodes or transfer to the higher resource so that no resource will be overloaded. However, several techniques are used for the management of workload cloud environment, but it is still a domain of research and development. Management of the load and scaling of cloud resources are some essential aspects of the cloud computing environment. A well-organized load balancing plan ensures efficient resource utilization.

The auto-scaling is a technique to include or terminate additional computing resources based on the scaling policies without involving humans.

Auto-Scaling Life Cycle

The auto-scaling life cycle has divided two types of provisioning, type A and B. type A is the process of a one-time setting, the same as SLA. The following are steps of type A process.

1. The auto-scale setting of cloud resource: In this process information store about targeted cloud resource, determine whether targeted resource scale up or down, notification setting.
2. Generate auto-scale profile: Link cloud customer profile with auto-scale cloud resource.
3. Capacity setting: In this step, to register minimum, maximum, and default values for the number of instances.
4. Auto-scaling rules preparing: In this step, define a trigger (time or metric) and a scale action (up or down).

Type B process is the periodic process, and states change as per pre-defined setting in the process A. Metric update, notification, and triggered action are parts of the type B process.

ADVANTAGES OF AUTO-SCALING IN CLOUD COMPUTING

The significant advantages of auto-scaling are better fault tolerance, high availability and cost management. Auto-scaling helpful for the failover process so that it has better fault tolerance. The cloud environment with auto-scaling can handle massive traffic. Auto-scaling can dynamically increase and decrease capacity as needed and provide the customer with a cost-effective solution.

Figure 2. Auto-scaling life cycle in the cloud environment

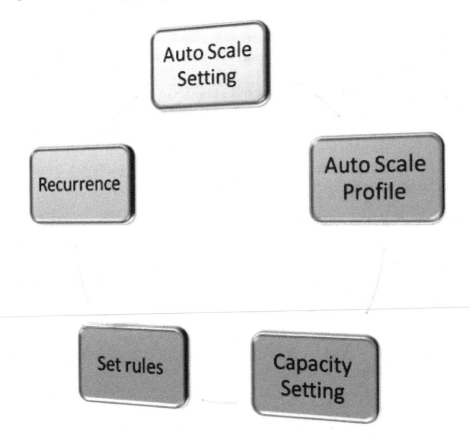

LIMITATION OF AUTO-SCALING IN CLOUD COMPUTING

Some limitations of the auto-scaling cloud computing environment are unreliable deployment, deployment speed, old application versions. When a particular time system moves to additional parallel resources (Horizontal scaling), It is a question parallel system is reliable or not, the time required to new deployment, and version of additional resources are some issues.

REFERENCES

Abawajy, J. (2018). *What is workload (cloud data center service provisioning: theoretical and practical approaches.* Retrieved from https://www.jnu.ac.in/content/LAB05/presentation/gian2018/day2.pdf

Bhargava, Sandeep, & Goya, Swatil. (2013). Dynamic Load Balancing in Cloud Using Live Migration of Virtual Machine. International Journal of Advanced Research in Computer Engineering & Technology, Vol. 2(8), 2472:2477

Calzarossa, Della Vedova, Massari, Petcu, Tabash, & Tessera. (2016). Workloads in the Clouds. *Principles of Performance and Reliability Modeling and Evaluation*, 1-27.

Evangelidisa, A., Parkera, D., & Bahsoona, R. (2018). Performance Modelling and Verification of Cloud-based Auto-Scaling Policies. [Preprint submitted Accepted Manuscript]. *Future Generation Computer Systems*, 12.

Katyal, M., & Mishra, A. (2013). A Comparative Study of Load Balancing Algorithms in Cloud Computing Environment. *International Journal of Distributed and Cloud Computing, 1*(2), 5-14.

Lorido-Botran, T., Miguel-Alonso, J., & Lozano, J. A. (2012). *Auto-scaling techniques for elastic applications in cloud environments.* Technical report, Department of Computer Architecture and Technology University of the Basque Country.

Rajput, R. S., & Pant, Anjali. (2018). Optimal Resource Management in the Cloud Environment-A Review. [IJCTM]. *International Journal of Converging Technologies and Management, 4*(1), 12–24.

Rajput, R. S., Goyal, D., & Pant, A. (2019). The Survival Analysis of Big Data Application Over Auto-scaling Cloud Environment. In A. Somani, S. Ramakrishna, A. Chaudhary, C. Choudhary, & B. Agarwal (Eds.), *Emerging Technologies in Computer Engineering: Microservices in Big Data Analytics. ICETCE 2019. Communications in Computer and Information Science* (Vol. 985, pp. 155–166). Singapore: Springer.

Rathore, J., Keswani, B., & Rathore, V. S. (2017). Analysis of Various Load Balancing Techniques in Cloud Computing: A Review. *Suresh Gyan Vihar University Journal of Engineering & Technology, 3*(2), 48–52.

Sharma, A., & Gupta, K. Amit and Goyal, Dinesh, An Optimized Task Scheduling in Cloud Computing Using Priority (April 20, 2018). Proceedings of 3rd International Conference on Internet of Things and Connected Technologies (ICIoTCT), 2018 held at Malaviya National Institute of Technology, Jaipur (India) on March 26-27, 2018. Available at SSRN: https://ssrn.com/abstract=3166077 or http://dx.doi.org/doi:10.2139srn.3166077

Swarnkar, Singh, & Shankar. (2013). A Survey of Load Balancing Techniques in Cloud Computing. *International Journal of Engineering Research & Technology, 2*(8), 800-804.

Vashistha, J., & Jayswal, A. K. (2013). Comparative Study of Load Balancing Algorithms. *IOSR Journal of Engineering, 3*(3), 45–50. doi:10.9790/3021-03324550

Chapter 6
Data Security and Privacy–Preserving in Cloud Computing Paradigm:
Survey and Open Issues

Abhineet Anand
ⓘD https://orcid.org/0000-0003-3505-8563
Chitkara University Institute of Engineering and Technology, Punjab, India

Arvindhan Muthusamy
Galgotias Universirty, India

ABSTRACT

Cloud computing is a new technique that has been widely spread recently due to the services provided to users according to their need. Being a pay-for-what-you-use service, it provides a much-encapsulated set of services. Cloud computing acts as a main attraction for the business owners. Whether they are big or small, they can choose from the required services. Management of heavy flow data is very likely to be managed under this with the confidentiality and security of the data attached. Having all these features may attract everyone, but every technique always comes with some issues. The main aim of this survey chapter is to gain a better understanding of security issues that can occur in cloud computing.

DOI: 10.4018/978-1-7998-1294-4.ch006

INTRODUCTION

Before coining of the system of cloud computing, there was centralized storage which used to contain all the data on the server side, in which if a client needed to acknowledge the data it has to establish a connection to the server side. After this centralized system, a distributed system came along where many systems which are connected together through the network can use shared resources.

Later, to overcome the disadvantages of both the system mentioned above cloud computing was introduced. Much before when the technology was not even up to mark to implement the cloud computing the idea was given by John McCarthy in 1961 at the speech at MIT. Hence, after some time the idea was able to be implemented by salesforce.com in 1999, as they provided some applications to the users using the internet through their website. In 2002, amazon web services provided the service of storage and computation to the users and started Elastic Compute Cloud in 2006 which was open to everybody and it was a truly commercial service. Google Apps started providing these services in 2009. After that many mainstream companies join the queue of providing different services using cloud computing as a platform. (Dong,et al., 2018) The main contributions of this article are summarized as follows:

1. An itemized examination of elements for edge figuring is condensed from the comprehensive point of view. A exhaustively audit of edge registering definition what's more, engineering are introduced.
2. The information security and protection necessities are outlined in light of five basic measurements, including the classification, accessibility, uprightness, verification and access control, and protection necessities.

CLOUD COMPUTING SERVICES

There are many ways in which cloud computing and services are defined. It consists of both the software and hardware components where software acts services provided to the user and hardware are the components connecting the server to the system to perform the services. Delivering various types of services like storage and access to data through the internet to the user instead of using hardware is the main motto of cloud. (Zhang, et.al 2018).

Computing. Due to the fast generation of data through the internet and the need for managing and access to data in a secure environment with other services are provided in cloud computing. According to NIST,the definition of cloud computing is "Cloud computing is a model for enabling a convenient, on-demand network access to a shared pool of configurable computing resources(e.g. networks, servers, storage, applications and services) that can be rapidly provisioned and released with minimal management effort or service provider interaction. Table 1 shows the major services in Cloud Computing .

Technologies Related To Cloud Computing

Grid Computing- It follows a distributed computing technique which proves very useful in following cloud computing services as resources are divided over the network and can be called when needed.

Utility Computing- It is the technique of cloud computing where one has to pay for the usage of the services when one needs to use other specific services rather than the basic ones.

Virtualization- This technique basically minimizes the use of hardware. It uses the server called virtual machine which helps in performing the tasks based over the virtualization that is collecting all the resources on different servers on one and performing the required tasks as and when needed.

Autonomic Computing- IBM coined this term in 2001, this is where the system itself takes the decision based on the statistics as required. (Li WenLI et.al.. 2015)

Main Characteristics of Cloud Computing Are

1-On-demand self-service- Different services provided to the user based on their needs that is storage, services provided by the software.

2-Broad network access- Many thick and thin clients can able to access the server equally and easily with a good speed.

3-Resource pooling- Gathering of many computer resources at one place to make it useful for multiple users providing multitasking.

4-Rapid elasticity- Availability of resources at any time as well as with same quality and quantity expanded as the user needed.

5-Measured services- Quality of the resources are optimized based on the services and it does not affect the quality of the data.

Types of Cloud Services: IaaS, PaaS, and SaaS

The cloud computing services fall into four broad categories: infrastructure as a service (IaaS), platform as a service (PaaS), serverless and software as a service (SaaS). These are being called as the cloud computing stack because they build on top of one another.

Figure 1.

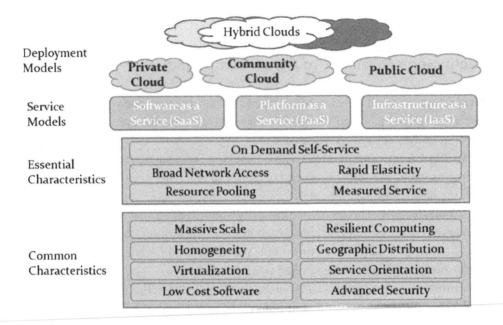

Infrastructure as a Service (IaaS)

Infrastructure as a service (IaaS) is an instant computing infrastructure, provisioned and managed over the internet. .It, let you pay only for what you use. It helps you avoid the expense and complexity of buying and managing your own physical servers and other data centre infrastructure. *(Fig.1).* each resource is offered as a respective service component, where you only need to rent a particular one for as long as you need it. A cloud computing service provider, such as Azure, manages the infrastructure, while you purchase, install, configure, and manage your own software. (Lakhwani kamlesh et,al.. 2018)

Platform as a Service (PaaS)

Platform as a service (PaaS) is an entire development and deployment environment in the cloud, it guards you resources that empower to deliver everything from simple cloud-based apps to sophisticated, cloud-enabled enterprise applications. You purchase the resources you need from a cloud service provider on a pay-as-you-go basis and sledge them over a secure Internet connection. It allows you to avert the expense and complexity of buying and contend software licenses, the fundamental application infrastructure and middleware.

Software as a Service (SaaS)

Software as a service (SaaS) allows users to *connect*. Common examples are email, calendaring and office tools (such as Microsoft Office 365) it provides an intact software solution which you purchase on a pay-as-you-go basis from a provider. Then, you rent the use of an app for your organization and your users connect to it over the Internet.

TOP BENEFITS OF CLOUD COMPUTING

Cloud computing is a big shift here are seven common reasons organizations are turning to cloud computing services:

Cost

Cloud computing eliminates the capital expense of buying hardware and software and setting up and running on-site data centres—the racks of servers, the round-the-clock electricity for power and cooling, the IT experts for managing the infrastructure. It adds up fast.

Speed

Most cloud computing services furnish self-service and on demand, so even huge amounts of computing resources can be provisioned in minutes, typically with just a few mouse clicks, giving businesses a lot of flexibility and taking the pressure off capacity planning.

Global Scale

The interest includes the ability to scale elastically. In cloud speak, that means dropship the right amount of IT resources—for example, more or less computing power, storage.

Productivity

On-site datacenters require a lot of "racking and stacking"—hardware set up, software patching and other tame IT management chores. Cloud computing abolish the need for many of these tasks, so IT teams can spend time to attaining more important business goals.

Performance

The biggest cloud computing services run on a worldwide network of secure data centres, which are regularly upgraded to the contemporary generation of fast and efficient computing hardware. This offers assorted benefits over a single corporate data centre, counting diminish network latency for applications and prominent economies of scale.

Security

Many cloud providers proffer a broad sies, technologies and controls that strengthen your security stance overall, helping protect your data, apps and infrastructure from potential warning.(V.Sakthivel et.al..2018)

USES OF CLOUD COMPUTING

You are probably using cloud computing right now, even if you don't realize it. If you use an online service to send an email, edit documents, watch movies or TV, listen to music, play games or store pictures and other files, it is likely that cloud computing is making it all possible behind the scenes. The first cloud computing services are barely a decade old, but already a variety of organizations—from tiny startups to global corporations, government agencies to non-profits—are embracing the technology for all sorts of reasons.

Here are a few examples of what is possible today with cloud services from a cloud provider:

Create New Apps And Services

Quickly erect, deploy and scale applications—web, mobile and API—on any platform. Ingress the resources you need to help meet execution, security and compliance requirements.

Test and Build Applications

Reduce application development cost and time by using cloud infrastructures that can easily be scaled up or down.

Store, Back Up and Recover Data

Fortify your data more cost-efficiently—and at enormous scale—by fetching your data over the Internet to an offsite cloud storage system that is approachable from any location and any device.

Analyze Data

Uniform your data across teams, divisions and locations in the cloud. Then use cloud services, such as machine learning and artificial intelligence, to bare insights for more informed decisions. Fortify your data more cost-efficiently—and at enormous scale—by fetching your data over the Internet to an offsite cloud storage system that is approachable from any location and any device.

Stream audio and video

Connect with your audience anywhere, anytime, on any device with high-definition video and audio with global distribution.

Embed intelligence

Services: on a public cloud, private cloud or hybrid cloud.

SECURITY ISSUES IN CLOUD COMPUTING

Every technique has its advantages and disadvantages, similarly, cloud computing deals with many security issues. Cloud storage faces many of these issues because it does not deal with the process of how the data is being saved and from where the data is coming from. (Fig.2) There are three main data security conditions that are needed to be fulfilled to avoid the issues-

1-**Confidentiality**- This deals with the protection of data in the cloud so that it cannot be changed due to malicious users or attacks.
2-**Integrity**-Integrity means wholeness of data that is data is not divided into different sections due to any attacks from outside.
3-**Availability**-Availability means data can be easily retrieved when required by the user and only the data are available.(Sara Alfatih Adam et.al.. 2016).

Figure 2.

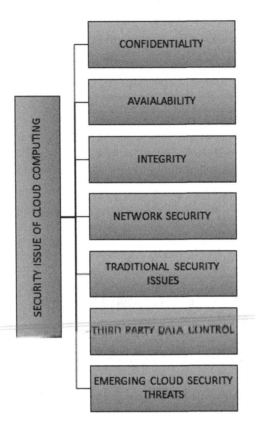

Every deployment models proposed by NIST has to deal with their own different issues of security. But the common issues that are faced by cloud computing as a whole are-

1-Confidentiality
2-Availability
3-Integrity
4-Traditional security issues
5-Network Security
6-Emerging cloud security threats
7-Third party data control

NETWORK SECURITY

Cloud security is gradually expanding many areas of security. Computer security, cryptography, network security, and information security. This security subject refers to a large set of policies applications, security infrastructure, technologies and controls deployed to protect data of the cloud computing. Cloud security surrounded a large range of security constraints from the user and the cloud provider's perspective. The end user's concerned with cloud provider's security policy decided that where the primary security provided. Provider's security policy decided where we store the data in the cloud. Who will access this data .cloud security era is different security. The computer security issue is that how we can provide the security in the physical computer. *(Fig.3)*. Much more security the access of control mange met of cloud assets and maintain the cloud security policy. The cloud security alliance is a non-profit organization. It makes proper guidelines of the framework, provides the security within the cloud environment. Network security describes the policies and procedure for cloud security.

MAIN IN THE MIDDLE

Man in the middle attack is the biggest issue for network security. It is also known as MITM. For MITM attack there are three victims needed. Sender, Receiver and eavesdropper/intruder. When the sender and receiver communicating to each other intruder will intercepting the message between the communications. Sender and Receiver don't know that anyone stole the message. Eavesdropper stole or get the message without knowing both parties. (Basel Saleh Al-Attab et.al. 2016).

Basically attack the MITM by eavesdropper operation is two types Passive and Active. In the passive the intruder may get the information/message does not change any content of the message. But in Active attack, the intruder will alter the message and then sent to the receiver which is sometimes may be harmful.

IP Spoofing: In the cloud network Security IP Spoofing is created by Internet protocol (IP).IP Protocol generates with a false source Internet address. From which other intruder computing device will take place. Sending the data over the internet IP is one major part. It contains the address of the computer system of the sender (I.P) . When the sender sends the packet over the network must have a header that contains the IP address of source. But the Intruder Changed the IP address between the transmissions. Receiver thought that this packet comes from another resource. So, it denied.

Figure 3.

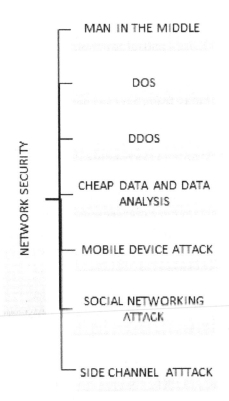

DNS Spoofing (Domain name server): DNS is domain name server spoofing. DNS Spoofing intruder generated a fake website which looks like a real DNS server. Intruder intention to get all the important information.

HTTP Spoofing: HTTP Spoofing is the type of MITM attack. HTTP stands for the Hypertext Transfer protocol used in the Internet service. HTTP is which used in the internet service. Before that HTTP is good for the Internet, it asked for login credentials. But today Now In this HTTP Spoofing is possible to man steal the data of the login credentials. *(*Fig.4*)*

HTTP/SSL Hijacking: **(Secure Socket Layer):** SSL Hijacking is the man middle attack. In the SSL Hijacking attacker creates false websites links. SSL Hijacking generates through SSL striping through victim computer. Whenever we use any website it started from HTTP. When SSL Hijacking if we search the attacker create own website of look like same, after that we all own information give to that website. HTTPS generally used to reliable communication between the client and the server.

Figure 4.

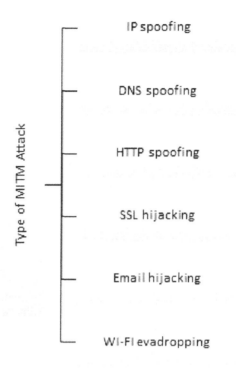

For secure communication between the client and the server. Every website linked started from HTTP:/.

Email hijacking: Email Hijacking is hacked by the unauthorized people or manipulation of an Email account.Nowadays Email is one of the most common communication media for anyone. Email is generally categorised in two different types of web services. Open web services in the open based web services provide the Email to anyone face. Closed based web Services: In the closed based web Services the email provided by the organization only its member. Email is widely used for communication due to its security. (Fig.5). The main reason behind to email hacked to get the client personal, confidential and sensitive information that email contains. Sometimes Email Hijacking is very harmful to loss of financial damage, personal life, and certain websites. Email hijacking attack three different types Spam, Virus, Phishing. (Sangeeta Sharma, 2015).

Spam: Spam email is also known as Junk email. This Spam and junk email are suspicious messages sent through the mail. These messages generally look commercial in nature. It contains a conventional link of a phishing website. That hosts malicious virus.

Figure 5.

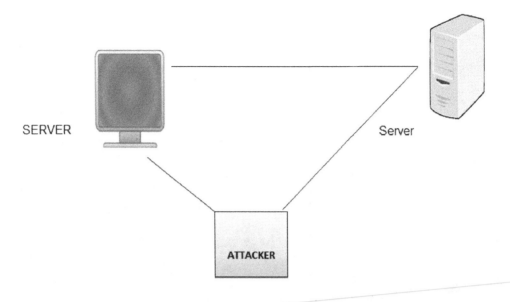

Vii us: Virus is a malicious code which harms the system or corrupts the system. This malicious set through the mail message. It activates when the action clicks on it an email message, it open with an email attachment to get infected message next time ransomware.

Phishing: phishing attack is common to attackman in the middle. In this attack, we verify the account . Usually, the email looks like a similar social network/marketing website /corporates website. In that website people login his information. Where we log in that website is a fake website to looks similar to the original. From there the intruder gets all information of credentials. A phishing attack is cyber-attack.

WIFI eavesdropping: Wi-Fi eavesdropping is the man in the middle attack. It is also called an evil twin attack. In this eavesdropping attack attacker attack unsuspecting victims connect to a malware Wi-Fi hotspots . This Wi-Fi eavesdropping performed in the public area where the people use public hotspots. Like a restaurant, park, hotels etc. The hacker Wi-Fi hotspots name is the same as the actual public hotspots name .whenever the person comes near about the malicious Wi-Fi hotspots reconnect automatically. .

Figure 6.

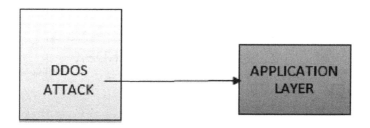

DENIAL OF SERVICES (DOS)

DOS attack is one of most common attack Man in the Middle Attack. Denial of service attack is a cyber-attack. In this attack to shut down the machine or network. Due to which the user can't access what they want. Dos attack to make a machine is inaccessible to its user. DOS accomplish by the flooding the target with the traffic. In the DOS attack, it does not get only the information or other assets. Its costs the victim deal time and money. In the DOS attack organization, the loss is big or high. DOS attack method is two types: Flooding services and crash services.

DISTRIBUTED DENIAL SERVICES (DDOS)

Distributed denial of services. Distribute denial service is a type of denial of service attack. In the Distributed DDOS the network traffic, or communicating path or server or the targeted system traffic. This attack occurs by the internet flooding traffic. Internet flooding traffic means that the targeted system gets more and more request from another computer. That is the reason the system goes shut down or crash.DDOS is totally different from the DOS. In the DDOS the system will get the request from the different IP address. So it is called DDOS. It is a malicious attempt to disturb or close the normal traffic of the targeted sever system. In the DDOS attack system server targeted from the more computer system.. Each one is turning into a bot. The attacker gets the remote control over the bot. Group of the bots are called the botnet.(Liu et al., 2015).

Application layer attack: - An application layer of attack of DDOS is sometimes called layer DDOS attack. The goal of the application layer attack is exhaust/denied to achiever the resource target. In the Application, layer human is interacting with the network layer through an application. (Fig.6) DDOS attacker attack the application

Figure 7.

Figure 8.

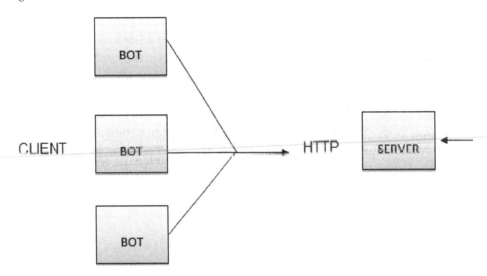

webpage or application layer process .The attacker attack on the application layer to disable the functionality of the application page or features. This attack is different from a network attack. There are many methods to attach to the application some is HTTP flood.

HTTP Flood: - It is a type of volumetric attack of DDOS. This attacked to design overcome a targeted server with HTTP requests. Once the targeted has been full of requests and cannot able to respond in normal traffics. (Fig.7) So denial of services takes palace to the actual users. HTTP flood in two types HTTP gets an HTTP post.

Volumetric Attack: - Volumetric attack is a basic type of DOS attack. A volumetric attack sends a larger amount of requests, or traffic for the targeted network system to overcome the bandwidths. In the volumetric attacks, the attacker sends the huge amount of traffic request to a targeted system to overcome the bandwidth capabilities.

Figure 9.

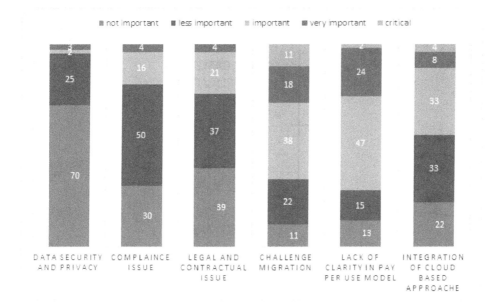

These attacks look like a flood to the target system. (Fig.8) It is getting more request causing the system will goes in slow down and stopping or denied the services.

Just like the example: - if any system has a speed of 100's of Gbps attacker attacks the over the 100's Gbps, the system stopped the services. It is generated from the single source attacker. There is a different method of volumetric attack achieve DNS amplification, UDP flood, TCP flood.(Fig. 9).

CHEAP DATA AND DATA ANALYSIS

Cloud Computing is the new generation computing system based on the internet. It provides easy services to use to accessing or fetching the data with the various cloud applications. It also provides the space to store and access e data from the remote area by using the cloud application .By the cloud services the user store the local data in the remote server. The remote server can be accessed or managed through cloud services.

Figure 10.

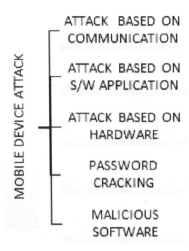

DATA SECURITY CHALLENGES

When the company moving towards the internet-based cloud services. One is a big challenge that data provides security and privacy. Data loss and leakage created lots of challenge or also impact on the business, origination, trust and broad.

1. ***SECURITY***: - In the real world security of any things very challenging .now days the internet is most popular. Through which globalization is possible. On the internet one of the big issues is that security of data (Fig.10).how we can secure its data when two organization sharing data resources, it might be a risk to misuse of data. So it's very necessary to secure communication channel, data storage, transmit, and process. This is also a big challenge for cloud computing to securing the data .for cloud computing to securing the data.

    1.1 ***Confidentiality***:-Confidential means that data is secured from the unauthorized person. Through it's we maintain the security of the data. In the confidentiality unauthorized person can't see the data or read. Data always maintain confidentially.

    1.2 *Integrity:-*It means that the data of the client not to be modified .it maintains the integrity of data.

    1.3 *Availability:* - Availability means data is always available when they want to access the data .this is the major issue of data security.

LOCALITY

In cloud computing, the client gets the data from the remote area .this data is distributed over the network region. In the data security to find the distributed data location is very difficult .when the data move from one place to another place laws of data changing can also change. So it generates data compliance and the data privacy laws. In the cloud custom always should know the location of the data which intimated by the service provider.

Integrity:- Integrity means to maintain the integrity of data Integrity of the data means that no one unauthorized person modified the data. So to maintain the security of data, must always maintain the integrity of data. In cloud computing, it always follows the ACID properties to maintain Data integrity Recent days web services finding lots of the problems with the transaction as it uses HTTP.HTTP service cannot support the guaranteed delivery. This thing can be handled by the transaction API itself.

Access control:- In the access control each and every organization make a data policy. In which they make a policy for the employee who will access the data or not. In the organization, they do not give permission to access all data for the employee. Every organization uses various encryption technique to secure accessing the data between the valid users. The organization provide the key only valid or authorized user.

Confidentiality:- Confidential means that the data is secured from the unauthorized person. In the cloud computing data is stored in the remote server, such as video, file pdf, and images etc. This data may be provided by single or multiple cloud providers. When the data store in the remote server, data confidentiality must be required.

Breaches: -Data breaches is one major security issue in cloud computing. In the cloud, many important documents stored in the cloud server .if its data is the intentional or unintentional release the private data or confidential information is called the data breach. In the data breach, an unauthorized accessed the confidential data or viewing the copied, or transmitted. In the data breaches most of the financial information health information, banking credit data, trade secret etc. Data breaches attack the unstructured data file, documents and important sensitive information .

Storage:-In the cloud computing the data storage reliability is an issue. This data store in the virtual machine. This virtual machine needs a physical infrastructure to stores the data which may cause a data security threat.

Data Centre Operation:-In the data Centre operation cloud computing application always to protects the user's data without any loss. If cloud computing cannot be managed properly. Then create a problem in storage and accessing the data. In that case, if the data is a loss, cloud providers are responsible for that.

Figure 11.

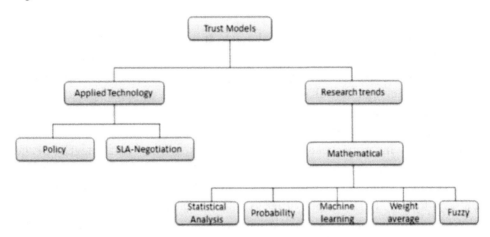

Segregation:-Segregation is the security threat of cloud computing. Segregation of data among many customers who accessed .Segregation separates the data for all individual customers.one of the major property of cloud computing is multitenancy. Through which the cloud gives permission to store or process the data by the multiple users on the cloud server. In cloud computing data, segregation is very difficult. If the data segregation fails in any circumstance may be the possibility of data intrusion .

MOBILE DEVICE ATTACKS

Mobile device attacks are common in these days. It is a handheld device which is mostly used for communication. The attacker always tried to attack the device (target) device and exploits targeting devices. Examples: - smartphone tablets and many other devices.

Mobile device attack are many types:-

An Attack Based on Communication

Attacks based on communication means that Attacks on the device by communication on the mobile device there are many different ways through communication (Fig .11)

- SMS \MMS Attacks
- GSM Attacks
- Wi-Fi Attacks

SMS Attack / Mms Attack

SMS attack is usually a common attack of the mobile device. Some Mobile device can't be managed binary SMS message. It tends to infect message block which causes to the device to restart. The device performed the denial services attack. Some are many devices whose mail address space is 32 character email address. It gives more than that space address that leads the "curse of silence" attack. It also leads the complete dysfunction. In the big city attack through DDOS. DDOS attack against the mobile device which performed to delays messaging to overloaded network. Another attack is performed through the MMS. On the MMS the attacker sends the attachment which is infected with a virus. When the receiver open that attachment the phone/mobile device is infected.

GSM Attacks

GSM is a technology using for communication telecommunication. It is developed by the ETSI standard. Which describe the second generation cellular network of telecommunication devices. In GSM there are three main things which we are using a mobile station, mobile equipment and subscriber identity module (SIM) Subscriber identity module is a smart card. SIM stores the specific subscriber Information with the encryption keys. Core Network which carries the function of mobile management of mobile is the roaming on the Network. The third one is the base station which handling the traffic and signalling between the station network and core network. GSM attack is widely used for against mobile communication. This does not depend on network weakness. GSM attackers include malware identity theft by sim cloning. Many more attacks performed on that., Some security issue find. Generally, the attacks exploit the GSM protocol. Most of the attacks the A5/1 and A5/2 cypher algorithm. This will be performed active and passive attacks.

Attacks Based on Software Application

Today software application attack is common. In the software application many malware viruses which affect the mobile devices when downloading the software application, it gets all the confidential information or bank credential information. Web browser mobile attack is popular. Web browser attack also considers in the software application. It is one of the emerging attacks for a mobile device. May mobile device have web attack by phishing malicious websites and software run in the mobile device.

ATTACK BASED ON H/W

Smartphones or mobiles devices contain different types of microchips, memory storage, board, server-H/w and Microprocessor.

H/w attack is generally two types:-

1.   Logical attack
2.   Physical attack

Logical attack: - In the logical attack mobiles devices usually browser vulnerabilities. Mobile devices further target due to the interaction between the browser and phone. The logical attack also performed by remote maintains. Remote configuration to other devices due to insufficiently protected interfaces to promote the attack.

Physical attack: - Physical attack when the data can be transfer through the wireless medium and interfaces allowing vulnerabilities in the Wi-Fi, Radio, BLE, many more. In this attack, the attacker obtains the user data password illegally. Basically the physical attack more attack on the memory. Memory store the many more unprotected data. An attacker may be able to read the data. The attacker manipulated the store data of the memory card.

Password cracking: - the University of Pennsylvania to finding the password cracking through smudge attack. In the pattern gesture to unlock the mobile device password or passcode.

Malicious software: -Mobile devices easily attack by malware software.Because mobile devices are the fixed point of access to the internet. Malicious software is a program that aims to harm the devices. Mobiles malware software specially design the code for mobile devices like smartphones, tablets and smartwatches. This malware software is written for the mobile operating system and mobile technology. This day's mobile malware security is a big issue for the industry. Attacks on mobile devices are gradual increases.

Wi-Fi attack: - Wi-Fi attacker attacks the mobile devices to eavesdrop the Wi-Fi communication. It gets the device information. (Like a password, username). Wi-Fi eavesdropping is not unique for smartphones. But they did harm attack because of Wi-Fi only uses the internet for communication. So the security of the wireless system is important. Before we secure the Wi-Fi by WEP Security keys. But WEP encryption n key is very small. This is the weakness of the WEP keys. These WEP keys are breakable. After the WEP keys the wireless communication is secured by the WAP security protocol WAP based on the [TKIP].WAP is a dynamic key encryption. In the mobile devices, the user might short encryption keys only one of the numeric short number. This is an attacker attack or succeeds in breakable by brute force attack.

BLE: - BLE mobile attack is one of the easier exploits vulnerable .in the mobile BLE attack attacker does not require to authentication .the attacker target is that used the serial port to control the phase. This virtual serial port contains in the vulnerable application .one more attack on the BLE. In which BLE must be reached in the range. The attacker sends via BLE. If the receiver phone signs the file, the virus is transmitted.(M. Sookhak et.al., 2017).

SOCIAL NETWORKING ATTACK

Social networking attack is a social platform where a large number of user's base like Twitter, Face book, outlook, Instagram and many more. This social platform gradually increases in the market. In this social networking, one of the big challenges is a security issue. Many of the attackers get sensitive information from their social media use against us. Social network threat is gradually increasing very fast now day's. This social media content the user's name, phone, location and other may business activities. In the social networking attack, there are many risks fakes identity theft, fake request, social sharing post, profile hacking, and fake apps or malicious software links. Attacker using may different method to do an attack on the user by social media network. Discuss below fake offering, fakes apps, Phishing attack, social networking infrastructure, evil twin, identity theft.(R. Roman et.al., 2018).

Fake offering: In the fake offering the attacker use the gift card and may other offers trick for the social network users. Users of the social media network join a fake group for the gift cards. This fake offering attack is recent increases very fast. In 2013 the 82% of the social media attack performed through fake offering. Users of the social media for finding the gift card they share the credential or phone number.

Fake Apps: In the social networking attacks the number of fake apps raised in 2013. These apps look like to be legitimate but it contains the malicious code payload. This apps is available free in the market. The user installs this app in the phone; it steals the data or crashes the mobile device.

Social Networking Infrastructure:-In social networking infrastructure we discuss the distributed denial of service attack. Before we are going to discuss the DDOS. We know about the DOS.DOS attack is the IP protocol attack. In which the users unable to access the resource of the system. DOS attack consumes all the computational resource, memory space, CPU time or bandwidth. DDOS is also a type of DOS but it more powerful than DOS .In the DOS attack attacker performed an attack from the one originating source. But in the DDOS attack, it performed from the multiple sources simultaneously. This launching attack is also called the bombards attack.

Evil Twin Attack: Evil twin attack is an impersonation. it means that an attacker is a fake person. This attack is growing fast. In this attacker impersonate people gets the companies' person profile information. The attacker creates an evil twin account on Face book, Fill the information, upload the picture and validate the Facebook account. When the Facebook account is created, it user id must be unique. When the ID is created impersonate people added several friends by sending request, people from the native palace, same schools, and joining the groups.

Identity theft:-identity theft is less dangerous and easier to perform from another attack.IN this attack attackers only gets the user information. This attack performed by the hijacking of Facebook Id. This identity theft not only for the consumer but also for the business and the organization.(S. K. Pasupuleti et,al., 2015).

SIDE CHANNEL ATTACK

Side Channel Attack is a type of cryptographic device attack. Most probably side channel reveal or out information of secret key which use in the encryption/decryption process. Also, side channel attack leakage the data from the physical implementation of the system. The leakage of data from many ways like that electronic leak sound, the power consumption etc.Side channel attack most attack in the cloud computing area. Where the attackers attack to finding the secure data, secret keys and services. In the side channel there are a different type of attack will perform on it there are many basic side channel occur.

Interprocess: In this Spy process and victim process executed in the same process.

Inter VM: This kind of channel produces when two operating systems run on the same CPU.

Side channel attack is divided into two types.

Active attack: In the active attack of side channel change the information of data by the attacker.(Younis et.al.,2014)

Passive attack: In the passive attack of side channel may observe, eavesdrops the information without changes the real content. Side channel are different based:-

CPU processing side channel: In the CPU side channel, the CPU shares the resources between two virtual machines. In the CPU side channel different two virtual machines run on the single CPU. Due to which the load on the CPU different in different operation. These differences of the load on the CPU leakage the information. (Q. Huang et.al., 2017)

Cache side channel: In the cache side-channel cache share among the different VM. Sharing of cache between the different VM causes the leaking of data. This cache side channel is divided into three parts L1, L2 and L3. L1 and L2 are shared between the line processor. But L3 is shared between all the Core processor. HAL. Through which get the pattern of accessing the L3 in different processor unit. In the cache side-channel traces of cache channel unit of indexes into the tables.

TRADITIONAL SECURITY ISSUES

VM Level Attack

Virtual machine looks like a real physical computer, It's just as the Architecture of the computer or emulation of the of a computer system. This virtual machine like a physical computer which runs an OS application environment software.(Hu W et al., 2013).

In the virtual machine, the hypervisor is specialized software, which emulates the PC client's hard disk Server, CPU, Network and different type of h/w resources. Virtual machine generally most useful for the resources. Hypervisors provide the environment emulate the more than one Virtual machine hardware platform that is different or isolates from each other (Fig.13) In the virtual machine, there is a different type of attack. The virtual machine is more secure than Operating system. But now the attacker is successful to find the weak parts of the virtual machine. From there they attack and break the security of the virtual machine. In this paper, we already discuss the hypervisors which are important for the Virtual machine. Attacker copied the virtual disk content and gain the unrestricted access of VM. The different issue for the Virtual Machine:

Mobility:- Virtual machine are not permanent physical. It emulates the hardware and software environments. So, the attackers do not take the palace to steal the physical host machine. The Virtual machine store the content in the file by hypervisors. Hypervisors allow copying the contents and the run on the physical machine That is the weak point of Virtual machine where the attacker takes palaces. An attacker can copy all contents where it flows through Network, accessing the contents by own computer machine. (Fig 14). The accessing of the content by not stealing the hard drive. If the one attacker gets the accessing of a virtual disk, the attacker defeats all security mechanism, password and offline attacks. The second attack of the virtual machine is that attacker destroy, corrupt or modify the file .virtual machine file always maintain the integrity file. Integrity means that the file should not modify. *Communication Attack*:-Communication attack one of the common attacks of virtual level attack. This attack is performed between the guest attacks. All

Figure 12.

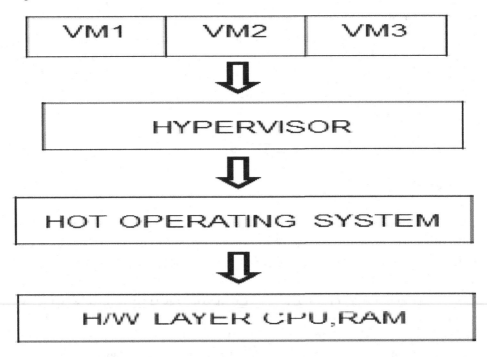

Figure 13.

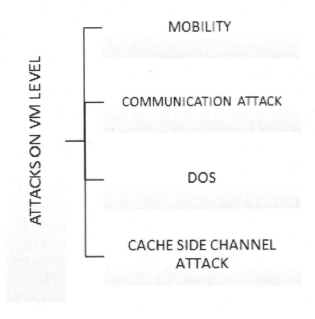

the Virtual machine connected with the same hypervisor through which the attacker used one VM access, control the VM. An attacker which access the VM through shared memory, network topology connection and the many other resources. When the VM, VM2 and VM3 attacker may or may not be authorized number to access .It May be a chance to access the unauthorized VM.

*Denial of services:-*Dos is one of the common threat for all the servers. When hypervisor not configured properties.one the Virtual machine consumed all resource, due to which the starving problem is created. Starving means that it takes a lot of time to perform the task. This starving problem for the other VM which run of some hypervisor.Dos attack main drawback is unable to function and process the hardware resource to extents equal interval of times. This problem is solved by a simple method. Hypervisor prevents any virtual machine 100%gaining of any resources, including May H/w component of the physical computer. Also, Hypervisor configured that when the attacker attack consumes 100% the resource. When the VM detected it system automatically restart the VM.VM is the small effect then the physical machine is restarting.

*Cache side channel attack:-*Virtual machine one more common attack is cache side-channel attack .cache side attack in the cloud computing due to the resource sharing.. This is proposed to detect and stop the guest virtual machine from the cache side-channel attack. Cache miss pattern is analysing and detecting the side channel attack. It's a two type's time driven cache attack, Trace-driven cache attack. (Liu et, al., 2014)

Phishing cloud provider:-

Phishing attacks are the common attack of cloud computing. In the phishing attack company have challenges to keep the information secure. Both company s and individual have challenges to keep the secure password, credit cards or other sensitive information. The attacker tries to access all the sensitive information by hacking email, social media, smartphone application, popup pages and any form of communication .they can steal the data from the different communication media. Phishing attack stealing the data via the Internet. In this attack, the attacker wants to do financial fraud .this attack now come under the criminal activity on the internet.

Phishing problem or issue is a big challenge for security. Attackers make a website same as company website page .user think that where they log in the credential page is secure or company page. (D. Zissis et. Al., 2012).

AUTHENTICATION AUTHORIZATION

Authentication is the process of identifying the user. This authentication process is verified by entity via Username and password. In the cloud, computing user wants to connect with cloud services their Own credential by using password and username .then prove that the user is identified and give the accessing the cloud services.(J.Lai et.al., 2013).

Network Eavesdropping:- Networking eavesdropping is performed in the network Layer. The intruder focus on the small packet which transmitted in the network from one computer to another computer. The intruder tried to read the content of the packet. This type of attack performed due to lack intruder tried to read the content of the packet. This type of attack performed due to lack called the Black Hat.

Brute Force Attacks*:* In the Brute force attack, the attacker always guessing the username and password. In some cases. The attacker known the username, they are trying to Guessing the password break the security.

Dictionary Attack*:* The intruder or attacker used the dictionary attack in the cloud for the identity or credential Dictionary attack is the form of the brute force attack. But it is a little different from brute force mechanism. This attack used forgetting the authentication. This dictionary attack based on the trying to find all possible string listing. This possible string is derived from a collection of list. Which store in dictionary attack. In this brute force, we are using the maximum possible number of attempt.

Cookies Reply Attack: -A cookies reply attack stolen cookies of clients by the attackers. It is reused by the attacker to perform the unauthorised accessing or translation. This cookie is stolen from the user endpoints. Cookies can also steal from the user machines using XSL, malware etc. (Kai Wei et,al., 2011).

Credential Theft: Credential theft is a credential based attack. In this process theft the credential information. The attacker uses the phishing concept to steal the credential information. This method is very easy for the attacker. This credential theft 'attacker also uses the phishing email sent through the mail.

AUTHORIZATION:-Authorization is the identification process to secure the data from the unauthorised accessing. Authorization is a plug-in model for a cloud computing provided the environment for the customer to control their own enterprise's data or information. This cloud Services provided to each and every customer of whose application deploy in the cloud. The customer registered their company information.

Some threat of authorization are:-

Elevation of Privileges:-In this attack the attacker logged in the system as a normal person having low-privilege. when the attacker gets successfully login, the attacker gets successfully login. The attacker gets high or roots privileges access to the system. Through is attacked attacker access the VM and data of the customer. In this attack attacker accessing more than one unauthorized access to many VM at the same time.(Ping Wang et,al., 2011)

Disclose the Confidential data:-Disclose the Confidential data, the attacker always trying to get the sensitive data. The attacker accesses the confidential data because of the failure accessing control operation.In this attack the data stored in many different palaces. In this threat, the attacker illegally accessing the data.

Data Tempering:-Data tempering is a threat. In which the Attacker change the data according to requirements. This kind of attack, the attacker accessing the stored data. Data tempering is also called the integrity attack.

Configuration stores attacked:-Configuration stores attack is unauthorised accessing of configuration file due to the failure of access operation mechanism. This configuration store attack on the integrity and confidentiality of configure files.

Attack on Administrator Interface: In the attack, the attack gets the unauthorized accessing of administrator interfaces.

Attack on plaintext configuration Secrets: In this Attacks the attacker successfully accesses the configure file and its secrets. The attacker also accessing the databases connection URL path. Through these attacks, the attacker gets the unauthorised access sensitive data of cloud-like customer databases.

CLOUD FORENSIC

Due to increase in a number of crimes over the internet and they being of different types, there was a need to accomplish this forensic cloud system to keep track of the data being collected through crimes over the years. Digital forensics is the application of science to the identification, collection. Examination and analysis of data while preserving the integrity of the information. And maintaining a strict chain of custody for the data. (Kent ET al.2006)Cloud computing is a model for enabling convenient, on-demand network access to a Shared pool of configurable resources (e.g. networks, servers, storage, applications and Services) that can rapidly be provisioned and released with minimal management effort or Service provider interaction. Cloud computing has five essential characteristics, I.e., on-demand Self-service, broad network access, resource pooling, rapid elasticity and measured service. It has three service models, i.e., Cloud Software as a Service,(SaaS), CloudPlatform as a Service(PaaS) and Cloud Infrastructure as a Service(IaaS). As it has four deployment models, i.e. private cloud, community cloud, public cloud and hybrid cloud.(Jing He et.al.,2012) Forensic Data Collection

1-Elastic, Static and Live Forensics
2-Evidence Segregation
3-Investigations in Virtualised Environment
4-Proactive preparations

Challenges in Cloud Forensics

Although it proved to be a very helpful concept in the area of cloud computing in the end, it also has some challenges. Few of them are-

1-Data collection in Cloud Forensics
2-In Elasticity of data
3-During Evidence Segregation
4 In a virtual environment in Cloud Forensics
5-In Internal Staffing
6-Regarding SLA
7-Regarding Multi-Jurisdiction and multi-tenancy

- In Data Collection in Cloud Forensics-Most faced a challenge in cloud forensics is data collection, due to improper service level agreements and different deployment models being followed and at different types of services causes the difficulty in retrieving data. Decreased in access to forensic data means the client has no knowledge of what is happening to their data(Y. Chang et. al., 2016)
- During Evidence Segregation-Evidence segregation works on resource pooling but the agreements established between different service providers to pool over one platform can be improper and can cause disadvantage to the data. Thus to make the segregation secure law should be enforced and the proper key should be introduced to access the forensic data to maintain the integrity of the data.(S. Habib et,al., 2011).
- In Virtual Environment in cloud forensics- Virtualized environment means data is many times replicated and reserved and as they use basically hypervisor two provide with different environments it is normal that the attackers would attack the hypervisors first. Law enforcement over this type of problems is not good which is providing attackers with the cause to attack the forensic data.(Dimitrios Zissis et,al., 2018)

○ Regarding SLA- Due to lack of knowledge of these agreements, i.e., SLA (service legal agreement), many times clients sign to them without knowing them which causes them to lose their information even in the legal way. Since law and regulation process is very slow over the cloud computing technology it causes only a problem to the client in every way.(Priya Govindaraj et. al., 2017)

EMERGING CLOUD SERVICE THREATS

Cloud computing being a cheaper option to store data many companies store most of their private data on the cloud and day to day of constant generation of data and need to store them safely and cheaply over the cloud is a most important feature required. However, as all the techniques have their disadvantages this technique feels a loss at times of cybercrimes where criminals breach the cloud services to get access to the sensitive data from the cloud. To prevent this type of breaches, cloud services databases should have a good architecture and security provided through different encryption techniques.(Yasir Ahmed Hamza et.al., 2013) though encryption can be considered a good method of protecting the data in encryption leak of the key is possible. In cloud computing, the databases also have copies stored of them so even when the database is breached the data will not get lost, but creating many copies of data can lead them to take a large amount of space.(Adeela Waqar et,al., 2012)

Different types of emerging cloud service threats are-

1-Side Channel Attack
2-Insider Organized Crime Threat
3-Increased Authentication Demands
4-Mash-Up Authorization

Side Channel Attack

Side channel in computer science is a channel which already exists in hardware and deals with the cache implementation and the attack followed by these side channel deals with the attack on the algorithms implementing security over the cloud. It gains information from the computer system itself and later attacks the system over their security encryption area. It can leak information through the encryption keys used in network security. Side channel attacks can be derived further in three classes-

1-Time-driven attacks

2-Trace-driven attacks

3-Access driven attacks

Time-driven attacks-This attack occurs when the attacker follows all the operations performed by the user in the time being, that is, it follows every step taken by the user and the total time duration it takes.(Peter Mell et.al., 2011)

Trace-driven attacks-In these attacks attacker mainly focuses on the cryptographic operations done on of user's system to attack it.

Access driven attacks-Access driven attacks are conducted when the attacker runs a program over the client or user's system causing any damages to the system settings. This attack mostly occurs on the Virtual Machine where co accessing parties exist over the same system or share the same platform.

Insider Organized Crime Threat

As the name suggests, the malicious insider organized crime threat is a properly organized threat by the user within the organization that is when a user within an organization uses its position or status for wrong use to carry on its theft. The main problem in these threats is that it is so small, catching the roots of this threat within an organization is the most difficult part of it all. To steal data-Since data can be of millions of dollars, collecting data through hacking can have many Advantages in the eyes of the hacker. (Sandeep K. Sood et. al.,2012)

INCREASED AUTHENTICATION DEMANDS

Meaning of authentication is confirming the identity of the user going to use the services, it is divided in two steps identification of the client and credentials by using a password or a secret key not known to others. Authentication demands increase when thin clients do not prefer installing the application but using the application online although this has its own security measures yet it can be proved to be a security issue because the licensed product is always more secure than the applications.

MASH-UP AUTHORIZATION

Mashup is a collection of different types of content using text, video, audio. A mashup can also include SaaS and contents on the website. Whereas Authorization is a process which provides access to the contents on the website or on other related content containing services for cloud computing. But this combination of the two terms or services can lead to various types of security issues like data leaks

THIRD PARTY DATA CONTROL

Third party control means giving all control of the cloud and its services being provided to the user is given to a third party to handle. They also have the legal power over the data of the clients and the services being used by them. This can lead to a lack of transparency over the data being controlled and gives all over control over the personal data of the client and can use it whatever the way they can There are many types of third party data control-

1-Due diligence
2-Audit ability
3-Contractual obligations
4-Transitive nature of contracts

1-Due diligence-It deals with the possibility that when the user or client leave the services of the company then what is the possible confirmation or guarantee that after leaving the enterprise its data has been deleted or not being leaked by that company or sold?

2-Auditability-It also deals with the transparency provided by the third party in control of data. It deals with the operations provided by the services and defines the regulation to perform audit dynamically but it has to be changed geographically.

3-Contractual obligations-There can be many legal obligations or conditions that can be added to the contract without letting the client know or there is a possibility that these conditions can be ignored by the client but later can lead to a problem for the user.

4-Transitive nature of contracts-It is also a possibility that the third party can have another subcontract with another party regarding services provided by them and this party cannot be trusted. Thus causing another security issue for the data of the client and over the operations performed on it.(Younis Y. A et,al., 2014).

CONCLUSION

Managing data and providing different types of services on the pay for what you need a basis on the internet is one of the most important roles of cloud computing. All types of businesses are using it, cloud computing has provided users with different types of deployment models on the basis of users requirements and also are divide by system models like a private, public and hybrid cloud.

But with many features also comes a security issue that one can face in cloud computing. Here, in this survey paper, we have taken in the note of many papers and managed to discuss some of the commonly known security issues that users are facing in cloud computing. As there is yet much further works is needed to be done in this field, this paper would help in knowing the issues of security and future work on solving issues can be done further. Hence, this paper helps in gathering the security issues at one place so that one can focus on the future work to solve it based on these data on how to solve them.

REFERENCES

Adam, S. A., Yousif, A., & Bashir, M. B. (2016). Multilevel Authentication Scheme for Cloud Computing. *International Journal of Grid and Distributed Computing*, *9*(9), 205–212. doi:10.14257/ijgdc.2016.9.9.18

Al-Attab, B. S., & Fadewar, H. S. (2016). Authentication Scheme for Insecure Networks in Cloud Computing. *IEEE International Conference on Global Trends in Signal Processing, Information Computing and Communication*, 158-163. 10.1109/ICGTSPICC.2016.7955289

Cao, N., Wang, C., Li, M., Ren, K., & Lou, W. (2016). Privacy-preserving multi-keyword ranked search over encrypted cloud data. *IEEE Transactions on Parallel and Distributed Systems*, *25*(1), 222–233. doi:10.1109/TPDS.2013.45

Chang, Y., & Liu, F. (2016). Network traffic and user behavior analysis of mobile reading applications. *International Conference on Information Science and Technology (ICIST)*, 142-146. 10.1109/ICIST.2016.7483400

Cisco Cloud Index Supplement. (2017). *Cloud readiness regional details white paper, 2016-2021*. White paper. Cisco.

González-Martínez, J. A., Bote-Lorenzo, M. L., Gómez-Sánchez, E., & Cano-Parra, R. (2015). Cloud computing and education: A state-of-the-art survey. *Computers & Education*, *80*, 132–151. doi:10.1016/j.compedu.2014.08.017

Habib, S., Ries, S., & Muhlhauser, M. (2011). Towards a trust management system for cloud computing, in Proc 10th IntConf Trust, Security Privacy. *Computer Communications*, 933939.

Hamza, Y. A., & Omar, M. D. (2013). Cloud Computing Security: Abuse and Nefarious Use of Cloud Computing. *International Journal of Computational Engineering Research*, *03*(6), 22–27.

He, J., Zhang, Y., Huang, G., Shi, J., & Cao, J. (2012). Distributed Data Possession For Securing Multiple Replicas In Geographically Dispersed Clouds. *Journal of Computer and System Sciences*, *78*(5), 1345–1358. doi:10.1016/j.jcss.2011.12.018

Hu, W. (2013). A Quantitative Study of Virtual Machine Live Migration. In *Proc. of the 2013 ACM Cloud and Autonomic Computing Conf.* ACM. 10.1145/2494621.2494622

Huang, Q., Yang, Y., & Wang, L. (2017). Secure data access control with cypher text update and computation outsourcing in fog computing for the internet of things. *IEEE Access: Practical Innovations, Open Solutions*, *5*, 12941–12950. doi:10.1109/ACCESS.2017.2727054

Lai, J., Deng, R., Guan, C., & Weng, J. (2013). Attribute-based encryption with verifiable outsourced decryption. *IEEE Transactions on Information Forensics and Security*, *8*(8), 1343–1354. doi:10.1109/TIFS.2013.2271848

Lakhwani, K., Kaur, R., & Kumar, P., & Thakur, M. (2018). An Extensive Survey on Data Authentication Schemes In Cloud Computing. *4th International Conference on Computing Sciences*. 10.1109/ICCS.2018.00016

Li, W., & Wan, X. L. (2015). An Analysis and Comparison for Public Cloud Technology and Market Development Trend in China. *5th IEEE International Conference on Cyber Security and Cloud Computing (CSCloud)/2018 4th IEEE International Conference on Edge Computing and Scalable Cloud (EdgeCom)*.

Liu, C., Zhu, L., Wang, M., & Tan, Y. (2014). Search pattern leakage in searchable encryption: Attacks and new construction. *Information Sciences*, *265*, 176–188. doi:10.1016/j.ins.2013.11.021

Liu, H., Ning, H., Xiong, Q., & Yang, L. T. (2015). Shared authority-based privacy-preserving authentication protocol in cloud computing. *IEEE Transactions on Parallel and Distributed Systems*, *26*(1), 241–251. doi:10.1109/TPDS.2014.2308218

Liu, W. (2012). *Research on Cloud Computing Security Problem and Strategy*. IEEE. doi:10.1109/CECNet.2012.6202020

Mahajan & Sharma. (2015). The Malicious Insider Threat in the Cloud. *International Journal of Engineering Research and General Science, 3*(2).

Mell, P., & Grance, T. (2011). The NIST Definition of Cloud Computing. NIST Special Publication 800-145, 1-7. doi:10.6028/NIST.SP.800-145

Mollah, M. B., Azad, M. A. K., & Vasilakos, A. (2017). Security and privacy challenges in mobile cloud computing: Survey and way ahead. *Journal of Network and Computer Applications, 84*, 34–54. doi:10.1016/j.jnca.2017.02.001

Pasupuleti, S. K., Ramalingam, S., & Buyya, R. (2016). An efficient and secure privacy-preserving approach for outsourced data of resource-constrained mobile devices in cloud computing. *Journal of Network and Computer Applications, 64*, 12–22. doi:10.1016/j.jnca.2015.11.023

Priya, G., & Jaisankar, N. (2017). A Review on Various Trust Models in Cloud Environment. *Journal of Engineering Science and Technology Review, 10*(2), 213–219. doi:10.25103/jestr.102.24

Roman, R., Lopez, J., & Mambo, M. (2018). Mobile edge computing, Fog et al.: A survey and analysis of security threats and challenges. *Future Generation Computer Systems, 78*(part 2), 680–698. doi:10.1016/j.future.2016.11.009

Shi, Y., Liu, J., Han, Z., Zheng, Q., Zhang, R., & Qiu, S. (2014). Attribute-based proxy re-encryption with keyword search. *PLoS One, 9*(12), e116325. doi:10.1371/journal.pone.0116325 PMID:25549257

Sood, S. K. (2012). A Combined Approach to Ensure Data Security in Cloud Computing. *Journal of Network and Computer Applications, 35*(6), 1831–1838. doi:10.1016/j.jnca.2012.07.007

Sookhak, M., Yu, F. R., Khan, M. K., Xiang, Y., & Buyya, R. (2017). Attribute-based data access control in mobile cloud computing:Taxonomy and open issues. *Future Generation Computer Systems, 72*, 273–287. doi:10.1016/j.future.2016.08.018

Wan, Z., Liu, J., & Deng, R. (2012). A hierarchical attribute-based solution for flexible and scalable access control in cloud computing. *IEEE Transactions on Information Forensics and Security, 7*(2), 743–754. doi:10.1109/TIFS.2011.2172209

Wang, P., & Qiu, J. (2011). *Evaluating Mechanism Trust Model Based on Behavior Result under Cloud Computing*. Fuzzy Systems and Knowledge Discovery.

Wang, S., Zhou, J., Liu, J. K., Yu, J., Chen, J., & Xie, W. (2016). An efficient file hierarchy attribute-based encryption scheme cloud computing. *IEEE Transactions on Information Forensics and Security, 11*(6), 1265–1277. doi:10.1109/TIFS.2016.2523941

Waqar, A., Raza, A., Abbas, H., & Khan, M. K. (2012). A Framework For Preservation of Cloud Users Data Privacy Using Dynamic Reconstruction Of Metadata. *Journal of Network and Computer Applications*.

Wei, K., & Tang, S. (2011). Trust Model Research in Cloud Computing Environment. *Computational Intelligence and Security, 2*, 411.

Yang, Y., Zhu, H., Lu, H., Weng, J., Zhang, Y., & Choo, K.-K. R. (2016). Choo, "Cloud-based data sharing with fine-grained proxy encryption. *Pervasive and Mobile Computing, 28*, 122–134. doi:10.1016/j.pmcj.2015.06.017

Yihui, D., Sun, L., Liu, D., Feng, M., & Miao, T. L. (2018). A Survey on Data Integrity Checking in Cloud. In *1st International Cognitive Cities Conference (IC3)*. IEEE.

Younis, Y. A., Kifayat, K., & Merabti, M. (2014). An access control model for cloud computing. *Journal of Information Security and Applications, 19*(1), 45-60.

Zhang, J., Zheng, L., Gong, L., & Gu, Z. (2018). A Survey on Security of Cloud Environment: Threats, Solutions, and Innovation. In *Third International Conference on Data Science in Cyberspace*. IEEE. 10.1109/DSC.2018.00145

Zhang, P., Chen, Z., Liu, J. K., Liang, K., & Liu, H. (2018). An efficient access control scheme with outsourcing capability and attribute update for fog computing. *Future Generation Computer Systems, 78*(part 2), 753–762. doi:10.1016/j.future.2016.12.015

Zissis, D., & Lekkas, D. (2012). Addressing cloud computing security issue. *Future Generation Computer Systems, 28*(3), 583–592. doi:10.1016/j.future.2010.12.006

Zissis, D., & Lekkas, D. (2018). Addressing Cloud Computing Security Issues. *Future Generation Computer Systems, 28*(3), 583–592. doi:10.1016/j.future.2010.12.006

Chapter 7

The Complex and Opaque Cloud Ecosystem:
Recommendations for IaaS Providers for a Successful Positioning in the Ecosystem

Reimar Weissbach
Technical University of Munich, Germany

Alexander Bogislav Herzfeldt
iD https://orcid.org/0000-0002-6601-6481
Technical University of Munich, Germany

Sebastian Floerecke
iD https://orcid.org/0000-0003-0489-8551
University of Passau, Germany

Christoph Ertl
iD https://orcid.org/0000-0002-5527-3888
Technical University of Munich, Germany

ABSTRACT

In the complex and opaque cloud business ecosystem, service providers face several challenges. The fastest growing field of IaaS is evolving towards a commodity market, resulting in an increasing price competition. By first examining current challenges for cloud service providers, giving a theoretical background on value facilitation with a focus on the areas of value creation, and describing a state-of-the-art cloud ecosystem model, a sound understanding of the current situation is established. The role of value facilitation and standardization as core capabilities for successful IaaS providers are discussed and identified as being crucial for successful long-term survival in the competitive ecosystem. Additionally, learnings from expert interviews are analyzed, and five concrete recommendations for IaaS providers are derived. These recommendations should serve the management of IaaS providers in order to compare, challenge, and potentially adapt their current business models.

DOI: 10.4018/978-1-7998-1294-4.ch007

INTRODUCTION

Scientific literature has come up with numerous definitions for cloud computing over the years, either with a stronger business or technical focus. The National Institute of Standards and Technology (NIST) has established a more technical definition that has become the standard both in theory and practice in the meantime. According to NIST, *[c]loud computing is a model for enabling ubiquitous, convenient, on-demand network access to a shared pool of configurable computing resources (e.g., networks, servers, storage, applications, and services) that can be rapidly provisioned and released with minimal management effort or service provider interaction.* (Mell & Grance, 2011, p. 2).

A closer look shows that the technology which enables cloud services is not new. Cloud computing is a combination of existing technologies and concepts such as virtualization, autonomic computing, grid computing and usage-based pricing (Zhang et al., 2010). Despite its low degree of novelty in technological terms, cloud computing has fundamentally changed the way IT resources are provided and utilized (Armbrust et al., 2010; Marston et al., 2011). Several scholars therefore see cloud computing as joint development of computing technology and new business models (Floerecke & Lehner, 2018b).

There have been two dominating developments of cloud computing in recent years. On the one hand, public clouds based on large-scale Internet data centers such as offered by Amazon Web Services or Microsoft and on the other hand smaller data centers that host clouds from different users. The latter type is usually found in metropolitan areas and efficiency gains are leveraged by joint management and administration (Zhou et al., 2017). This chapter focuses on the first type, the large-scale cloud computing service providers.

The introduction of cloud computing resulted in an expansion and also in some circumstances replacement of traditional value chains in IT service provision by network-like relations, forming a complex business ecosystem (Böhm et al., 2010; Leimeister et al., 2010). The main trigger for the emergence of the cloud ecosystem was that cloud computing became an enabler for new, innovative business models (Böhm et al., 2011; Iyer & Henderson, 2012). However, research on cloud computing has rather focused on the technical aspects so far. Less consideration has been given to the major changes within the business perspective of IT provisioning (Herzfeldt et al., 2018).

A business ecosystem represents an environment for systemic innovations, where different companies cooperate to deliver customer solutions (Adner, 2017; Moore, 1993). According to the biological ecosystem perspective by Moore (1993), an organization cannot actively choose to be part of an ecosystem or not. Each organization that provides or uses any cloud service or product automatically becomes part of the cloud ecosystem. As organizations continuously enter and leave the business ecosystem, relationships are formed, renewed and dissolved, a business ecosystem thus is highly dynamic (Basole et al., 2015).

As customers have high expectations regarding cloud services, new providers are offering bundled solutions built on offerings from multiple other providers. This development is especially supported by cloud services on different layers (IaaS, PaaS, SaaS), but also by the increasingly modular structure within each layer, the growing degree of standardization and on-demand self-service (Floerecke & Lehner, 2016). Infrastructure as a Service (IaaS) can be seen as the basic layer of cloud services delivering infrastructure services to customers via networks. These services include hardware (e.g.,computation, network, storing) and software (e.g., operating systems) components (Mell & Grance, 2011). A frontrunner for IaaS is Amazon Web Services' Elastic Compute Cloud Service. The second layer of cloud computing services, Platform as a Service (PaaS), offers online access to an environment providing required resources to build applications. Necessary services are e.g., design, development, testing, deployment, and operating tools offering access to programming libraries and different languages (Velte et al., 2010). One of the leading PaaS platforms is for example Azure by Microsoft. On top of that, Software as a Service (SaaS) offers a ready-to-use software directly to the end customer, embedded in the underlying platform and utilizing the available and suitable infrastructure (Mell & Grance, 2011). If applicable, customers can almost instantaneously start using the respective software, such as Office365 from Microsoft.

The model of having a one-stop provision of IT-related requests changes for the end customer towards a web of vendors. Here, since services are bundled and resold, end customers will not have full transparency on the service or service components (Floerecke & Lehner, 2016). Most important is the interoperability between the offerings of all involved cloud service providers of a bundled service, which proves to be very challenging because of missing global interface standards in the current cloud computing ecosystem (Floerecke & Lehner, 2018b).

Important reasons for the popularity of cloud computing – flexibility, scalability and often also cost reduction – are beneficial for the end customer who monetizes on these advantages compared to previous computing paradigms. On the other side of the coin, the providers have to take the involved risks that come with the promise of constant availability and high performance. In this situation, providers are continuously threatened by new market entrants and confronted with price pressure (Herzfeldt et al., 2018). Especially for IaaS providers, price pressure has evolved as a dominating threat since basic public IaaS services are being commoditized, leading to the price as being the primordial buying criteria for clients (Floerecke & Lehner, 2018a). As a consequence, the market for IaaS is consolidating more and more around the so called hyperscalers. The dominating hyperscalers are Alibaba, Amazon Web Services

(AWS), Google and Microsoft, whose market share accumulated to 75% in 2017, with an outlook for further strong growth (Costello & Hippold, 2018).

In this competitive high-risk environment for cloud service providers, the capability of facilitation proves to be a success requirement in attracting customers (Herzfeldt et al., 2019). Facilitation is the capability to predict and plan for future demands to create resources upfront before future customer engagements. This helps providers to offer the engagement at reduced costs (Grönroos, 2017; Grönroos & Voima, 2013). The different types of cloud service providers make use of value facilitation in different ways. Large-scale cloud providers such as Alibaba or Microsoft offer mainly standardized services that can be purchased on-demand and without personal interaction via self-service on the respective website – they are thus clearly a value facilitator where the value finally is created by the customer alone and mainly independently. The smaller providers that also operate locally on the other hand engage with their customers already in an early stage. A dedicated development and design process is used to jointly create a customer-specific solution and value is co-created by the provider and the customer mostly based on individual contract negotiations (Herzfeldt et al., 2019).

In this contribution, the authors will discuss how facilitation can help cloud providers to counter challenges such as price competition and service availability, first. It will be explained how facilitation needs to balance standardization and innovation and how to differentiate as a cloud service provider from competitors with a combination of both. Second, the authors will deliver some new insights on further components of the business model, in particular the value proposition, from a multitude of expert interviews conducted with cloud service providers in the time from end of 2017 to the end of 2018. Based on these, the authors suggest five recommendations for cloud service providers with a focus on IaaS on how to successfully position themselves in the cloud ecosystem. According to Gartner, IaaS is the fastest growing Cloud Computing business segment globally with an increase of 27.6% in 2019 (Costello & Hippold, 2018). Additionally, the amount of research investigating the reasons for the business success is very limited in this segment, compared to SaaS and PaaS (Floerecke & Lehner, 2018b).

The contribution will build on the **Pa**ssau **C**loud Computing **E**cosystem (PaCE Model) to create an understanding for the distributed and increasingly nontransparent cloud ecosystem as well as to highlight challenges and requirements for the roles in the dynamic ecosystem. Several of the companies being part of the cloud ecosystem offer a variety of services and products (Böhm, et al., 2010; Floerecke and Lehner, 2016). In order to capture these sets of service and product portfolios, it is required and also beneficial to apply a role concept. A role in the ecosystem context is defined as a *[...] set of similar services offered by market players to similar customers* (Böhm, et al. 2010, p. 133).

The PaCE model comprises 26 roles and includes the basic service flows between those roles. It is particularly a research framework supporting the detailed and goal-oriented analysis of cloud business models. The PaCE model thus tackles a problematic of past research, namely that examinations of cloud computing business models did not consider that the cloud computing ecosystem consists of a multitude of companies with an increased degree of heterogeneity. This increased degree of heterogeneity is characterized by e.g., offering a portfolio of services comprising IaaS, PaaS and SaaS, but also act as an integrator, aggregator or consultant (Floerecke & Lehner, 2016). Consequently, an undifferentiated analysis of business models neglecting the different roles of the cloud ecosystem has a low level of explanatory significance (Floerecke & Lehner, 2018b).

BACKGROUND

Challenges for Cloud Service Providers

The above-mentioned characteristics of cloud computing as being a new provisioning paradigm rather than a new technology in combination with the highly competitive market environment currently observable make the business perspective a crucial part for cloud service providers. Main challenges to be addressed in this section are establishing an understanding of their customers' business needs, designing and managing service-oriented business models (Floerecke, 2018), implementing an on-demand self-service with convincing and profitable pricing models and scalability as well as facing a heavy price competition in the market (Floerecke & Lehner, 2018b). This is a challenge for providers of IaaS in particular, because basic IaaS services have become a commodity, similar to electricity, water, gas and telephony, over the recent years. Here, the price has, similar to other utility markets, turned into the main decision criterion for end customers (Floerecke & Lehner, 2018b, 2018a).

As described above, cloud service providers have to understand what their customers want and need as well as how they want to pay for it first (Bogataj Habjan & Pucihar, 2017). This is prerequisite for any business offering and especially for a cloud service that also allows the customer to easily integrate it in the existing IT landscape as well as business processes (Böhm et al., 2010). After having established a sound understanding of customers' needs, cloud service providers have to design service-oriented business models (Marston et al., 2011). With a successful go-to-market, the providers also need to ensure a reliable and efficient management of these services. As studies have shown, both are a very challenging task for many cloud service providers (Floerecke, 2018). Main reasons slowing down customer adoption of cloud offerings are lacking business model innovation and problems in showing attractive business cases for end customers. This is surprising as the expected value propositions for both SMEs as well as larger companies are quite similar with for example, low CAPEX, scalability capabilities, and pooling of resources (Clohessy et al., 2016).One advantage of cloud offerings is that the nature of cloud computing offers a broad range of business models. The perspective of the business model component *revenue streams* alone shows multiple models currently observable, such as licensing, pay-per-use, recurrent subscription models (Clohessy et al., 2016). Per definition, cloud service providers additionally need to implement characteristics such as self-service, rapid scalability, pay-as-you-go pricing and on-demand services in their offerings, to distinguish from their traditional counterpart of on-premise IT offerings (Mell & Grance, 2011). As reality shows, common web-based offerings are frequently advertised as cloud services for marketing purposes, without meeting the key characteristics of cloud services (Floerecke, 2018). This strategy of rebranding existing offerings under the name of cloud services is also referred to as *cloud washing* (Adamov & Erguvan, 2009).

One of the main criteria for business executives when making sourcing decisions regarding cloud computing are costs (Buyya et al.,2009). Apparently, customers even show a tendency towards a lower willingness to pay for cloud computing services in comparison with traditional IT services (Oliveira et al., 2014). This automatically increases price pressure and price competition amongst the different providers in the cloud ecosystem. With a focus on customer value, cloud service providers also face technical challenges as customers demand security, a high and also scalable performance, bandwidth and reliability as well as adherence to specific IT policies and regulations (Marston et al., 2011).

Security is a prerequisite for customers when using cloud services and needs to be one primary dimension providers have to ensure. Applying Herzberg's two factor theory (Herzberg et al., 1959) to cloud computing adoption, security can be seen as a switching inhibitor coming from traditional on-premise IT solutions, due to the fact that cyber security is seen as a key risk for customers (Park & Ryoo, 2013; Ye & Potter, 2011). Perceived security often goes hand-in-hand with adherence to IT policies, which can be industry-specific as well as regional-specific. As the cloud services often play a crucial role for customers' business performance, service level agreements (SLAs) are commonly used to agree on a certain minimum of availability and reliability. Usually, annual uptime percentage is agreed as being higher than 99.9% throughout 24 hours on 365 days per year (Buyya et al., 2009; Marston et al., 2011). Ensuring this level of reliability in combination with on-demand scalability can be a technical challenge for cloud service providers.

Since cloud computing services are usually offered in a modular approach, there is most often a basis set of standard modules or components which is supplemented by several individual modules to conclude a solution solving a specific customer need (Zhang & Zhou, 2009). The composition of a solution based on standardized as well as individualized modules also allows for a strongly increased cost-efficiency – one of the key decision criteria when choosing a service provider (Buyya et al., 2009). Standardization is one key factor for making cloud computing cost-efficient since it enables scalability. This infers that cloud service providers have to strive for maximal standardization for their standardized modules in order to achieve highest operational efficiency as well as effectiveness, which is prerequisite to survive in the price competition. Ideally, standardization is increased over time as service providers learn from past customer engagements and thus optimize their offering. Especially for IaaS providers, standardization is crucial to leverage economies of scale in order to be able to survive in the current price competition. Hence, small providers have a disadvantage compared to hyperscalers, due to the fact that they do not have large data centers. In the recent past, this led to an ongoing trend of consolidation (Floerecke & Lehner, 2018a). Finding the optimal offering in terms of standardization and individualization can be challenging and thus a competitive advantage for successful providers.

Value Facilitation

To tackle challenges that cloud service providers are facing, provision of a competitive value proposition is crucial. Thus, providers need to co-create with their customers to integrate resources into their services. This means that providers and customers should not be seen in their dyadic roles of a consumer that uses up value that the producer created but both should rather be seen as co-creators (Lusch & Nambisan, 2015). This concept of co-creation applies the service-dominant logic (Vargo & Lusch, 2004, 2008). For the case of cloud computing, resources are integrated from the provider as well as the customer when provisioning a service. The focus of co-creation is on the customer value, as the whole process aims to increase customer well-being. The role of the cloud service provider in the value co-creation process is the proposition of a valuable service. The customer on the other hand can perceive the enhanced well-being in the process of value-in-use, meaning acquisition, usage and disposal of services (Herzfeldt et al., 2019).

Researchers suggest value facilitation – building up resources prior to future customer engagements (Grönroos, 2017; Grönroos & Voima, 2013). Accordingly, value creation then takes place throughout three successive spheres with the provider sphere of *value facilitation*, the joint sphere of *value-co-creation*, and finally the consumer sphere (value-in-use). The cloud service provider facilitates the value-creation process with the customer by building up resources such as knowledge, experience and pre-defined services in advance. These resources need to be built up in a way that they support the customers' value-in-use sphere best. As described, value facilitation by the provider can take place without direct customer interaction whereas value-creation then takes place through the interaction of the provider with the customer. Therefore, both parties need to integrate their respective resources. The provider also plays a part in the value-in-use sphere where he indirectly acts as a value facilitator by significantly shaping and influencing the customer value through the previous value co-creation (Grönroos, 2017; Grönroos & Voima, 2013).

For cloud service providers and especially IaaS providers, value facilitation is a core capability. It is a crucial lever for standardization to enable scalability leading to a superior competitive advantage. Literature from the resource-based view of the firm gives insights in the different facets of facilitation capabilities. According to most studies, IT resources can be categorized in physical characteristics, human characteristics and organizational characteristics (Gupta et al., 2018). Looking at the first characteristic of IT infrastructure flexibility, it can be concluded, that having technical resources will not result per se in a competitive advantage but rather the usage of infrastructure creates value for a firm.

The Cloud Business Ecosystem

Business ecosystems were initially a matter of research by drawing the analogy to biological ecosystems and describe the structure and behavior of organizations that are interacting in a respective network. In a business ecosystem *[…] companies coevolve capabilities around a new innovation: they work co-operatively and competitively to support new products, satisfy customer needs, and eventually incorporate the next round of innovations* (Moore, 1993, p.76). Even though there is no commonly agreed definition of business ecosystems yet (Adner, 2017; Rong et al., 2018), the core of business ecosystems consists of loosely coupled parties that interact as partners, complementors, contractors, competitors and customers. Around this core, there is a periphery consisting of additional actors leading to dynamic developments of the ecosystem (Iansiti & Levien, 2004; Moore, 2006). Actors in a business ecosystem do not deliberately choose to take part in it but rather automatically are a part by utilizing or providing resources. Involved parties thus enter and leave a business ecosystem continuously turning it into a highly dynamic system (Basole et al., 2015; Moore, 1993).

The cloud ecosystem has been continuously expanding with regard to the number of organizations, roles and service linkages, and has become increasingly complex and nontransparent (Floerecke & Lehner, 2015; Herzfeldt et al., 2018). To gain an overview and improve transparency in this field, several attempts have been made to formally describe the cloud computing ecosystem by the means of a model. However, the proposed models show considerable differences with regard to their constructs (e.g., number of roles, types of relationships, scope of the model) and their form of presentation (e.g., non-standardized graph-based models and process models) (Floerecke & Lehner, 2016). Beyond this background, Floerecke and Lehner (2016) developed a revised cloud-specific ecosystem model named **Pa**ssau **C**loud **C**omputing **E**cosystem Model (PaCE Model). It serves as a theoretical model abstracting the cloud ecosystem observable in reality and can particularly be used as a research framework supporting a goal-oriented and fine granular analysis of cloud business models (Floerecke & Lehner, 2018b).

According to Böhm et al., 2010 (p.133), a role is a *[...] set of similar services offered by market players to similar customers*. The PaCE Model describes 26 roles for the organizations that are active in the cloud ecosystem and further clusters these roles in five groups: clients, vendors, hybrid roles, support roles and environment. Emphasis is on the stereotypical relationships that members of each roles establish over time (see: Figure 1: The Passau Cloud Ecosystem Model).

Clients are the only participants in the ecosystem, which do not deliver services or products to other members of the ecosystem. They are the origin and end point of a request respectively product/service delivery. Vendors on the other hand provide specific services or products to their clients. Vendors include, amongst others, hardware developers, network operators, software vendors or physical infrastructure vendors and examples for vendors with a broad offering portfolio are Microsoft or Telekom. The hybrid roles are vendors as well as clients at the same time. Typical hybrid roles are for example the market place operator who provides the platforms on which other players offer their cloud services, application provider, platform provider, service bundler and service integrator. Examples are Salesforce, that primarily acts as application and platform provider or Amazon Web Services, with an offering in almost every category. Ecosystem participants that can be categorized as support offer non-technological services such as consulting, trainings or also certifications, e.g., Accenture with its consulting unit or TÜV with a focus on certifications. Members of the cluster environment of the ecosystem can be located in the periphery of the ecosystem but have a significant influence on the business ecosystem and are also influenced by it themselves. Here the actors mostly are non-profit organizations. Roles comprise of legislators, research institutes or standard developers such as the US Congress as a legislator and ISO or IEEE as standard developers (Floerecke & Lehner, 2016). This contribution focuses on and gives recommendations for the role of the infrastructure provider (H5) in the PaCE model, mainly providing virtual computing, storage and networking resources to platform providers, application providers and end customers.

Figure 1: The Passau Cloud Ecosystem Model (PaCE Model)

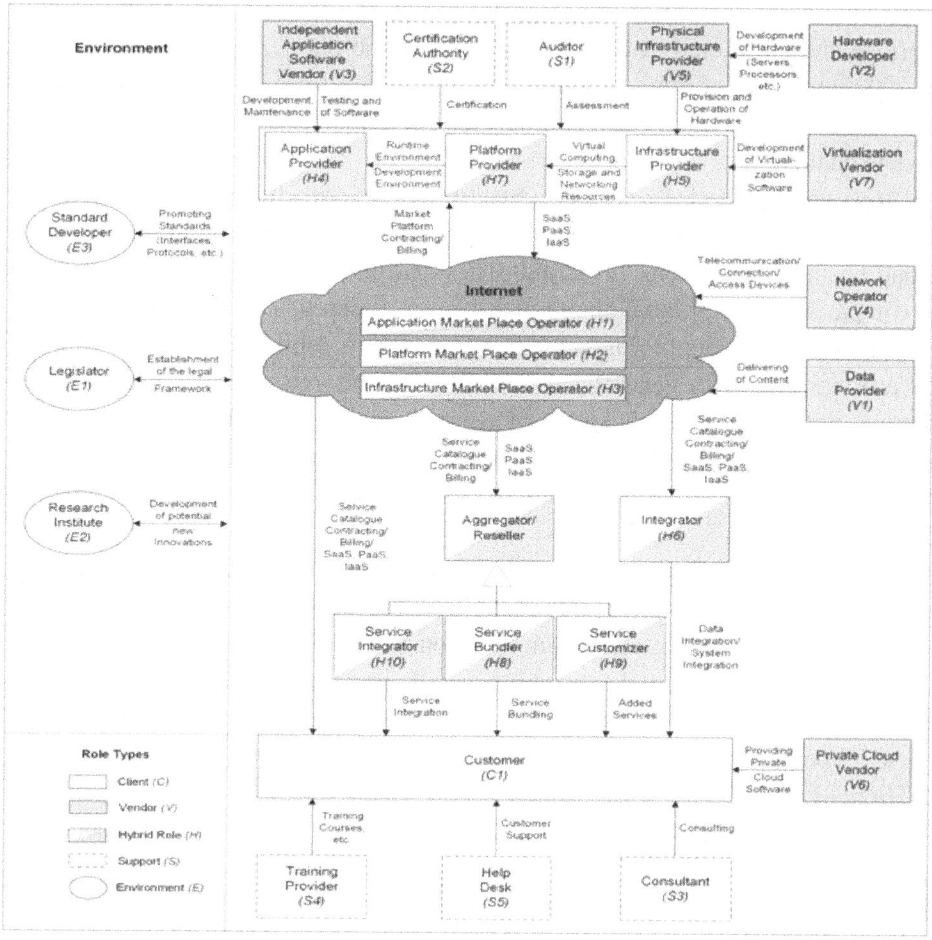

METHODS AND DATA COLLECTION

In order to analyze what customers really want and how to be economically successful in the cloud business ecosystem, this contribution takes the provider perspective based on the PaCE model as described above.

For the component of key resources, the resource-based view of a firm is applied. A resource in this context is defined as *[...] anything which could be thought of as a strength or weakness of a given firm* (Wernerfelt, 1984, p.172). In the context of the resource-based view, resources are generally clustered in capabilities, assets and competencies in order to examine on what a certain competitive advantage is based on (Barney, 1991).

The insights and recommendations in this contribution are based on 40 interviews conducted in the time from end of 2017 to end of 2018. The interviews were in German and conducted in-person as well as on the phone, with a duration of 30 to 100 minutes. According to Sturges & Hanrahan (2004), there is no significant difference when conducting expert interviews in-person or on the phone with regard to data quality.

As a sample, experts from cloud service providers with different size, geographic reach and target markets, experience in their role, number of occupied roles in the cloud business ecosystem, focus industries and perception of relevance of cloud in comparison to traditional on premise were considered. The heterogeneity of the companies allows identifying contrasting as well as replicated results leading to conclusions that can be generalized (Yin, 2014). In order to select the right interview partners within the selected cloud provider organizations two criteria were applied: A person was considered suitable when being in a managerial position and being responsible for the initial development or continuous adaptation of a company's business models.

In the interview series we wanted to identify business model characteristics for cloud service providers that enable a long-term business success, whereas different roles in the cloud business ecosystem were considered. Special focus was laid on the three core roles in the cloud ecosystem, namely providers of IaaS, PaaS and SaaS. These form the heart of the whole cloud business and are forecasted to account for about 70 percent of the overall turnover of the cloud ecosystem in 2019 (Costello & Hippold, 2018).

For the conduction, a semi-structured interview guide was developed. Key questions were focused on, e.g., value propositions, resources, partners, channels and costs. Questions were looking to provide insights into how the companies designed the individual business model components and with what intention these components were designed in a specific way. Besides that, it was asked what direct competitors were doing in comparison, what success factors they could observe, and which mistakes should be avoided. In addition, it was specifically asked which changes the companies were planning regarding their business model components and which reasoning lead to these changes.

The interview guide was revised in an iterative process involving discussions among researchers as well as two subsequent test interviews with practitioners. Finally, the pre-tested interview guide comprised open questions that aside of being focused on the Business Model Canvas (Osterwalder & Pigneur, 2010) gave the interviewees enough space to think and answer without constraints or being tied to predefined answering options. The data collection was deemed sufficient after observing answers being repetitive and not adding new aspects anymore.

Results, namely business model characteristics that allow for long-term business success, were directly taken from the experts participating in the interviews. Consequently, experiences and opinions of the experts were essential for the conclusions, even if those may not automatically depict the actual situation or the overall strategy of the respective company. Consciously and in line with this approach, no objective organizational information was analyzed and statistically related to key figures of the organization. Main reason was the lacking availability to qualitative as well as quantitative data for all considered companies. However, research has shown (Grunert & Sørensen, 1996; Hoffmann & Schlosser, 2001; Leidecker & Bruno, 1984) that the subjective impression and opinion of particularly senior managers of successful providers regarding business success factors mainly are in line with the objective factors. All companies were able to grow their revenue over the course of the past years and are thus seen as successful. On the other hand, companies with stagnating or declining revenue were consciously not selected to be part of this study. The decisive parameter measuring business success was thus chosen to be revenue growth, which is the proxy most frequently used for measuring business success of particularly small or medium-sized companies in the scientific context, due to the expected high correlation of growth and business (Chandler & Hanks, 1993; Chandler & Jansen, 1992; Cox et al., 2002; Kim et al., 2004; Mendelson, 2000).

Finally, the results were evaluated with the qualitative data analysis software MAXQDA in two phases, namely open coding and axial coding, as suggested in relevant literature (Corbin & Strauss, 1990). First, a line-by-line evaluation of the interviews was conducted until a general agreement among the researchers was established. Second, the derived codes were consolidated by means of axial coding (Corbin & Strauss, 1990) resulting in a set of main codes that represent the cloud business model characteristics. This process was characterized by recoding data, combining or splitting clusters and creating new or dropping current clusters.

In the evaluation process, an aspect was considered as crucial for business success in case it was articulated as such by multiple interviewed experts or, in case of being mentioned only once, the underlying arguments were convincing. Additionally, aspects were considered if they occurred being very important during the process of data analysis of a specific case or also in the cross-reference comparison. The conclusions were not statistically evaluated, which is in line with recommendations form relevant literature (Corbin & Strauss, 1990).

The data collection allowed for multiple success-driving business model characteristics for the three key roles of the cloud business ecosystem, namely IaaS, PaaS as well as SaaS providers. However, this contribution focuses on the business model characteristics directly relatable to IaaS providers and their role in the cloud business ecosystem. This role is clearly the role where the least research has been conducted on, even though it is currently the fastest growing cloud computing business segment globally. In the following, five central as well as surprising conclusions that also contradict commonly agreed cloud characteristics for cloud business models are described and recommendations for IaaS providers are derived.

POSITIONING IN THE CLOUD ECOSYSTEM AS AN IAAS PROVIDER – WHAT CUSTOMERS REALLY WANT

Based on 40 interviews with experts as described above, five key learnings are described in the following, using representative expert statements (translated into English from German by the authors).

Offering Fixed Prices for Cloud Service Usage

In the literature, cloud services are mainly used in connection with pay-as-you-go pricing models (Marston et al., 2011; Mell & Grance, 2011). However, our insights reveal that this does not apply for all customer scenarios and requirements in practice. Several customers prefer fixed prices for a public cloud service usage, although it contradicts the basic logic of cloud computing. For this preference, clients have various reasons: First, public cloud services are actually not designed for permanent operation as they normally exceed the costs of on-premise solutions in the long run. Instead, public cloud services should be considered as a way out of load peaks to a temporary extension or as an environment for short testing scenarios. To summarize, public cloud means to go fast in and fast out. Consequently, a fixed price model is desired when the customer already has a precise knowledge what he expects. As a practitioner stated: *Let's say I have a specific use case, it obviously is like that, since I know exactly what I need and I can also buy it, that I get a price discount [...] when I buy this and this and that service for three years [...].*

A second reason that many companies are not capable to use cloud services on a pay-as-you-go basis are limitations in available budget, because budget is signed-off internally. Therefore, they have to know in advance which costs occur. An expert mentioned specifically that *it sounds very nice having the pay-per-use principle, but a company always has to plan a budget. Especially in the public domain, money has to be requested for specific purposes so you can't just go there and say I request five million, but it could also be that I only need one or I might also use six. No company is going to do that.*

Third, many buyers are still opting for fix prices similarly as they have done before. An expert said that *[customers] want a fixed price. They want a fixed monthly price where they can say this is it and they get a certain functionality or feature set and they get a certain security with it.*

Besides that, customers often lack the required know-how to be able to use IT resources in a flexible way and leverage the advantages of cloud computing in this regard. A usage-based pricing model thus is not beneficial for those customers, as an expert confirmed: *[…] small and medium-sized companies can neither handle flexible billing models nor are they able to book resources flexibly in a way that they gain additional value from it.*

In conclusion, it is important for IaaS providers to additionally offer pricing models based on fixed prices. In these cases, usually, the customers end up paying a regular fee, even if they have used fewer resources in retrospect. In the end, this is of advantage for the provider, as he gains a long-term bond with a customer and guaranteed ongoing revenue streams.

Extending Pure IaaS Services with Managed Services

The experts stated that there is a high potential for managed services. Managed services are usually on top of typical IaaS services and include services such as update, cyber security, monitoring or backup services. The service scope can range from individual items to even a complete IT outsourcing. An illustrative example for a managed service is the operation of a webserver by the provider whereby customers can exclusively focus on deploying their website without dealing with the underlying IT. As an IaaS expert described his experience: *The human factor is the bottleneck in [the customer's] IT. […] After two, three months of collaboration with the client, you will always notice that they have a shortage in IT personnel, so then […] add-on managed services are booked.*

Especially among firms that were former IT outsourcing customers, a high demand for managed services is identified, the reason also being lacking skillset amongst their own employees. These companies are used to the provider being responsible for the complete IT operation, as an expert explained: *So we believe that the customer per se is advised best if he knows that we manage his cloud for him, so we do everything and he can just use it like electricity. So they have it and they can enjoy the benefits of cloud services, but they don't have to deal with it, since the main problems of our clients are the lacking skill sets – meaning they don't have the people, they don't have the training, and they don't have the resources to keep up themselves. It actually requires a significant amount of knowledge to be well positioned here.*

Adapting the Sales Strategy By Providing Personal Sale And Self-Service

The prerequisite for providing self-service is that the service portfolio is depicted in great detail but in simple terms using the language of the target market on the provider's website. This way, a customer is enabled to get all the information he needs for his purchase decision. Further, the ordering process itself has to be straightforward and transparent. Moreover, it is very important for customers that cloud services are made available promptly after they placed the order. A time lag of hours or even days between order and receipt is considered too long. Nevertheless, it remains necessary to offer additional individual support. This is of particular relevance as some customers have difficulties using self-service due to a lack of skills.

Some providers believe that each type of cloud service can be sold by self-service without considering the size of the client company. However, we find: *Let's say it like this, these purely pay-per-use cases where I enter my credit card and that's it, this is more on the smaller scale. [...] So, no company, such as Adidas or the likes, is going to send somebody with his credit card and say, just go and use it. So there will always be contracts, there are contract negotiations and so on [...].*

Moreover, the acceptance of self-services decreases from IaaS toward SaaS. A reason for this is that SaaS services often have to be integrated in the customers' business processes and IT landscapes.

Overall, the self-service is useful when providing standardized cloud services for customers with no need for individual adjustment as another expert described: *[...] the projects are not really a simple infrastructure-as-a-service, click, click, click and sold, but we conceptually design a holistic package based on infrastructure, consulting and managed services.*

Therefore, providers have to develop their selling strategy in accordance with their target group: If they target medium-sized and large companies and offer more than standardized, basic IaaS services, it is mandatory to additionally offer the possibility to engage in negotiations with the provider. This has a major advantage, as the provider gets to know the customers that are on his platform.

Having the Leading Certificates

Cloud providers need to have for their country of operation relevant certificates. Certificates are commonly demanded as a prerequisite within tendering processes. They serve as an instrument to attract clients by transferring confidence from the certificate issuer to the corresponding cloud provider. The experts compared it with the private environment: everybody prefers to buy from a trusted online shop. Hence, decision makers feel more secure and protected by selecting a certified cloud provider. An expert talked about his experience: *So, without [certificates] it is also going to be hard to survive in the market. That's what also makes it very hard for the smaller players that obviously can't get certified since it costs money. No matter what the certificates actually mean, but the bottom line is that a customer wants to buy things in a trusted shop. That's exactly the same as when we shop privately. And of course, that's the same in industry or for large enterprises. [...] Actually, it is mainly used to protect the job of the decision makers. So that when he decides, he can say ok, they are ISO certified, they are SOC certified and C5 and I don't know what.*

The experts mentioned C5, ISO 27000, SOC, GGPA and ISO 9001 as most relevant certifications in the cloud field. Overall, four different categories of important certificates were identified: certificates proving that (1) single employees have a skill set in a specific area, (2) a provider is suitable and allowed to work with a specific sensitive industry like the banking industry, (3) internal cloud services are fully compatible with cloud services of a third-party provider, and finally (4) providers fulfill compliance and data security requirements within their data centers.

Orchestrate Various Cloud Services

The experts identified the increasing importance of multi-cloud management. The idea of multi cloud management is to be a broker for IaaS services of other providers. For many IaaS providers, who have problems to compete with the leading hyper scalers, this is a promising way to collectively benefit by cooperation. Many cloud service providers use services from various providers anyhow. This can be explained by the following: First, several SaaS services have to be developed for IaaS platform of the respective provider. Second, single employees often order IaaS services for temporary use by paying with their firm's credit card. Company executives in many cases do thus not know which clouds are used throughout the company. Third, customers fear vendor lock-in. An expert mentioned this as follows: *[...] I think it is mainly a question of what each business unit wants. Meaning, you have a marketing department that says they want Adobe Experience Manager. This works very well on Microsoft Azure, so now we have Azure in the company. Then, somebody in the DevOps area says he is working with data analytics so he wants AWS since they are currently strong there. And all of a sudden you already have two clouds in your company. And then you obviously have Salesforce, the third cloud which is always there. Managing this is really, really hard.*

It is evident that the management of the different clouds poses a challenge for clients, which creates a high demand for a working solution. Multi-cloud management provides a range of advantages to clients: (1) It serves as a viable exit strategy for customers to avoid vendor lock-in. (2) Managers are provided with a concise overview of the different available providers and associated prices. On that basis, clients can transfer workloads to the IaaS service which is currently the cheapest. (3) Managers can monitor which clouds are currently used, which workloads run on which IaaS service and which costs occur. (4) Clients are encouraged to use multiple clouds and decide which IaaS service is most efficient for each individual application. (5) Despite using IaaS service from various providers, customers achieve a desired single point of contact. An IaaS provider willing to offer such a multi-cloud management system is required to have a high level of competence in other clouds. Some IaaS providers are encouraging the compatibility of their IaaS services with those of other provides, as they figure that they are unable to compete as single player. Few providers even go so far as to locate their data centers in close proximity and establish a high-speed connection between their data centers in order to support efficient data transfer. In contrast, other players try to prevent their data to become interoperable and thereby complicate the establishment of a working multi-cloud management. Offering multi-cloud management can hence be challenging but is expected to be of competitive advantage as an expert explained: *I believe that the next big step will be the ability to offer multi cloud management. Meaning, that there are multiple software providers that concentrate on establishing the connection to the respective clouds. I believe it will be extremely challenging since all the cloud providers don't simply lay their cards on the table. Staying on top all the time is going to be a bit tricky, but if you have a solution here, this would be very, very sexy. I think this is the sweet spot at the moment.*

DISCUSSION

Practical Implications – Recommendations for IaaS Providers

This contribution is meant to be useful for practitioners by giving concrete recommendations for IaaS providers, that can be used for implementation for the different components of their business model. Besides concluding that value facilitation and standardization are key capabilities for IaaS providers, five recommendations can be given based on the results of 40 expert interviews in the time range from end of 2017 to end of 2018.

1. Offering fixed prices for cloud service usage besides pay-per-use pricing models
2. Extending pure IaaS services with managed services
3. Adapting the sales strategy by providing personal sale and self-service
4. Possessing the leading certificates
5. Supporting multi-cloud management

First, it is argued, that IaaS providers should not only focus on the cloud-inherent pay-as-you-go pricing and payment strategies. Besides, conventional fixed pricing models need to be considered and offered as many customers lack the IT skillset to have an overview over potential costs, require budget security and have their internal processes optimized for fixed pricing models from the past.

Second, IaaS providers should offer managed services besides the pure IaaS service. Many customers want to focus on their core business. They are used to outsourcing their IT and demand a holistic offering including managed services.

Third, besides a self-service approach, IaaS providers should adapt their sales strategy by also offering personal sales, especially if there is a focus on mid-sized and large companies as customers. Oftentimes, customers require a holistic offering package and want a personal consulting and pricing option. Especially in combination with the above-mentioned recommendation of offering managed services, an individual pricing becomes more important.

Fourth, it is crucial to possess the leading certificates if an IaaS provider wants to survive in the market and sell services to large clients and potentially participate in public tenders. Certificates such as e.g., ISO 27001 or the likes transport a certain level of trust and reliability that the customer relies on. In a competitive market, not possessing the fundamental certificates can be a disqualifying criterion.

Fifth, enabling and offering multi-cloud management could be a key competitive advantage in future. Thus, IaaS providers need to be able to offer their own services as well as orchestrate workload balancing between different providers at the same time. Parallel developments in companies lead to using multiple clouds in the same firm for different purposes. In addition, companies often want to avoid vendor lock-in.

LIMITATIONS AND FUTURE RESEARCH

As usual for empirical research, cross-sectional data is employed, meaning that conclusions from this research might change or even lose significance in the long-term. Longitudinal research could mitigate this constraint over time and back up the conclusions drawn in this contribution.

Additionally, recommendations given in this contribution are mainly based on learnings from expert interviews of nationally and internationally active companies in Germany. Nevertheless, this limitation could be overcome completely by conducting a replication with a global reach of experts, ideally in connection with longitudinal data to confirm or observe changes for the given recommendations and conclusions over time.

Moreover, all recommendations and conclusions presented in this contribution are based on management literature research as well as expert interviews. Either is cross-tested nor validated which could be another interesting subject for future research.

Lastly, it is necessary to identify the business model characteristics influencing the success of the further roles being part of the PaCE Model.

REFERENCES

Adamov, A., & Erguvan, M. (2009). The Truth about Cloud Computing as New Paradigm in IT. *3rd International Conference on Application of Information and Communication Technologies.* 10.1109/ICAICT.2009.5372585

Adner, R. (2017). Ecosystem as Structure. *An Actionable Construct for Strategy.*, *43*(1), 39–58. doi:10.1177/0149206316678451

Appelrath, H.-J., Kagermann, H., & Krcmar, H. (2014). *Future Business Clouds.* Academic Press.

Armbrust, M., Fox, A., Griffith, R., Joseph, A. D., Katz, R., Konwinski, A., ... Zaharia, M. (2010). A View of Cloud Computing. *Communications of the ACM,* *53*(4), 50–58. doi:10.1145/1721654.1721672

Barney, J. (1991). Firm Resources and Sustained Competive Advantage. *Journal of Management, 17*(1), 99–120. doi:10.1177/014920639101700108

Basole, R. C., Russell, M. G., Huhtamäki, J., Rubens, N., Still, K., & Park, H. (2015). Understanding Business Ecosystem Dynamics. *ACM Transactions on Management Information Systems, 6*(2), 1–32. doi:10.1145/2724730

Bogataj Habjan, K., & Pucihar, A. (2017). The Importance of Business Model Factors for Cloud Computing Adoption: Role of Previous Experiences. *Organizacija, 50*(3), 255–272. doi:10.1515/orga-2017-0013

Böhm, M., Koleva, G., Leimeister, S., Riedl, C., & Krcmar, H. (2010). Towards a Generic Value Network for Cloud Computing. *Conference: Economics of Grids, Clouds, Systems, and Services, 7th International Workshop.* 10.1007/978-3-642-35194-5

Böhm, M., Leimeister, S., Riedl, C., & Krcmar, H. (2011). Cloud Computing - Outsourcing 2.0 or a new Business Model for IT Provisioning. In F. Keuper, C. Oecking, & A. Degenhardt (Eds.), *Application Management* (pp. 31–56). Gabler. doi:10.1007/978-3-8349-6492-2_2

Buyya, R., Shin, C., Venugopal, S., Broberg, J., & Brandic, I. (2009). Cloud computing and emerging IT platforms: Vision, hype, and reality for delivering computing as the 5th utility. *Future Generation Computer Systems, 25*(6), 599–616. doi:10.1016/j.future.2008.12.001

Chandler, G. N., & Hanks, S. H. (1993). Measuring the Performance of Emerging Businesses: A Validation Study. *Journal of Business Venturing, 8*(5), 391–408. doi:10.1016/0883-9026(93)90021-V

Chandler, G. N., & Jansen, E. (1992). The Founder's Self-Assessed Competence and Venture Performance. *Journal of Business Venturing, 7*(3), 223–236. doi:10.1016/0883-9026(92)90028-P

Clohessy, T., Acton, T., Morgan, L., & Conboy, K. (2016). The times they are a-changin for ICT service provision: A cloud computing business model perspective. *24th European Conference on Information Systems ECIS,* 1–15. Retrieved from https://www.scopus.com/inward/record.uri?eid=2-s2.0-84995803001&partnerID=40&md5=802997b159b74d6b206feb56124f9b95

Corbin, J., & Strauss, A. (1990). Grounded Theory Research: Procedures, Canons and Evaluative Criteria. *Qualitative Sociology, 19*(6), 418–427.

Costello, K., & Hippold, S. (2018). Gartner Forecasts Worldwide Public Cloud Revenue to Grow 17.3 Percent in 2019. Stamford, CT: Academic Press.

Cox, L., Camp, S., & Ensley, M. (2002). Does It Pay to Grow? The Impact of Growth on Profitability and Wealth Creation. Babson College/Kauffman Foundation Entrepreneurship Research Conference, Boulder, CO.

Dillon, T., Wu, C., & Chang, E. (2010). Cloud Computing : Issues and Challenges. *24th IEEE International Conference on Advanced Information Networking and Applications*, 27–33. 10.1109/AINA.2010.187

Floerecke, S. (2018). Success Factors of SaaS Providers' Business Models – An Exploratory Multiple-Case Study. IESS 2018: Exploring Service Science, 193-207.

Floerecke, S., & Lehner, F. (2015). A Revised Model of the Cloud Computing Ecosystem. *12th International Conference on Economics of Grids, Clouds, Systems, and Services*. 10.1007/978-3-319-43177-2

Floerecke, S., & Lehner, F. (2016). Cloud Computing Ecosystem model: Refinement and Evaluation. *Twenty-Fourth European Conference on Information Systems (ECIS)*.

Floerecke, S., & Lehner, F. (2018a). Business Model Characteristics for Local IaaS Providers for Counteracting the Dominance of Hyperscalers. *International Conference on the Economics of Grids, Clouds, Systems, and Services*, 137–150.

Floerecke, S., & Lehner, F. (2018b). Success-Driving Business Model Characteristics of IaaS and PaaS Providers. *International Journal on Cloud Computing: Services and Architecture*, *08*(06). doi:10.5121/ijccsa.2018.8601

Grönroos, C. (2017). On Value and Value Creation in Service: A Management Perspective. *Journal of Creating Value*, *3*(2), 125–141. doi:10.1177/2394964317727196

Grönroos, C., & Voima, P. (2013). Critical service logic: Making sense of value creation and co-creation. *Journal of the Academy of Marketing Science*, *41*(2), 133–150. doi:10.100711747-012-0308-3

Grunert, K. G., & Sørensen, E. (1996). Perceived and actual key success factors: A study of the yoghurt market in Denmark, Germany and the United Kingdom. Aarhus, Denmark: Academic Press.

Gupta, S., Kumar, S., Singh, S. K., Foropon, C., & Chandra, C. (2018). Role of cloud ERP on the performance of an organization: Contingent resource-based view perspective. *International Journal of Logistics Management*, *29*(2), 659–675. doi:10.1108/IJLM-07-2017-0192

Hentschel, R., & Leyh, C. (2016). Cloud Computing: Gestern, heute, morgen. *HMD Praxis der Wirtschaftsinformatik*, *53*(5), 563–579.

Herzberg, F., Mausner, B., & Snyderman, B. (1959). *The Motivation to Work*. New York: John Wiley.

Herzfeldt, A., Floerecke, S., Ertl, C., & Krcmar, H. (2018). The Role of Value Facilitation Regarding Cloud Service Provider Profitability in the Cloud Ecosystem. Multidiscplinary Approaches to Service-Oriented Engineering. doi:10.4018/978-1-5225-5951-1.ch006

Herzfeldt, A., Floerecke, S., Ertl, C., & Krcmar, H. (2019). Examining the Antecedents of Cloud Service Profitability. *International Journal of Cloud Applications and Computing*, *9*(4), 37–65. doi:10.4018/IJCAC.2019100103

Hoffmann, W. H., & Schlosser, R. (2001). Success Factors of Strategic Alliances in Small and Medium-Sized Enterprises - An Empirical Study. *Long Range Planning*, *34*(3), 357–381. doi:10.1016/S0024-6301(01)00041-3

Iansiti, M., & Levien, R. (2004). *The Keystone Advantage: What the Dynamics of Business Ecosystems Mean for Strategy, Innovation and Sustainability*. Boston: Harvard Business School Press.

Iyer, B. R., & Henderson, J. C. (2012). Business Value from Clouds: Learning from users. *MIS Quarterly Executive*, *11*(1).

Kim, G., Shin, B., Kim, K. K., & Lee, H. (2011). IT capabilities, process-oriented dynamic capabilities, and firm financial performance. *Journal of the Association for Information Systems*, *12*(7), 487–517. doi:10.17705/1jais.00270

Kim, H., Hoskisson, R. E., & Wan, W. P. (2004). Power Dependence, Diversification Strategy, and Performance in Keiretsu Member Firms. *Strategic Management Journal*, *25*(7), 613–636. doi:10.1002mj.395

Leidecker, J. K., & Bruno, A. V. (1984). Identifying and Using Critical Success Factors. *Long Range Planning*, *17*(1), 23–32. doi:10.1016/0024-6301(84)90163-8

Leimeister, S., Böhm, M., Riedl, C., & Krcmar, H. (2010). The Business Perspective of Cloud Computing: Actors, Roles and Value Networks. *European Conference on Information Systems (ECIS)*, 12. Retrieved from http://aisel.aisnet.org/cgi/viewcontent.cgi?article=1082&context=ecis2010

Lusch, R., & Nambisan, S. (2015). Service innovation: A service-dominant logic perspective. *Management Information Systems Quarterly*, *39*(1), 155–176. doi:10.25300/MISQ/2015/39.1.07

Marston, S., Li, Z., Bandyopadhyay, S., Zhang, J., & Ghalsasi, A. (2011). Cloud computing - The business perspective. *Decision Support Systems*, *51*(1), 176–189. doi:10.1016/j.dss.2010.12.006

Mell, P. M., & Grance, T. (2011). The NIST Definition of Cloud Computing. *Special Publication (NIST SP) - 800-145.*

Mendelson, H. (2000). Organizational Architecture and Success in the Information Technology Industry. *Management Science, 46*(4), 513–529. doi:10.1287/mnsc.46.4.513.12060

Moore, J. F. (1993). Predators and prey: A new ecology of competition. *Harvard Business Review, 71*(3), 75–86.

Moore, J. F. (2006). *Business ecosystems and the view from the firm.* The Antitrust Bulletin. doi:10.1177/0003603X0605100103

Oliveira, T., Thomas, M., & Espadanal, M. (2014). Assessing the determinants of cloud computing adoption: An analysis of the manufacturing and services sectors. *Information & Management, 51*(5), 497–510. doi:10.1016/j.im.2014.03.006

Osterwalder, A., & Pigneur, Y. (2010). *Business Model Generation: A Handbook for Visionaries, Game Changers, and Challengers.* John Wiley & Sons.

Park, S. C., & Ryoo, S. Y. (2013). An empirical investigation of end-users' switching toward cloud computing: A two factor theory perspective. *Computers in Human Behavior, 29*(1), 160–179. doi:10.1016/j.chb.2012.07.032

Rong, K., Lin, Y., Li, B., Burström, T., Butel, L., & Yu, J. (2018). Business ecosystem research agenda: More dynamic, more embedded, and more internationalized. *Asian Business & Management, 17*(3), 167–182. doi:10.105741291-018-0038-6

Russo, M. V., & Fouts, P. (1997). Resource-based perspective on corporate environmental performance and profitability. *Academy of Management Journal, 40*(3), 534–559.

Sturges, J. E., & Hanrahan, K. J. (2004). Comparing Telephone and Face-to-Face Qualitative Interviewing: A Research Note. *Qualitative Research, 4*(1), 107–118. doi:10.1177/1468794104041110

Vargo, S. L., & Lusch, R. F. (2004). Evolving to a New Dominant Logic for Marketing. *Journal of Marketing, 68*, 1–17. doi:10.1509/jmkg.68.1.1.24036

Vargo, S. L., & Lusch, R. F. (2008). Service-Dominant Logic: Continuing the Evolution. *Journal of the Academy of Marketing Science, 36*(1), 1–10. doi:10.100711747-007-0069-6

Veit, D., Clemons, E., Benlian, A., Buxmann, P., Hess, T., Kundisch, D., ... Spann, M. (2014). Business Models - An Information Systems Research Agenda. *Business & Information Systems Engineering*, 6(1), 45–53. doi:10.100712599-013-0308-y

Velte, A. T., Velte, T. J., & Elsenpeter, R. (2010). Cloud Computing: A practical Approach. *Journal of the Electrochemical Society*, *129*. Retrieved from http://scholar.google.com/scholar?hl=en&btnG=Search&q=intitle:No+Title#0

Wernerfelt, B. (1984). A resource-based view of the firm. *Strategic Management Journal*, *5*(2), 171–180. doi:10.1002mj.4250050207

Ye, C., & Potter, R. (2011). The Role of Habit in Post-Adoption Switching of Personal Information Technologies: An Empirical Investigation. *Communications of the Association for Information Systems*, *28*, 585–610. doi:10.17705/1CAIS.02835

Yin, R. K. (2014). *Case Study Research: Design and Methods.* doi:10.3138/cjpe.30.1.108

Zhang, L.-J., & Zhou, Q. (2009). *CCOA: Cloud Computing Open Architecture.* Conference: IEEE International Conference on Web Services, Los Angeles, CA.

Zhang, Q., Cheng, L., & Boutaba, R. (2010). Cloud Computing: State of the Art and Research Challenges. *Journal of Internet Services and Applications*, *1*(2), 7–18. doi:10.100713174-010-0007-6

Zhou, R., Li, Z., Wu, C., & Huang, Z. (2017). *An Efficient Cloud Market Mechanism for Computing Jobs with Soft Deadlines.* Academic Press.

KEY TERMS AND DEFINITIONS

Business Ecosystem: A business ecosystem generally represents a pertinent scope for systemic innovations where different interrelated and interdependent companies cooperate in order to mutually deliver customer solutions.

Business Model: A business model is made up of several constitutive components acting as a tool for depicting, innovating and evaluating the business logic of an organization.

Cloud Computing: Cloud computing is a new technology mix based operations model where computing services (both hardware and software) are delivered on-demand to customers over a network in a self-service fashion, independent of device and location. The literature distinguishes between three main service models (Infrastructure-as-a-Service, Platform-as-a-Service and Software-as-a-Service) and four deployment models (public, hybrid, private and community).

Managed Services: Managed services are the extension of offering pure cloud services towards the customer. Whereas a cloud service provision is e.g., Infrastructure-as-a-Service (IaaS), the managed service could be managing a web server based on the given infrastructure.

Resource-Based View: The resource-based view analyzes and interprets internal resources of an organization and emphasizes resources and capabilities in formulating strategy to achieve sustainable competitive advantages.

Value Co-Creation: Value co-creation is a joint process that takes place on a co-creation platform involving a service provider and a customer, where the service provider's service (production) process and the customer's consumption and value creation process merge into one process of direct interactions.

Value Facilitation: The way a service provider contributes to the customer's value creation by offering resources representing potential value-in-use.

Compilation of References

10 . Best Learning Management Systems For Your Company. (n.d.). Retrieved April 25, 2019, from https://learning-management.financesonline.com/top-10-learning-management-software-solutions-for-your-company/

Aazam, M., Harras, K. A., & Zeadally, S. (2019). Fog Computing for 5G Tactile Industrial Internet of Things: QoE-Aware Resource Allocation Model. *IEEE Transactions on Industrial Informatics*, *15*(5), 3085–3092. doi:10.1109/TII.2019.2902574

Abawajy, J. (2018). *What is workload (cloud data center service provisioning: theoretical and practical approaches.* Retrieved from https://www.jnu.ac.in/content/LAB05/presentation/gian2018/day2.pdf

Adamov, A., & Erguvan, M. (2009). The Truth about Cloud Computing as New Paradigm in IT. *3rd International Conference on Application of Information and Communication Technologies.* 10.1109/ICAICT.2009.5372585

Adam, S. A., Yousif, A., & Bashir, M. B. (2016). Multilevel Authentication Scheme for Cloud Computing. *International Journal of Grid and Distributed Computing*, *9*(9), 205–212. doi:10.14257/ijgdc.2016.9.9.18

Adner, R. (2017). Ecosystem as Structure. *An Actionable Construct for Strategy.*, *43*(1), 39–58. doi:10.1177/0149206316678451

Agarwal, M. (2017). *Cloud Computing : A Paradigm Shift in the Way of Computing.* doi:10.5815/ijmecs.2017.12.05

Agrawal, D., Das, S., & El Abbadi, A. (2011, March). Big data and cloud computing: current state and future opportunities. In *Proceedings of the 14th International Conference on Extending Database Technology* (pp. 530-533). ACM. 10.1145/1951365.1951432

Ahmad, I., Bakht, H., & Mohan, U. (2017). Cloud Computing – A Comprehensive Definition. *Journal of Computing and Management Studies*, *1*(1). Retrieved from https://journals.indexcopernicus.com/api/file/viewByFileId/234155.pdf

Ahuja, V. (2000). Building trust in electronic commerce. *IT Professional*, *2*(3), 61–63. doi:10.1109/6294.846215

Al-Attab, B. S., & Fadewar, H. S. (2016). Authentication Scheme for Insecure Networks in Cloud Computing. *IEEE International Conference on Global Trends in Signal Processing, Information Computing and Communication*, 158-163. 10.1109/ICGTSPICC.2016.7955289

Alharkan, T., & Martin, P. (2012). Idsaas: Intrusion detection system as a service in public clouds. *Proceedings of the 2012 12th IEEE/ACM International Symposium on Cluster, Cloud and Grid Computing (ccgrid 2012)*. 10.1109/CCGrid.2012.81

Aljumah, A., & Ahanger, T. A. (2018). Fog computing and security issues: A review. *2018 7th International Conference on Computers Communications and Control (ICCCC)*, 237–239. 10.1109/ICCCC.2018.8390464

Almudarra, F., & Qureshi, B. (2015). Issues in adopting agile development principles for mobile cloud computing applications. *Procedia Computer Science*, *52*, 1133–1140. doi:10.1016/j.procs.2015.05.131

Amazon Web Services. (2019). Retrieved from https://aws.amazon.com/

Amazon. (2019). *Amazon - Cloud Products*. Retrieved April 15, 2019, from Amazon Web Services website: https://aws.amazon.com/products/?nc2=h_m1

Appelrath, H.-J., Kagermann, H., & Kremar, H. (2014). *Future Business Clouds*. Academic Press.

Armbrust, M., Fox, A., Griffith, R., Joseph, A. D., Katz, R., Konwinski, A., ... Zaharia, M. (2010). A View of Cloud Computing. *Communications of the ACM*, *53*(4), 50–58. doi:10.1145/1721654.1721672

Banzai, T., Koizumi, H., Kanbayashi, R., Imada, T., Hanawa, T., & Sato, M. (2010, May). D-cloud: Design of a software testing environment for reliable distributed systems using cloud computing technology. In *2010 10th IEEE/ACM International Conference on Cluster, Cloud and Grid Computing* (pp. 631-636). IEEE.

Barney, J. (1991). Firm Resources and Sustained Competive Advantage. *Journal of Management*, *17*(1), 99–120. doi:10.1177/014920639101700108

Basole, R. C., Russell, M. G., Huhtamäki, J., Rubens, N., Still, K., & Park, H. (2015). Understanding Business Ecosystem Dynamics. *ACM Transactions on Management Information Systems*, *6*(2), 1–32. doi:10.1145/2724730

Bertion, E., Paci, F., & Ferrini, R. (2009). Privacy-Preserving Digital Identity Management for Cloud Computing. IEEE Computer Society Data Engineering Bulletin, 1-4.

Bhargava, Sandeep, & Goya, Swatil. (2013). Dynamic Load Balancing in Cloud Using Live Migration of Virtual Machine. International Journal of Advanced Research in Computer Engineering & Technology, Vol. 2(8), 2472:2477

Bogataj Habjan, K., & Pucihar, A. (2017). The Importance of Business Model Factors for Cloud Computing Adoption: Role of Previous Experiences. *Organizacija*, *50*(3), 255–272. doi:10.1515/orga-2017-0013

Böhm, M., Koleva, G., Leimeister, S., Riedl, C., & Krcmar, H. (2010). Towards a Generic Value Network for Cloud Computing. *Conference: Economics of Grids, Clouds, Systems, and Services, 7th International Workshop*. 10.1007/978-3-642-35194-5

Böhm, M., Leimeister, S., Riedl, C., & Krcmar, H. (2011). Cloud Computing - Outsourcing 2.0 or a new Business Model for IT Provisioning. In F. Keuper, C. Oecking, & A. Degenhardt (Eds.), *Application Management* (pp. 31–56). Gabler. doi:10.1007/978-3-8349-6492-2_2

Bojanova, I., & Zhang, J. (2013). *Guest editors' introduction*. Retrieved from www.hibu.com

Borko Furht, A. E. (2010). *Handbook of Cloud*. doi:10.1007/978-1-4419-6524-0

Briscoe, G., & Marinos, A. (2009). Digital Ecosystems in the Clouds: Towards Community Cloud Computing. *3rd IEEE International Conference on Digital Ecosystems and Technologies (DEST 2009)*, 103–108. Retrieved from https://arxiv.org/pdf/0903.0694.pdf

Burney, A. M. A., Asif, M., & Abbas, Z. (2016). Forensics Issues in Cloud Computing. *Forensics Issues in Cloud Computing Article in Journal of Computer and Communications*, 4, 63–69. doi:10.4236/jcc.2016.410007

Butt, S. A., Abbas, S. A., & Ahsan, M. (2016). Software development life cycle & software quality measuring types. *Asian Journal of Mathematics and Computer Research*, 112-122.

Butt, S. A. (2016). Analysis of unfair means cases in computer-based examination systems. *Pacific Science Review B. Humanities and Social Sciences*, 2(2), 75–79.

Butt, S. A. (2016). Study of agile methodology with the cloud. *Pacific Science Review B. Humanities and Social Sciences*, 2(1), 22–28.

Butt, S. A., & Jamal, T. (2017). Frequent change request from user to handle cost on project in agile model. *Proc. of Asia Pacific Journal of Multidisciplinary Research*, 5(2), 26–42.

Butt, S. A., Tariq, M. I., Jamal, T., Ali, A., Martinez, J. L. D., & De-La-Hoz-Franco, E. (2019). Predictive Variables for Agile Development Merging Cloud Computing Services. *IEEE Access: Practical Innovations, Open Solutions*, 7, 99273–99282. doi:10.1109/ACCESS.2019.2929169

Buyya, R., Garg, S. K., & Calheiros, R. N. (2011, December). *SLA-oriented resource provisioning for cloud computing: Challenges, architecture, and solutions. In 2011 international conference on cloud and service computing* (pp. 1–10). IEEE.

Buyya, R., Shin, C., Venugopal, S., Broberg, J., & Brandic, I. (2009). Cloud computing and emerging IT platforms: Vision, hype, and reality for delivering computing as the 5th utility. *Future Generation Computer Systems*, 25(6), 599–616. doi:10.1016/j.future.2008.12.001

Calzarossa, Della Vedova, Massari, Petcu, Tabash, & Tessera. (2016). Workloads in the Clouds. *Principles of Performance and Reliability Modeling and Evaluation*, 1-27.

Cao, N., Wang, C., Li, M., Ren, K., & Lou, W. (2016). Privacy-preserving multi-keyword ranked search over encrypted cloud data. *IEEE Transactions on Parallel and Distributed Systems*, 25(1), 222–233. doi:10.1109/TPDS.2013.45

Chandler, G. N., & Hanks, S. H. (1993). Measuring the Performance of Emerging Businesses: A Validation Study. *Journal of Business Venturing*, 8(5), 391–408. doi:10.1016/0883-9026(93)90021-V

Chandler, G. N., & Jansen, E. (1992). The Founder's Self-Assessed Competence and Venture Performance. *Journal of Business Venturing*, 7(3), 223–236. doi:10.1016/0883-9026(92)90028-P

Chang, Y., & Liu, F. (2016). Network traffic and user behavior analysis of mobile reading applications. *International Conference on Information Science and Technology (ICIST)*, 142-146. 10.1109/ICIST.2016.7483400

Chellappa, R. (1997). *Cloud computing: an Emerging paradigm for computing*. Dallas, TX: INFORMS.

Chen, D., & Zhao, H. (2012). *Data security and privacy protection issues in cloud computing*. Paper presented at the 2012 International Conference on Computer Science and Electronics Engineering. 10.1109/ICCSEE.2012.193

Chong, Y. N. (2019). Cloud Computing Challenges in a General Perspective. *Journal of Computing and Management Studies*, 3. Retrieved from https://64243b79-a-62cb3a1a-s-sites.googlegroups.com/site/jcomandman/NYC1319.pdf?attachauth=ANoY7cpjpe_BJkPXryTjeGoKmFInLc1svcZgVi3YHbpmKciM65WNCc_gYPdNSzs5jNaAa5U GOinNbxpNUmijXcxh2CfD0aAjt3_6IiUznVmi548SdKo235rNmchw56ps9in45z-Q8J3IjXqmHegSzVPRmduNdr0O442

Choosing a Cloud Platform | Managed Cloud by Rackspace. (n.d.). Retrieved April 15, 2019, from https://www.rackspace.com/cloud

Cisco Cloud Index Supplement. (2017). *Cloud readiness regional details white paper, 2016-2021*. White paper. Cisco.

Cito, J., Leitner, P., Fritz, T., & Gall, H. C. (2015, August). The making of cloud applications: An empirical study on software development for the cloud. In *Proceedings of the 2015 10th Joint Meeting on Foundations of Software Engineering* (pp. 393-403). ACM. 10.1145/2786805.2786826

Clohessy, T., Acton, T., Morgan, L., & Conboy, K. (2016). The times they are a-changin for ICT service provision: A cloud computing business model perspective. *24th European Conference on Information Systems ECIS*, 1–15. Retrieved from https://www.scopus.com/inward/record.uri?eid=2-s2.0-84995803001&partnerID=40&md5=802997b159b74d6b206feb56124f9b95

Cloud Computing and its Evolution Over Time 1969 to 2015. (n.d.). Retrieved April 1, 2019, from https://infooptics.com/cloud-computing-evolution-time/

Cloud Computing History timeline | Timetoast timelines. (n.d.). Retrieved April 1, 2019, from https://media.timetoast.com/timelines/cloud-computing-history

Cloud Marketplace - Hybrid Cloud Computing | Dell EMC US. (n.d.). Retrieved April 15, 2019, from https://www.dellemc.com/en-us/cloud/hybrid-cloud-computing/index.htm

Cloud Service Provider Resources from Intel. (n.d.). Retrieved April 15, 2019, from https://www.intel.com/content/www/us/en/cloud-computing/cloud-service-provider-resources.html

Cloud, G. (n.d.). *Future of Cloud Computing Survey*. Retrieved April 25, 2019, from https://cloud.google.com/future-cloud-computing/

Corbin, J., & Strauss, A. (1990). Grounded Theory Research: Procedures, Canons and Evaluative Criteria. *Qualitative Sociology, 19*(6), 418–427.

Costa, M., Crowcroft, J., Castro, M., Rowstron, A., Zhou, L., Zhang, L., & Barham, P. (2005). *Vigilante: End-to-end containment of internet worms*. Paper presented at the ACM SIGOPS Operating Systems Review. 10.1145/1095810.1095824

Costello, K., & Hippold, S. (2018). Gartner Forecasts Worldwide Public Cloud Revenue to Grow 17.3 Percent in 2019. Stamford, CT: Academic Press.

Cox, L., Camp, S., & Ensley, M. (2002). Does It Pay to Grow? The Impact of Growth on Profitability and Wealth Creation. Babson College/Kauffman Foundation Entrepreneurship Research Conference, Boulder, CO.

CSA. (2011). STAR (security, trust and assurance registry) program. *Cloud Security Alliance*. Accessed on 16 Oct. 2012 https://cloudsecurityalliance.org/star/

da Silva, E. A. N., & Lucredio, D. (2012, September). Software engineering for the cloud: A research roadmap. In *2012 26th Brazilian Symposium on Software Engineering* (pp. 71-80). IEEE. 10.1109/SBES.2012.12

Data Center Providers. (n.d.). Retrieved April 25, 2019, from https://www.datacenters.com/providers

Dhar, P. (2012). *Cloud computing and its applications in the world of networking*. Retrieved from www.IJCSI.org

Dhar, S. (2012). From outsourcing to Cloud computing: Evolution of IT services. *Management Research Review, 35*(8), 664–675. doi:10.1108/01409171211247677

Dikaiakos, M. D., Katsaros, D., Mehra, P., Pallis, G., & Vakali, A. (2009). Cloud computing: Distributed internet computing for IT and scientific research. *IEEE Internet Computing, 13*(5), 10–13. doi:10.1109/MIC.2009.103

Dillon, T., Wu, C., & Chang, E. (2010). Cloud Computing : Issues and Challenges. *24th IEEE International Conference on Advanced Information Networking and Applications, 27–33.* 10.1109/AINA.2010.187

Dunlap, G. W., King, S. T., Cinar, S., Basrai, M. A., & Chen, P. M. (2002). ReVirt: Enabling intrusion analysis through virtual-machine logging and replay. *ACM SIGOPS Operating Systems Review, 36*(SI), 211-224.

Dynasis. (n.d.). *Cloud-Computing-Public-Private-and-Hybrid.* Retrieved from www.DynaSis. com/ITility

Egele, M., Kruegel, C., Kirda, E., Yin, H., & Song, D. (2007). *Dynamic spyware analysis.* Academic Press.

Elbadawi, K., & Al-Shaer, E. (2009). TimeVM: A Framework for online intrusion mitigation and fast recovery using multi-time-lag traffic replay. *Proceedings of the 4th International Symposium on Information, Computer, and Communications Security.* 10.1145/1533057.1533077

EM360. (2018). *Top 10 most interesting data centre providers in the world | EM360.* Retrieved April 25, 2019, from https://www.em360tech.com/tech-news/top-ten/top-10-interesting-data-centre-providers-world/

Erickson, J., Lyytinen, K., & Siau, K. (2005). Agile modeling, agile software development, and extreme programming: The state of research. *Journal of Database Management, 16*(4), 88–100. doi:10.4018/jdm.2005100105

Erl, T., Puttini, R., & Mahmood, Z. (2013). *Cloud computing : concepts, technology, & architecture.* Retrieved from https://books.google.com.pk/books/about/Cloud_Computing. html?id=czCiJ6sbhpAC&source=kp_book_description&redir_esc=y

Evangelidisa, A., Parkera, D., & Bahsoona, R. (2018). Performance Modelling and Verification of Cloud-based Auto-Scaling Policies. [Preprint submitted Accepted Manuscript]. *Future Generation Computer Systems*, 12.

Feldman, S. (2000). The changing face of e-commerce: Extending the boundaries of the possible. *IEEE Internet Computing, 4*(3), 82–83. doi:10.1109/MIC.2000.845395

Floerecke, S. (2018). Success Factors of SaaS Providers' Business Models – An Exploratory Multiple-Case Study. IESS 2018: Exploring Service Science, 193-207.

Floerecke, S., & Lehner, F. (2015). A Revised Model of the Cloud Computing Ecosystem. *12th International Conference on Economics of Grids, Clouds, Systems, and Services.* 10.1007/978-3-319-43177-2

Floerecke, S., & Lehner, F. (2016). Cloud Computing Ecosystem model: Refinement and Evaluation. *Twenty-Fourth European Conference on Information Systems (ECIS).*

Floerecke, S., & Lehner, F. (2018a). Business Model Characteristics for Local IaaS Providers for Counteracting the Dominance of Hyperscalers. *International Conference on the Economics of Grids, Clouds, Systems, and Services*, 137–150.

Floerecke, S., & Lehner, F. (2018b). Success-Driving Business Model Characteristics of Iaas and Paas Providers. *International Journal on Cloud Computing: Services and Architecture*, *08*(06). doi:10.5121/ijccsa.2018.8601

Foote. (2017). *A Brief History of Cloud Computing*. Retrieved April 10, 2019, from DATAVERSITY website: https://www.dataversity.net/brief-history-cloud-computing/

Fucci, D., Erdogmus, H., Turhan, B., Oivo, M., & Juristo, N. (2016). A dissection of the test-driven development process: Does it really matter to test-first or to test-last? *IEEE Transactions on Software Engineering*, *43*(7), 597–614. doi:10.1109/TSE.2016.2616877

Future of cloud computing: 5 insights from new global research | Google Cloud Blog. (2019). Retrieved April 27, 2019, from Google website: https://cloud.google.com/blog/topics/research/future-of-cloud-computing-5-insights-from-new-global-research

García, A. L., & Cusumano, M. A. (2006). *The Evolution of the Cloud The Work, Progress and Outlook of Cloud Infrastructure*. Retrieved from https://dspace.mit.edu/bitstream/handle/1721.1/100311/932065967-MIT.pdf;sequence=1

Garfinkel, T., & Rosenblum, M. (2003). *A Virtual Machine Introspection Based Architecture for Intrusion Detection*. Paper presented at the Ndss. Google Cloud. Retrieved from https://cloud.google.com/

Ghilic-Micu, B., Stoica, M., & Uscatu, C. R. (2014). Cloud Computing and Agile Organization Development. *Informatica Economica, 18*(4).

González-Martínez, J. A., Bote-Lorenzo, M. L., Gómez-Sánchez, E., & Cano-Parra, R. (2015). Cloud computing and education: A state-of-the-art survey. *Computers & Education, 80*, 132–151. doi:10.1016/j.compedu.2014.08.017

Gorelik, E. (2013). *Cloud Computing Models*. Retrieved from http://web.mit.edu/smadnick/www/wp/2013-01.pdf

Grönroos, C. (2017). On Value and Value Creation in Service: A Management Perspective. *Journal of Creating Value*, *3*(2), 125–141. doi:10.1177/2394964317727196

Grönroos, C., & Voima, P. (2013). Critical service logic: Making sense of value creation and co-creation. *Journal of the Academy of Marketing Science*, *41*(2), 133–150. doi:10.100711747-012-0308-3

Grunert, K. G., & Sørensen, E. (1996). Perceived and actual key success factors: A study of the yoghurt market in Denmark, Germany and the United Kingdom. Aarhus, Denmark: Academic Press.

Guha, R., & Al-Dabass, D. (2010, December). Impact of web 2.0 and cloud computing platform on software engineering. In *2010 International Symposium on Electronic System Design*(pp. 213-218). IEEE. 10.1109/ISED.2010.48

Gupta, G., & Pathak, D. (2016). *Cloud Computing:"Secured Service Provider for data mining*. International Journal Of Engineering And Computer Science.

Gupta, S., Kumar, S., Singh, S. K., Foropon, C., & Chandra, C. (2018). Role of cloud ERP on the performance of an organization: Contingent resource-based view perspective. *International Journal of Logistics Management, 29*(2), 659–675. doi:10.1108/IJLM-07-2017-0192

Habib, S., Ries, S., & Muhlhauser, M. (2011). Towards a trust management system for cloud computing, in Proc 10th IntConf Trust, Security Privacy. *Computer Communications,* 933939.

Haig-Smith, T., & Tanner, M. (2016). Cloud Computing as an Enabler of Agile Global Software Development. *Issues in Informing Science & Information Technology, 13.*

Hamza, Y. A., & Omar, M. D. (2013). Cloud Computing Security: Abuse and Nefarious Use of Cloud Computing. *International Journal of Computational Engineering Research, 03*(6), 22–27.

Hashmi, S. I., Clerc, V., Razavian, M., Manteli, C., Tamburri, D. A., Lago, P., ... Richardson, I. (2011, August). Using the cloud to facilitate global software development challenges. In *2011 IEEE Sixth International Conference on Global Software Engineering Workshop* (pp. 70-77). IEEE. 10.1109/ICGSE-W.2011.19

Hawedi, M., Talhi, C., & Boucheneb, H. (2018). Security as a service for public cloud tenants (SaaS). *Procedia Computer Science, 130,* 1025–1030. doi:10.1016/j.procs.2018.04.143

Heidari, S., & Buyya, R. (2019). Quality of Service (QoS)-driven resource provisioning for large-scale graph processing in cloud computing environments: Graph Processing-as-a-Service (GPaaS). *Future Generation Computer Systems, 96,* 490–501. doi:10.1016/j.future.2019.02.048

He, J., Zhang, Y., Huang, G., Shi, J., & Cao, J. (2012). Distributed Data Possession For Securing Multiple Replicas In Geographically Dispersed Clouds. *Journal of Computer and System Sciences, 78*(5), 1345–1358. doi:10.1016/j.jcss.2011.12.018

Hentschel, R., & Leyh, C. (2016). Cloud Computing: Gestern, heute, morgen. *HMD Praxis der Wirtschaftsinformatik, 53*(5), 563–579.

Hentschel, R., Leyh, C., & Petznick, A. (2018). Current cloud challenges in Germany: The perspective of cloud service providers. *Journal of Cloud Computing, 7*(1), 5. doi:10.118613677-018-0107-6

Herzberg, F., Mausner, B., & Snyderman, B. (1959). *The Motivation to Work.* New York: John Wiley.

Herzfeldt, A., Floerecke, S., Ertl, C., & Krcmar, H. (2018). The Role of Value Facilitation Regarding Cloud Service Provider Profitability in the Cloud Ecosystem. *Multidiscplinary Approaches to Service-Oriented Engineering.* doi:10.4018/978-1-5225-5951-1.ch006

Herzfeldt, A., Floerecke, S., Ertl, C., & Krcmar, H. (2019). Examining the Antecedents of Cloud Service Profitability. *International Journal of Cloud Applications and Computing, 9*(4), 37–65. doi:10.4018/IJCAC.2019100103

Hill, R. (2013). Guide to Cloud Computer - Principles and Practice. Computer Communications and Networks. doi:10.1007/978-1-4613-1041-9

Hille, M., Klemm, D., & Lemmermann, L. (2017). *Cloud Computing: Vendor & Service Provider Comparison*. Retrieved from https://www.reply.com/Documents/Crisp_Vendor_Universe_Cloud Computing_250118_REPLY_englischeVersion_FINAL.pdf

Hod, Ss., & Professor, C. S. E. A., & Sri Venkateswara, M. (2012). Cloud computing : SAAS. *GESJ: Computer Science and Telecommunications, 4*(36). Retrieved from https://fenix.tecnico.ulisboa.pt/downloadFile/1126518382178096/1986.pdf

Hoffmann, W. H., & Schlosser, R. (2001). Success Factors of Strategic Alliances in Small and Medium-Sized Enterprises - An Empirical Study. *Long Range Planning, 34*(3), 357–381. doi:10.1016/S0024-6301(01)00041-3

Huang, C.-Y., Hsu, P.-C., & Tzeng, G.-H. (2012). *Evaluating Cloud Computing Based Telecommunications Service Quality Enhancement by Using a New Hybrid MCDM Model*. doi:10.1007/978-3-642-29977-3_52

Huang, D., & Wu, H. (2017). *Mobile cloud computing : foundations and service models*. Retrieved from https://books.google.com.pk/books/about/Mobile_Cloud_Computing.html?id=1q2fAQAACAAJ&source=kp_book_description&redir_esc=y

Huang, Q., Yang, Y., & Wang, L. (2017). Secure data access control with cypher text update and computation outsourcing in fog computing for the internet of things. *IEEE Access: Practical Innovations, Open Solutions, 5*, 12941–12950. doi:10.1109/ACCESS.2017.2727054

Huth, A., & Cebula, J. (2011). *The Basics of Cloud Computing*. Retrieved from http://csrc.nist.gov/publications/drafts/800-145/Draft-SP-800-145_cloud-definition.pdf

Hu, W. (2013). A Quantitative Study of Virtual Machine Live Migration. In *Proc. of the 2013 ACM Cloud and Autonomic Computing Conf.* ACM. 10.1145/2494621.2494622

Ian Mitchell, J. A. (n.d.). *Cloud Security- The definitive guide to managing risk in the new ICT landscape*. Academic Press.

Iansiti, M., & Levien, R. (2004). *The Keystone Advantage: What the Dynamics of Business Ecosystems Mean for Strategy, Innovation and Sustainability*. Boston: Harvard Business School Press.

IBM Cloud Team. (2019). *IBM Cloud services | IBM Cloud*. Retrieved April 15, 2019, from IBM website: https://www.ibm.com/cloud/services

Ibrahim, M. H., & Darwish, N. R. (2015). Investigation of Adherence Degree of Agile Requirements Engineering Practices in Non-Agile Software Development Organizations. *International Journal of Advanced Computer Science and Applications, 6*(1).

Info, J. D., & Deyo, J. (2008). *Software as a Service (SaaS) A look at the migration of applications to the web*. Retrieved from http://www.isy.vcu.edu/~jsutherl/Info658/SAAS-JER.pdf

Iyer, B. R., & Henderson, J. C. (2012). Business Value from Clouds: Learning from users. *MIS Quarterly Executive, 11*(1).

Jadeja, Y., & Modi, K. (2012). Cloud computing - Concepts, architecture, and challenges. *2012 International Conference on Computing, Electronics, and Electrical Technologies, ICCEET 2012*, 877–880. 10.1109/ICCEET.2012.6203873

Jajodia, S., Kant, K., Samarati, P., Singhal, A., Swarup, V., & Wang, C. (2014). Securing Mission-Centric Operations in the Cloud. Secure Cloud Computing. doi:10.1007/978-1-4614-9278-8

Jinno, M., & Tsukishima, Y. (2009, March). Virtualized optical network (VON) for agile cloud computing environment. In *2009 Conference on Optical Fiber Communication-incudes post-deadline papers* (pp. 1-3). IEEE. 10.1364/OFC.2009.OMG1

Jin, Y., & Wen, Y. (2017). When cloud media meets network function virtualization: Challenges and applications. *IEEE MultiMedia*.

Jonas, E., Schleier-Smith, J., Sreekanti, V., Tsai, C.-C., Khandelwal, A., Pu, Q., … Gonzalez, J. E. (2019). *Cloud Programming Simplified: A Berkeley View on Serverless Computing*. Academic Press.

Juncai, S., & Shao, Q. (2011). Based on Cloud Computing E-commerce Models and ItsSecurity. *International Journal of e-Education, e-Business, e- Management Learning*, *1*(2), 175.

Karim, S., Soomro, T. R., & Aqil Burney, S. M. (2018). *Spatiotemporal Aspects of Big Data*. Applied Computer Systems. doi:10.2478/acss-2018-0012

Katherine, A. V., & Alagarsamy, K. (2012). Software testing in cloud platform: A survey. *International Journal of Computers and Applications*, *46*(6), 21–25.

Katherine, A. V., & Alagarsamy, K. (2012). Software testing in the cloud platform: A survey. *International Journal of Computers and Applications*, *46*(6), 21–25.

Katyal, M., & Mishra, A. (2013). A Comparative Study of Load Balancing Algorithms in Cloud Computing Environment. *International Journal of Distributed and Cloud Computing, 1*(2), 5-14.

Kavis, M. (2014). *Architecting the cloud : design decisions for cloud computing service models* (1st ed.). SaaS, PaaS, and IaaS. doi:10.1002/9781118691779

Kim, G., Shin, B., Kim, K. K., & Lee, H. (2011). IT capabilities, process-oriented dynamic capabilities, and firm financial performance. *Journal of the Association for Information Systems*, *12*(7), 487–517. doi:10.17705/1jais.00270

Kim, H., Hoskisson, R. E., & Wan, W. P. (2004). Power Dependence, Diversification Strategy, and Performance in Keiretsu Member Firms. *Strategic Management Journal*, *25*(7), 613–636. doi:10.1002mj.395

King, D., Chung, H. M., Lee, J. K., & Turban, E. (1999). *Electronic commerce: A managerial perspective*. Prentice Hall PTR.

Krasteva, I., Stavros, S., & Ilieva, S. (2013). Agile model-driven modernization to the service cloud. *The Eighth International Conference on Internet and Web Applications and Services (ICIW 2013)*.

Kumar, M. (2014). Software as a service for efficient Cloud Computing. *International Journal of Research in Engineering and Technology, 3*(1), 2321–7308. Retrieved from http://www.ijret.org

Kumar, N., Kumar Kushwaha, S., & Kumar, A. (2014). Cloud Computing Services and its Application Nitin. *Advance in Electronic and Electric Engineering, 4*(1), 107–112. Retrieved from http://www.ripublication.com/aeee.htm

Kumar, R., & Charu, S. (2015). Comparison between cloud computing, grid computing, cluster computing and virtualization. *International Journal of Modern Computer Science and Applications, 3*(1), 42–47.

Lai, J., Deng, R., Guan, C., & Weng, J. (2013). Attribute-based encryption with verifiable outsourced decryption. *IEEE Transactions on Information Forensics and Security, 8*(8), 1343–1354. doi:10.1109/TIFS.2013.2271848

Lakhwani, K., Kaur, R., & Kumar, P., & Thakur, M. (2018). An Extensive Survey on Data Authentication Schemes In Cloud Computing. *4th International Conference on Computing Sciences*. 10.1109/ICCS.2018.00016

Leidecker, J. K., & Bruno, A. V. (1984). Identifying and Using Critical Success Factors. *Long Range Planning, 17*(1), 23–32. doi:10.1016/0024-6301(84)90163-8

Leimeister, S., Böhm, M., Riedl, C., & Krcmar, H. (2010). The Business Perspective of Cloud Computing: Actors, Roles and Value Networks. *European Conference on Information Systems (ECIS)*, 12. Retrieved from http://aisel.aisnet.org/cgi/viewcontent.cgi?article=1082&context=ecis2010

Lele, A. (2019a). Cloud Computing. In *Disruptive Technologies for the Militaries and Security* (pp. 165–185). Systems and Technologies. doi:10.1007/978-981-13-3384-2_10

Lenart, A. (2011). *ERP in the Cloud – Benefits, and Challenges*. doi:10.1007/978-3-642-25676-9_4

Li, W., & Wan, X. L. (2015). An Analysis and Comparison for Public Cloud Technology and Market Development Trend in China. *5th IEEE International Conference on Cyber Security and Cloud Computing (CSCloud)/2018 4th IEEE International Conference on Edge Computing and Scalable Cloud (EdgeCom)*.

Liu, F., Tong, J., Mao, J., Bohn, R., Messina, J., Badger, L., & Leaf, D. (2011). NIST cloud computing reference architecture. *NIST special publication, 500*(2011), 1-28.

Liu, C., Zhu, L., Wang, M., & Tan, Y. (2014). Search pattern leakage in searchable encryption: Attacks and new construction. *Information Sciences, 265*, 176–188. doi:10.1016/j.ins.2013.11.021

Liu, H., Ning, H., Xiong, Q., & Yang, L. T. (2015). Shared authority-based privacy-preserving authentication protocol in cloud computing. *IEEE Transactions on Parallel and Distributed Systems, 26*(1), 241–251. doi:10.1109/TPDS.2014.2308218

Liu, K., Wang, H., & Yao, Y. (2016). On storing and retrieving geospatial big-data in the cloud. *Proceedings of the Second ACM SIGSPATIALInternational Workshop on the Use of GIS in Emergency Management - EM-GIS '16.* 10.1145/3017611.3017627

Liu, W. (2012). *Research on Cloud Computing Security Problem and Strategy.* IEEE. doi:10.1109/CECNet.2012.6202020

Lorido-Botran, T., Miguel-Alonso, J., & Lozano, J. A. (2012). *Auto-scaling techniques for elastic applications in cloud environments.* Technical report, Department of Computer Architecture and Technology University of the Basque Country.

Lusch, R., & Nambisan, S. (2015). Service innovation: A service-dominant logic perspective. *Management Information Systems Quarterly, 39*(1), 155–176. doi:10.25300/MISQ/2015/39.1.07

Maciá Pérez, F., Berna-Martinez, J. V., Marcos-Jorquera, D., Lorenzo Fonseca, I., & Ferrándiz Colmeiro, A. (2012). *Cloud agile manufacturing.* Academic Press.

Mahajan & Sharma. (2015). The Malicious Insider Threat in the Cloud. *International Journal of Engineering Research and General Science, 3*(2).

Mansouri, Y., Toosi, A. N., & Buyya, R. (2017). *Cost optimization for dynamic replication and migration of data in cloud data centers.* IEEE Transactions on Cloud Computing.

Marston, S., Li, Z., Bandyopadhyay, S., Zhang, J., & Ghalsasi, A. (2011). Cloud computing - The business perspective. *Decision Support Systems, 51*(1), 176–189. doi:10.1016/j.dss.2010.12.006

Mather, T., Kumaraswamy, S., & Latif, S. (2009). *Cloud security and privacy: an enterprise perspective on risks and compliance.* O'Reilly Media, Inc.

Mell, P. M., & Grance, T. (2011). The NIST Definition of Cloud Computing. *Special Publication (NIST SP) - 800-145.*

Mell, P., & Grance, T. (2011). *The NIST definition of cloud computing.* Academic Press.

Mell, P., & Grance, T. (2011). The NIST Definition of Cloud Computing. NIST Special Publication 800-145, 1-7. doi:10.6028/NIST.SP.800-145

Mendelson, H. (2000). Organizational Architecture and Success in the Information Technology Industry. *Management Science, 46*(4), 513–529. doi:10.1287/mnsc.46.4.513.12060

Merlino, G., Dautov, R., Distefano, S., & Bruneo, D. (2019). Enabling Workload Engineering in Edge, Fog, and Cloud Computing through OpenStack-based Middleware. *ACM Transactions on Internet Technology, 19*(2), 1–22. doi:10.1145/3309705

Microsoft Azure. (2019). Retrieved from https://azure.microsoft.com/en-us/

Mike, W. (2019). *Best cloud backup of 2019 | TechRadar*. Retrieved April 25, 2019, from https://www.techradar.com/news/best-cloud-backup

Mirashe, S. P., & Kalyankar, N. V. (2010). Cloud Computing. *Communications of the ACM*, *51*(7), 9. doi:10.1145/358438.349303

Mohagheghi, P., & Sæther, T. (2011, July). Software engineering challenges for migration to the service cloud paradigm: Ongoing work in the remics project. In *2011 IEEE World Congress on Services* (pp. 507-514). IEEE. 10.1109/SERVICES.2011.26

Mollah, M. B., Azad, M. A. K., & Vasilakos, A. (2017). Security and privacy challenges in mobile cloud computing: Survey and way ahead. *Journal of Network and Computer Applications*, *84*, 34–54. doi:10.1016/j.jnca.2017.02.001

Mont, M. C., Pearson, S., & Bramhall, P. (2003). *Towards accountable management of identity and privacy: Sticky policies and enforceable tracing services*. Paper presented at the 14th International Workshop on Database and Expert Systems Applications. 10.1109/DEXA.2003.1232051

Moore, J. F. (1993). Predators and prey: A new ecology of competition. *Harvard Business Review*, *71*(3), 75–86.

Moore, J. F. (2006). *Business ecosystems and the view from the firm*. The Antitrust Bulletin. doi:10.1177/0003603X0605100103

Munz, F. (2011). *Middleware and cloud computing*. Retrieved from https://books.google.com.pk/books/about/Middleware_and_Cloud_Computing.html?id=xStaYgEACAAJ&source=kp_book_description&redir_esc=y

Nate, D. (2019). *Best cloud storage of 2019: free, paid and business options | TechRadar*. Retrieved April 25, 2019, from https://www.techradar.com/news/the-best-cloud-storage

Nazir, M., Bhardwaj, N., Chawda, R., & Mishra, R. (2015). *Cloud Computing: Current Research Challenges*. doi:10.9790/0661/0811422

Nazir, A., Raana, A., & Khan, M. F. (2013). Cloud Computing ensembles Agile Development Methodologies for Successful Project Development. *International Journal of Modern Education and Computer Science*, *5*(11), 28–35. doi:10.5815/ijmecs.2013.11.04

Neto, P. (2011). Demystifying Cloud Computing. *Proceeding of Doctoral Symposium on Informatics Engineering*, *24*, 16–21.

Nguyen, T. D., Nguyen, T. T. T., & Misra, S. (2014). *Cloud-Based ERP Solution for Modern Education in Vietnam*. doi:10.1007/978-3-319-12778-1_18

Nicholas, F. (2019). *Best disaster recovery service | TechRadar*. Retrieved April 25, 2019, from https://www.techradar.com/best/best-disaster-recovery-service

Nick Antonopoulos, L. G. (2010). *Cloud Computing - Principles, Systems, and Applications*. Springer. doi:10.1007/978-1-84996-241-4

Ning, Z., Kong, X., Xia, F., Hou, W., & Wang, X. (2019). Green and Sustainable Cloud of Things: Enabling Collaborative Edge Computing. *IEEE Communications Magazine*, *57*(1), 72–78. doi:10.1109/MCOM.2018.1700895

Ohlhorst, F. J. (2018). *The Best Disaster Recovery-as-a-Service (DRaaS) Solutions for 2019*. Retrieved April 25, 2019, from https://www.pcmag.com/roundup/342348/the-best-disaster-recovery-as-a-service-draas-solutions

Oliveira, T., Thomas, M., & Espadanal, M. (2014). Assessing the determinants of cloud computing adoption: An analysis of the manufacturing and services sectors. *Information & Management*, *51*(5), 497–510. doi:10.1016/j.im.2014.03.006

Osterwalder, A., & Pigneur, Y. (2010). *Business Model Generation: A Handbook for Visionaries, Game Changers, and Challengers*. John Wiley & Sons.

Padilla, R. S., Milton, S. K., & Johnson, L. W. (2015). Components of service value in business-to-business Cloud Computing. *Journal of Cloud Computing*, *4*(1), 15. doi:10.118613677-015-0040-x

Park, S. C., & Ryoo, S. Y. (2013). An empirical investigation of end-users' switching toward cloud computing: A two factor theory perspective. *Computers in Human Behavior*, *29*(1), 160–179. doi:10.1016/j.chb.2012.07.032

Pasupuleti, S. K., Ramalingam, S., & Buyya, R. (2016). An efficient and secure privacy-preserving approach for outsourced data of resource-constrained mobile devices in cloud computing. *Journal of Network and Computer Applications*, *64*, 12–22. doi:10.1016/j.jnca.2015.11.023

Patidar, S., Rane, D., & Jain, P. (2011, December). Challenges of software development on cloud platform. In *2011 World Congress on Information and Communication Technologies*(pp. 1009-1013). IEEE. 10.1109/WICT.2011.6141386

Pawar, P. S., Sajjad, A., Dimitrakos, T., & Chadwick, D. W. (2015). *Security-as-a-service in multi-cloud and federated cloud environments.* Paper presented at the IFIP international conference on trust management. 10.1007/978-3-319-18491-3_21

Piper, B., & Clinton, D. (2019). *AWS certified solutions architect : study guide : Associate (SAA-C01) exam* (2nd ed.). Retrieved from https://books.google.com.pk/books/about/AWS_Certified_Solutions_Architect_Study.html?id=ocmGDwAAQBAJ&source=kp_book_description&redir_esc=y

Popović, K., & Hocenski, Ž. (2010). *Cloud computing security issues and challenges.* Paper presented at the The 33rd International Convention MIPRO.

Priya, G., & Jaisankar, N. (2017). A Review on Various Trust Models in Cloud Environment. *Journal of Engineering Science and Technology Review*, *10*(2), 213–219. doi:10.25103/jestr.102.24

Products & Services | Google Cloud. (n.d.). Retrieved April 1, 2019, from https://cloud.google.com/products/

Qian, L., Luo, Z., Du, Y., & Guo, L. (2009). *Cloud Computing: An Overview*. Springer. doi:10.1007/978-3-642-10665-1_63

Rafaels, R. (2015). *Cloud computing : from beginning to end, cloud technology, design, and migration methodologies explained* (revised). Retrieved from https://books.google.com.pk/books/about/Cloud_Computing.html?id=dGFWrgEACAAJ&source=kp_book_description&redir_esc=y

Raj, G., Yadav, K., & Jaiswal, A. (2015, February). Emphasis on testing assimilation using cloud computing for improvised agile SCRUM framework. In *2015 International Conference on Futuristic Trends on Computational Analysis and Knowledge Management (ABLAZE)* (pp. 219-225). IEEE. 10.1109/ABLAZE.2015.7154995

Rajput, R. S., & Pant, Anjali. (2018). Optimal Resource Management in the Cloud Environment-A Review. [IJCTM]. *International Journal of Converging Technologies and Management, 4*(1), 12–24.

Rajput, R. S., Goyal, D., & Pant, A. (2019). The Survival Analysis of Big Data Application Over Auto-scaling Cloud Environment. In A. Somani, S. Ramakrishna, A. Chaudhary, C. Choudhary, & B. Agarwal (Eds.), *Emerging Technologies in Computer Engineering: Microservices in Big Data Analytics. ICETCE 2019. Communications in Computer and Information Science* (Vol. 985, pp. 155–166). Singapore: Springer.

Rashid, A., & Chaturvedi, A. (2019). Cloud Computing Characteristics and Services: A Brief Review Proposing an Innovative Approach for Dynamic Resource Scaling Especially in Multi-tenancy Cases On Cloud Networks View project Cloud Computing Characteristics and Services: A Brief Review. *International Journal of Computer Sciences and Engineering*. doi:10.26438/ijcse/v7i2.421426

Rathore, J., Keswani, B., & Rathore, V. S. (2017). Analysis of Various Load Balancing Techniques in Cloud Computing: A Review. *Suresh Gyan Vihar University Journal of Engineering & Technology, 3*(2), 48–52.

Riahi, G. (2015). E-learning systems based on cloud computing: A review. *Procedia Computer Science, 62*(Scse), 352–359. doi:10.1016/j.procs.2015.08.415

Rizvi, S., Ryoo, J., Kissell, J., Aiken, W., & Liu, Y. (2018). A security evaluation framework for cloud security auditing. *The Journal of Supercomputing, 74*(11), 5774–5796. doi:10.100711227-017-2055-1

Roman, R., Lopez, J., & Mambo, M. (2018). Mobile edge computing, Fog et al.: A survey and analysis of security threats and challenges. *Future Generation Computer Systems, 78*(part 2), 680–698. doi:10.1016/j.future.2016.11.009

Rong, K., Lin, Y., Li, B., Burström, T., Butel, L., & Yu, J. (2018). Business ecosystem research agenda: More dynamic, more embedded, and more internationalized. *Asian Business & Management, 17*(3), 167–182. doi:10.105741291-018-0038-6

Russo, M. V., & Fouts, P. (1997). Resource-based perspective on corporate environmental performance and profitability. *Academy of Management Journal, 40*(3), 534–559.

Saleh, A. A. E. (2012). A proposed framework based on cloud computing for enhancing e-commerce applications. *International Journal of Computers and Applications, 59*(5).

Salmon, J. (2008). Clouded in uncertainty–the legal pitfalls of cloud computing. *Computing*, 24.

Samlinson, E., & Usha, M. (2013). *User-centric trust based identity as a service for federated cloud environment.* Paper presented at the 2013 Fourth International Conference on Computing, Communications and Networking Technologies (ICCCNT). 10.1109/ICCCNT.2013.6726636

Sareen, P. (2013). Cloud Computing: Types, Architecture, Applications, Concerns, Virtualization, and Role of IT Governance in Cloud. *International Journal of Advanced Research in Computer Science and Software Engineering, 3*. Retrieved from www.ijarcsse.com

Schafer, J. B., Konstan, J. A., & Riedl, J. (2001). E-commerce recommendation applications. *Data Mining and Knowledge Discovery, 5*(1-2), 115–153. doi:10.1023/A:1009804230409

Sehgal, N. K., & Bhatt, P. C. P. (2018). Cloud computing: Concepts and practices. In *Cloud Computing*. Concepts and Practices. doi:10.1007/978-3-319-77839-6_3

Sen, J. (2015). Security and privacy issues in cloud computing. In Cloud Technology: Concepts, Methodologies, Tools, and Applications (pp. 1585-1630). IGI Global.

Sharma, A., & Gupta, K. Amit and Goyal, Dinesh, An Optimized Task Scheduling in Cloud Computing Using Priority (April 20, 2018). Proceedings of 3rd International Conference on Internet of Things and Connected Technologies (ICIoTCT), 2018 held at Malaviya National Institute of Technology, Jaipur (India) on March 26-27, 2018. Available at SSRN: https://ssrn.com/abstract=3166077 or http://dx.doi.org/ doi:10.2139srn.3166077

Sharma, D. H., Dhote, C., & Potey, M. M. (2016). Identity and access management as security-as-a-service from clouds. *Procedia Computer Science, 79*, 170–174. doi:10.1016/j.procs.2016.03.117

Shi, Y., Liu, J., Han, Z., Zheng, Q., Zhang, R., & Qiu, S. (2014). Attribute-based proxy re-encryption with keyword search. *PLoS One, 9*(12), e116325. doi:10.1371/journal.pone.0116325 PMID:25549257

Singh, S., & Chana, I. (2016). A survey on resource scheduling in cloud computing: Issues and challenges. *Journal of Grid Computing, 14*(2), 217–264. doi:10.100710723-015-9359-2

Sood, S. K. (2012). A combined approach to ensure data security in cloud computing. *Journal of Network and Computer Applications, 35*(6), 1831–1838. doi:10.1016/j.jnca.2012.07.007

Sookhak, M., Yu, F. R., Khan, M. K., Xiang, Y., & Buyya, R. (2017). Attribute-based data access control in mobile cloud computing:Taxonomy and open issues. *Future Generation Computer Systems, 72*, 273–287. doi:10.1016/j.future.2016.08.018

Soomro, T. R., & Sarwar, M. (2012). Green Computing : From Current to Future Trends. *International Journal of Social, Behavioral, Educational, Economic, Business and Industrial Engineering, 6*(3), 326–329. Retrieved from http://waset.org/Publications?p=63

Soomro, T. R., & Wahba, H. (2010). Perspectives of cloud computing: An overview. *14th International Business Information Management Association Conference, IBIMA 2010, 2,* 631–637. Retrieved from http://www.scopus.com/inward/record.url?eid=2-s2.0-84905099773&partnerID =40&md5=f69f5d8565b11d01a6c44676249ac1dd

Sturges, J. E., & Hanrahan, K. J. (2004). Comparing Telephone and Face-to-Face Qualitative Interviewing: A Research Note. *Qualitative Research, 4*(1), 107–118. doi:10.1177/1468794104041110

Sullivan, D. (2010). *The Definitive Guide to Cloud Computing* (Vol. 1). Retrieved from http://www.realtimepublishers.com/book?id=157

Swarnkar, Singh, & Shankar. (2013). A Survey of Load Balancing Techniques in Cloud Computing. *International Journal of Engineering Research & Technology, 2*(8), 800-804.

Systems Kerridge Commercial. (2016). *A History of Cloud Computing Timeline.* Retrieved March 28, 2019, from Industry Insights website: https://blog.kerridgecs.com/a-history-of-cloud-computing-timeline

Takabi, H., Joshi, J. B., & Ahn, G.-J. (2010). Security and privacy challenges in cloud computing environments. *IEEE Security and Privacy, 8*(6), 24–31. doi:10.1109/MSP.2010.186

technavio. (2018). *Top 10 Data Center Companies in the World 2018 | Global Data Center Market Report - Technavio.* Retrieved April 25, 2019, from https://blog.technavio.com/blog/top-10-data-center-companies

The Four Types of Cloud Computing Models. (n.d.). Retrieved April 15, 2019, from https://www.paranet.com/blog/bid/128265/The-Four-Types-of-Cloud-Computing-Models

Top 10 Security Concerns for Cloud-Based Services. (2015). Retrieved from https://www.imperva.com/blog/top-10-cloud-security-concerns/

Tupakula, U., Varadharajan, V., & Akku, N. (2011). *Intrusion detection techniques for infrastructure as a service cloud.* Paper presented at the 2011 IEEE Ninth International Conference on Dependable, Autonomic and Secure Computing. 10.1109/DASC.2011.128

Types of Cloud Computing Explained | GlobalDots. (n.d.). Retrieved April 15, 2019, from https://www.globaldots.com/cloud-computing-types-of-cloud/

Vaquero, L. M., Rodero-Merino, L., Caceres, J., & Lindner, M. (2008). A break in the clouds: Towards a cloud definition. *Computer Communication Review, 39*(1), 50–55. doi:10.1145/1496091.1496100

Vargo, S. L., & Lusch, R. F. (2004). Evolving to a New Dominant Logic for Marketing. *Journal of Marketing, 68,* 1–17. doi:10.1509/jmkg.68.1.1.24036

Vargo, S. L., & Lusch, R. F. (2008). Service-Dominant Logic: Continuing the Evolution. *Journal of the Academy of Marketing Science*, *36*(1), 1–10. doi:10.100711747-007-0069-6

Vashistha, J., & Jayswal, A. K. (2013). Comparative Study of Load Balancing Algorithms. *IOSR Journal of Engineering*, *3*(3), 45–50. doi:10.9790/3021-03324550

Vecchiola, C., Pandey, S., & Buyya, R. (2009, December). High-performance cloud computing: A view of scientific applications. In *2009 10th International Symposium on Pervasive Systems, Algorithms, and Networks* (pp. 4-16). IEEE. 10.1109/I-SPAN.2009.150

Veit, D., Clemons, E., Benlian, A., Buxmann, P., Hess, T., Kundisch, D., ... Spann, M. (2014). Business Models - An Information Systems Research Agenda. *Business & Information Systems Engineering*, *6*(1), 45–53. doi:10.100712599-013-0308-y

Velte, A. T., Velte, T. J., & Elsenpeter, R. (2010). Cloud Computing: A practical Approach. *Journal of the Electrochemical Society*, *129*. Retrieved from http://scholar.google.com/scholar?hl=en&btnG=Search&q=intitle:No+Title#0

Wang, P., & Qiu, J. (2011). *Evaluating Mechanism Trust Model Based on Behavior Result under Cloud Computing*. Fuzzy Systems and Knowledge Discovery.

Wang, S., Zhou, J., Liu, J. K., Yu, T., Chen, J., & Xie, W. (2016). An efficient file hierarchy attribute-based encryption scheme cloud computing. *IEEE Transactions on Information Forensics and Security*, *11*(6), 1265–1277. doi:10.1109/TIFS.2016.2523941

Wan, Z., Liu, J., & Deng, R. (2012). A hierarchical attribute-based solution for flexible and scalable access control in cloud computing. *IEEE Transactions on Information Forensics and Security*, *7*(2), 743–754. doi:10.1109/TIFS.2011.2172209

Waqar, A., Raza, A., Abbas, H., & Khan, M. K. (2012). A Framework For Preservation of Cloud Users Data Privacy Using Dynamic Reconstruction Of Metadata. *Journal of Network and Computer Applications*.

Wei, K., & Tang, S. (2011). Trust Model Research in Cloud Computing Environment. *Computational Intelligence and Security*, *2*, 411.

Wernerfelt, B. (1984). A resource-based view of the firm. *Strategic Management Journal*, *5*(2), 171–180. doi:10.1002mj.4250050207

White, C. (2013). *Cloud computing timeline illustrates cloud's past, predicts its future*. Retrieved April 10, 2019, from TechTarget website: https://searchcloudcomputing.techtarget.com/feature/Cloud-computing-timeline-illustrates-clouds-past-predicts-its-future

White, T. (2015). Hadoop: The definitive guide. In *Online* (4th ed.; Vol. 54). Academic Press.

Wittig, M., Wittig, A., & Whaley, B. (2018). *Amazon Web Services in action* (2nd ed.). Retrieved from https://books.google.com.pk/books/about/Amazon_Web_Services_in_Action.html?id=-LRotAEACAAJ&source=kp_book_description&redir_esc=y

Xu, X. (2012). From cloud computing to cloud manufacturing. *Robotics and Computer-integrated Manufacturing, 28*(1), 75–86. doi:10.1016/j.rcim.2011.07.002

Yang, Y., Chen, X., Wang, G., & Cao, L. (2014). *An identity and access management architecture in cloud.* Paper presented at the 2014 Seventh International Symposium on Computational Intelligence and Design. 10.1109/ISCID.2014.221

Yang, Y., Zhu, H., Lu, H., Weng, J., Zhang, Y., & Choo, K.-K. R. (2016). Choo, "Cloud-based data sharing with fine-grained proxy encryption. *Pervasive and Mobile Computing, 28,* 122–134. doi:10.1016/j.pmcj.2015.06.017

Ye, C., & Potter, R. (2011). The Role of Habit in Post-Adoption Switching of Personal Information Technologies: An Empirical Investigation. *Communications of the Association for Information Systems, 28,* 585–610. doi:10.17705/1CAIS.02835

Yihui, D., Sun, L., Liu, D., Feng, M.,& Miao, T. L. (2018). A Survey on Data Integrity Checking in Cloud. In *1st International Cognitive Cities Conference (IC3).* IEEE.

Yin, R. K. (2014). *Case Study Research: Design and Methods.* doi:10.3138/cjpe.30.1.108

Younas, M., Ghani, I., Jawawi, D. N., & Khan, M. M. (2016). A Framework for agile development in cloud computing environment. *Journal of Internet Computing and Services 2016.*

Younis, Y. A., Kifayat, K., & Merabti, M. (2014). An access control model for cloud computing. *Journal of Information Security and Applications, 19*(1), 45-60.

Zhang, L.-J., & Zhou, Q. (2009). *CCOA: Cloud Computing Open Architecture.* Conference: IEEE International Conference on Web Services, Los Angeles, CA.

Zhang, J., Zhang, J.-A., & Sun, P. (2010). Trust evaluation model based on cloud model for C2C electronic commerce. *Comput. Syst. Appl, 19*(11), 83–87.

Zhang, J., Zheng, L., Gong, L., & Gu, Z. (2018). A Survey on Security of Cloud Environment: Threats, Solutions, and Innovation. In *Third International Conference on Data Science in Cyberspace.* IEEE. 10.1109/DSC.2018.00145

Zhang, L., Luo, Y., Tao, F., Li, B. H., Ren, L., Zhang, X., ... Liu, Y. (2014). Cloud manufacturing: A new manufacturing paradigm. *Enterprise Information Systems, 8*(2), 167–187. doi:10.1080/17517575.2012.683812

Zhang, P., Chen, Z., Liu, J. K., Liang, K., & Liu, H. (2018). An efficient access control scheme with outsourcing capability and attribute update for fog computing. *Future Generation Computer Systems, 78*(part 2), 753–762. doi:10.1016/j.future.2016.12.015

Zhang, Q., Cheng, L., & Boutaba, R. (2010). Cloud Computing: State of the Art and Research Challenges. *Journal of Internet Services and Applications, 1*(2), 7–18. doi:10.100713174-010-0007-6

Zhan, Z.-H., Liu, X.-F., Gong, Y.-J., Zhang, J., Chung, H. S.-H., & Li, Y. (2015). Cloud Computing Resource Scheduling and a Survey of Its Evolutionary Approaches. *ACM Computing Surveys*, *47*(4), 1–33. doi:10.1145/2788397

Zhou, R., Li, Z., Wu, C., & Huang, Z. (2017). *An Efficient Cloud Market Mechanism for Computing Jobs with Soft Deadlines*. Academic Press.

Zissis, D., & Lekkas, D. (2012). Addressing cloud computing security issues. *Future Generation Computer Systems*, *28*(3), 583–592. doi:10.1016/j.future.2010.12.006

About the Contributors

Saikat Gochhait is presently working with Symbiosis Institute of Digital and Telecom Management (constituent of Symbiosis International: Deemed University). Ph.D thesis was awarded with Doctoral Bursary Award in 2010 from Coventry University, UK., Deusto International Tuning Academy (DITA) Scholarships from University of Deusto, Spain, and Taiwan Research Fellowship 2019 from Ministry of Foreign Affairs. Post Doctoral fellow from University of Extremadura, Spain in 2018.

* * *

Arshad Ali received the PhD degree in Computer Science and telecommunication jointly from the Institute of Telecom SudParis and UPMC (Paris VI) in 2013. He worked as a post-doctoral researcher at Orange Labs, Paris for 1 year. Currently, he is working as an assistant professor in the Computer Science & Information Technology Department at the University of Lahore, Pakistan. His research interests are in the areas of delay/disruption tolerant networks, wireless mobile ad hoc networks, network coding, Software metrics and supervised learning.

Abhineet Anand, with his 18+ years of academic and administrative experience, his research includes the following field of endeavor: Decision Tree, nearest neighbor method, Clustering, Rule induction, Optical Fiber Switching in Wavelength Multiplexing, Automata Theory. He has published more than 16 Scopus indexed papers, 16 paper in International conference, 8 Intentional Journal, 3 National Journal, and 3 National Conference. He has been part 12 special session at various conferences at international level as session chair/co-chair, contributed at 20 different conferences as Technical Program Committee member. His expertise also includes reviewer at more than 25 conferences and Publication group.

Christoph Ertl is an external research assistant at the Chair of Information Systems at Munich University of Technology. He is currently working as Vice President Financial Management at Munich Airport International. His research focus encompasses public sector organizations and their challenges in management accounting.

Sebastian Floerecke graduated with both a Bachelor's and a Master's degree in Information Systems at Technical University of Munich (Germany) in 2011 and 2014, respectively. During his studies, he worked as a student assistant at the Chair for Information Systems (Prof. Dr. Helmut Krcmar) in the research fields of product service systems and enterprise architecture management. In late 2014, he joined the Chair of Information Systems (with focus on Information and IT Service Management) of University of Passau held by Professor Franz Lehner as research associate and doctoral candidate. In October 2019, he finished his doctoral thesis on cloud computing business models and ecosystems. Currently, he is working as IT Solution Manager at Munich International Airport. His research has been published in international journals, including Electronic Markets and International Journal of Service Science, Management, Engineering, and Technology (IJSSMET), and international conferences, such as European Conference on Information Systems and Internationale Tagung Wirtschaftsinformatik..

Charu Gandhi is a PhD in Computer Science from Kurukshetra University, Haryana, India. She has more than ten years of teaching experience. She is currently an Associate Professor at Jaypee Institute of Information Technology, Noida, India. She has published several papers in national and international conferences and journals. Her areas of interest include wireless networks, mobile ad hoc networks, QoS routing in MANETs, clustering techniques, energy efficiency and secure routing for MANETs, distributed and parallel computing.

Dinesh Goyal is Director Porima Institute of Engineering and Technology and former Dean Academics in the Suresh Gyan Vihar University. Dr. Goyal acquired experience of 16 years in Teaching, Research, and Administration. His research areas are Image Processing and Information Security. He has published more than 100 research papers in international publications followed by 21 papers presented in conferences and earned one full patent three provisional patents. He is the editor of numbers of books with prestigious publishers. He has organized four conferences and five workshops and also completed three consultancy and sponsored research projects. He has supervised eight doctoral students. He is a fellow member of IEEE and former president of the Computer Society of India, Jaipur chapter.

Alexander Herzfeldt earned his PhD in Management Information Systems from Munich University of Technology in 2014. He researched profitability of cloud service providers in his dissertation project. After finishing his PhD, Alexander started as consultant for a German-based private equity company. Today, he is working as project manager at Siemens Management Consulting focusing on strategy and M&A projects in both the oil and gas (service) and digital factory industries. His research interests include service engineering and finance/accounting topics in service businesses.

Saadia Karim is pursuing her PhD in Computer Science from CCSIS, IoBM. She holds MS degree in Computer Science from Muhammad Ali Jinnah University (MAJU) and Bachelor (Honors) degree in Computer Science (BSCS) from Sir Syed University of Engineering & Technology, Karachi (SSUET). She has served at IoBM as IT person and also Adjunct Faculty in CS department, where she taught ERP and SAP to the masters' students. She has more than 4.5 years of academic experience and 7 years of experience as a Software Programmer and Team Lead in IT. Her fields of interests are Artificial Intelligence, Machine Learning, Big Data, and Fuzzy Set Theory. She has published her research work in national and International Journals.

Shweta Kaushik received her BE degree in Computer Science and Engineering from Uttar Pradesh Technical University, Lucknow, India in 2010 and MTech degree in Computer Science and Engineering from Jaypee Institute of Information Technology (JIIT) Noida, India in 2012. She is pursuing her PhD degree in Cloud Computing from Jaypee Institute of Information Technology (JIIT), Noida, India. In 2012, she joined the Department of Computer Science and Information Technology, UPTU as an Assistant Professor. Since August 2015, she has been with the Department of Master of Computer Application, Indraprastha University (IP) Delhi, where she was an Assistant Professor. Her current research interests include cloud computing, network security, distributed system, algorithms and big data. She is a member of ACM.

Mujahid Rafiq is working as a lecturer at Superior University Lahore. He is also doing his Ph.D. in Computer Science from the University of Lahore, Pakistan. He is an active researcher and has several publications in Conferences and Journals. He is a Certified Cyber Security Professional. His Interest lies in Computer and Network Security, Cloud Computing and Human-Computer Interaction Domain.

Ravindra Kumar Singh Rajput is an Assistant Professor in Computer Science with the Department of Mathematics, Statistics and Computer Science, G. B. Pant University of Agriculture & Technology, Pantnagar, Uttarakhand, India, and also pursuing Ph.D. in Computer Science from Suresh Gyan Vihar University, Jaipur. Before joining G. B. Pant University, he has worked with Modi Olivetti limited, Spice Mobile, National informatics Center and Hindustan Aeronautics limited. His research interests include Cloud Computing, System Reliability, Internet-based application development, and Data Mining. He has attended five national and international conferences, and published more than twenty research articles, book chapters with prestigious publishers. He is also developed more than twenty software applications for government and business organizations.

Tariq Rahim Soomro, Professor and Dean College of Computer Science & Information Systems, Institute of Business Management, has received BSc (Hons) and M.Sc degrees in Computer Science from University of Sindh, Jamshoro, Pakistan and his Ph.D. in Computer Applications from Zhejiang University, Hangzhou, China. He has more than 25 years of extensive and diverse experience as an administrator, computer programmer, researcher and teacher. As an administrator, He served as Coordinator, Head of Department, Head of Faculty, Dean of Faculty, Head of Academic Affairs and having wide experience in accreditation related matters, including ABET, HEC Pakistan and Ministry of Higher Education and Scientific Research, United Arab Emirates (UAE). He has published over 80 peer-reviewed papers. He is Senior Member of IEEE, IEEE Computer Society and IEEE Geosciences & RS Society since 2005 and IEEE Member since 2000. He has been active member of IEEE Karachi Section (Region 10), served as Chair GOLD affinity Group, Member Executive Committee 2014 & 2017 and Branch Councilor. He is member Task Force on Arabic Script IDNs by Middle East Strategy Working Group (MESWG) of ICANN and Member Editorial Board "Journal of Geosciences and Geomatics" and also served as Technical Program Committee Member of several International conferences. He also received the ISOC Fellowship to the IETF for 68th Internet Engineering Task Force (IETF) Meeting. Detail view. He is currently serving as Vice-Chair, IEEE Karachi Section and R10 Computer Society Area Coordinator for Southern Area.

Reimar Weißbach holds a M.Sc. and a B.Sc. in Mechanical Engineering as well as a B.Sc. in Management & Technology from Technical University of Munich (TUM). After finishing his studies with research projects at Massachusetts Institute of Technology (MIT), Reimar started as a strategy consultant for Siemens Management Consulting with a focus on digital strategy projects. His research interests include numerical modeling and method development, additive manufacturing and novel business models.

Index

Ensure Quality Research is Introduced to the Academic Community

Become an IGI Global Reviewer for Authored Book Projects

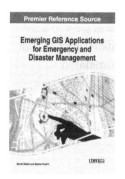

Premier Reference Source

Emerging GIS Applications for Emergency and Disaster Management

Premier Reference Source

Managerial Strategies and Green Solutions for Project Sustainability

Premier Reference Source

Comparative Approaches to Using R and Python for Statistical Data Analysis

Premier Reference Source

Solutions for High-Touch Communications in a High-Tech World

The overall success of an authored book project is dependent on quality and timely reviews.

In this competitive age of scholarly publishing, constructive and timely feedback significantly expedites the turnaround time of manuscripts from submission to acceptance, allowing the publication and discovery of forward-thinking research at a much more expeditious rate. Several IGI Global authored book projects are currently seeking highly-qualified experts in the field to fill vacancies on their respective editorial review boards:

Applications and Inquiries may be sent to:
development@igi-global.com

Applicants must have a doctorate (or an equivalent degree) as well as publishing and reviewing experience. Reviewers are asked to complete the open-ended evaluation questions with as much detail as possible in a timely, collegial, and constructive manner. All reviewers' tenures run for one-year terms on the editorial review boards and are expected to complete at least three reviews per term. Upon successful completion of this term, reviewers can be considered for an additional term.

If you have a colleague that may be interested in this opportunity, we encourage you to share this information with them.